Communications
in Computer and Information Science 422

T0213706

Cornelia Zehbold (Ed.)

S-BPM ONE – Application Studies and Work in Progress

6th International Conference, S-BPM ONE 2014
Eichstätt, Germany, April 22-23, 2014
Proceedings

 Springer

Volume Editor

Cornelia Zehbold
Technische Hochschule Ingolstadt
Esplanade 10
85049 Ingolstadt, Germany
E-mail: cornelia.zehbold@thi.de

ISSN 1865-0929
ISBN 978-3-319-06190-0
DOI 10.1007/978-3-319-06191-7
Springer Cham Heidelberg New York Dordrecht London

e-ISSN 1865-0937
e-ISBN 978-3-319-06191-7

Library of Congress Control Number: Applied for

Typesetting: Camera-ready by author, data conversion by Scientific Publishing Services, Chennai, India

Printed on acid-free paper

Springer is part of Springer Science+Business Media (www.springer.com)

Preface

The S-BPM ONE conference series started out in 2009 with the objective of establishing a platform where scientists, developers, practitioners, and educators can come together, share, and expand their expertise in the area of (S-) BPM.

Since then an increasing community involving the above-mentioned target groups has been contributing to the conference. These people make the events a very interactive meeting point with valuable input and lively discussions.

S-BPM ONE 2014, as the sixth event, was again able to attract many people to submit papers and to participate. Like 2012 in Vienna, the proceedings are provided in two volumes. For this CCIS volume, 14 papers have been selected from the application-oriented and early research submissions to the conference. They underwent the same rigorous peer-review process as those published in LNBIP 170. Authors contributed work in progress as well as application studies. The variety of topics ranges from model elicitation over strategic alignment to the application of S-BPM in different domains like software effort estimation, production planning, and education. Demos of running systems and a poster session complemented the paper presentations.

Organizing a successful conference needs many people valuably contributing in various ways:

- The keynote speakers, giving inspiring speeches
- The authors of the contributions presenting their work
- The members of the international Program Committee carefully reviewing papers and giving constructive comments
- The session chairs moderating the presentations and interaction between participants

We also thank the Collegium Willibaldinum for hosting S-BPM ONE 2014 in their impressive baroque building, and the many helping hands for guiding us through the whole program of the event. Special thanks goes to the Institute of Innovative Process Management (I2PM, www.i2pm.net), the umbrella institution of the overall S-BPM ONE conference series and related projects like Open S-BPM.

Last but not least, we thank Aliaksandr Birukou and Leonie Kunz from Springer for their assistance and support in publishing these proceedings.

April 2014   Cornelia Zehbold

Preface

Organization

Steering Committee

Albert Fleischmann   Metasonic AG, Germany
Werner Schmidt   Technische Hochschule Ingolstadt, Germany
Christian Stary   Universität Linz, Austria

Executive Committee

Conference Chairs

Alexandros Nanopoulos   Katholische Universität Eichstätt-Ingolstadt, Germany
Werner Schmidt   Technische Hochschule Ingolstadt, Germany

Organizing Chairs

Armin Felbermayr   Katholische Universität Eichstätt-Ingolstadt, Germany
Florian Wallner   Technische Hochschule Ingolstadt, Germany

Program Committee

Alexandros Nanopoulos (Chair)   Katholische Universität Eichstätt-Ingolstadt, Germany
Werner Schmidt (Chair)   Technische Hochschule Ingolstadt, Germany
Reza Barkhi   University of Grenoble-LIG, France
Jörg Becker   Westfälische Wilhelms-Universität Münster, Germany
Noureddine Belkhatir   University of Grenoble-LIG, France
Onur Demirors   Middle East Technical University Ankara, Turkey
Herbert Fischer   University of Applied Sciences Deggendorf, Germany
Peter Forbrig   University of Rostock, Germany
Andreas Gadatsch   Hochschule Bonn-Rhein-Sieg, Germany
Alexander Gromoff   Moscow National Research University, Higher School of Economics (HSE), Russia

Christian Huemer	Technical University of Vienna, Austria
Ebba Thora Hvannberg	University of Iceland, Iceland
Mikhail Komarov	National Research University of Higher School of Economics, Russia
John Krogstie	Norwegian University of Science and Technology, Norway
Matthias Kurz	Datev eG, Germany
Juhnyoung Lee	IBM T.J. Watson Research Center, USA
Franz Lehner	University of Passau, Germany
Jan Mendling	Wirtschaftsuniversität Wien, Austria
Tansel Özyer	TOBB Economics and Technology University Ankara, Turkey
Adrian Paschke	Freie Universität Berlin, Germany
Manfred Reichert	Ulm University, Germany
Wolfgang Renninger	University of Applied Sciences Amberg-Weiden, Germany
Susanne Robra-Bissantz	Technical University of Braunschweig, Germany
Gustavo Rossi	LIFIA Universidad Nacional de La Plata, Argentina
Detlef Seese	Karlsruhe Institute of Technology (KIT), Germany
Robert Singer	FH Joanneum University of Applied Sciences, Austria
Christian Stary	Johannes Kepler University Linz, Austria
Armin Stein	Westfälische Wilhelms-Universität Münster, Germany
Victor Taratoukhine	National Research University Higher School of Education, Russia
Alexandra Totter	ByElement GmbH, Switzerland
Eric Tsui	The Hong Kong Polytechnic University, China
Oktay Türetken	Eindhoven University of Technology, The Netherlands
Jan Verelst	Universiteit Antwerpen, Belgium
Jan vom Brocke	University of Liechtenstein, Liechtenstein
Guido Wirtz	University of Bamberg, Germany
Cornelia Zehbold	Technische Hochschule Ingolstadt, Germany

Sponsoring Institutions

ConsSys IT AG, Cham, Switzerland
IANES (Interactive Acquisition, Negotiation and Enactment of Subject-Oriented Business Process Knowledge) – EU FP 7 Marie Curie IAPP
IFG Ingolstadt AöR, Ingolstadt, Germany
INFOMEDIAservices GmbH, Vienna, Austria

IngolStadtLandPlus - Initiative Regionalmanagement Region Ingolstadt e.V.
Katholische Universität Eichstätt-Ingolstadt
Maihiro GmbH, Ismaning, Germany
METASONIC AG, Pfaffenhofen-Hettenshausen, Germany
Technische Hochschule Ingolstadt Business School, Germany
VALIAL Solution GmbH, Ilmmünster, Germany

 maɪhɪro

ɪanes

IFG Ingolstadt AöR
Ein Unternehmen der Stadt Ingolstadt

Technische Hochschule
Ingolstadt
Business School

Table of Contents

Long Papers

Separation of Concerns in Model Elicitation – Role-Based Actor-Driven
Business Process Modeling   3
   Stefan Oppl and Thomas Rothschädl

TicTacTuned – Subject-Oriented Business Process Model Elicitation . . .   21
   Boris Sobočan, Nils Meyer, and Christoph Fleischmann

An Interactional View of Context in Business Processes   42
   Udo Kannengiesser, Alexandra Totter, and David Bonaldi

Exploration of a Method for COSMIC Size Estimation from S-BPM   55
   Murat Salmanoğlu, Onur Demirörs, and Oktay Türetken

Applying the Strategy-Oriented Business Process Modeling to
S-BPM   67
   Matthias Lederer, Matthias Kurz, and Ulricke Lembcke

Using Meta Processes for the Structured Discovery and Self-learning
Improvement of S-BPM Processes   85
   Christoph Fleischmann and Gerhard Stein

Managing Knowledge-Intensive Business Processes by Harnessing
Collective Practical Experience without Codification   107
   Andreas Fink and Simon Vogt

Short Papers

Abstract Layers in PASS – A Concept Draft   125
   Matthes Elstermann and Jivka Ovtcharova

An Editing Concept for PASS Layers   137
   Matthes Elstermann and Jivka Ovtcharova

Complex Adaptive Systems Theory in the Context of Business Process
Management   147
   Eray Uluhan and Mehmet N. Aydin

Architecting the Enterprise along Communication Paradigm Using the
TOGAF® Framework   157
   Ramtin Mesbahipour, André Nursinski, and Michael Spiller

Production Planning for SMEs – Implementation of Production
Planning with Subject-Oriented Business Process Management
(S-BPM)   164
    Christoph Piller and DI Walter Wölfel

Can We Use S-BPM for Modeling Collaboration Scripts?   174
    Kai Michael Höver and Max Mühlhäuser

3D Progressive Education Environment for S-BPM   188
    Georg Weichhart, Johanna Pirker, Christian Gütl, and
    Christian Stary

Author Index   199

Long Papers

Model elicitation and application of S-BPM in different domains are the major topics addressed by the long papers of this volume.

Stefan Oppl and Thomas Rothschädl present concepts and a prototype for model visualization and modeling support according to different roles using distributed tangible tabletop interfaces.

Model elicitation is also the focus of the contribution by Boris Sobočan, Nils Meyer, and Christoph Fleischmann. They propose an S-BPM-based method for building, validating and improving processes in organizations.

Udo Kannengiesser, Alexandra Totter, and David Bonaldi develop a subject-oriented model for the alignment of individual contextual views of workers and business process experts as the basis of a framework for developing methods and tools to consider interactional context in business process descriptions.

Murat Salmanoğlu, Onur Demirörs, and Oktay Türetken use S-BPM to explore a method for estimating software development effort with the COSMIC functional size measurement.

An approach linking strategy maps with BPMN and S-BPM process models in order to close the strategy-to-operation gap is proposed in the paper by Matthias Lederer, Matthias Kurz, and Ulricke Lembcke.

Christoph Fleischmann and Gerhard Stein introduce an S-BPM meta process for structured discovery, design, execution, and improvement of S-BPM processes, enabling self-organization of process participants.

Andreas Fink and Simon Vogt close the section with their contribution on the support of knowledge-intensive, collaborative business processes, without having knowledge linguistically encoded for transfer.

Separation of Concerns in Model Elicitation – Role-Based Actor-Driven Business Process Modeling

Stefan Oppl[1] and Thomas Rothschädl[2]

[1] Department of Business Information Systems – Communications Engineering
Kepler University of Linz, Linz, Austria
stefan.oppl@jku.at
http://www.ce.jku.at
[2] Metasonic AG, Münchner Straße 29, Hettenshausen, 85276 Pfaffenhofen, Germany
thomas.rothschaedl@metasonic.de
http://www.metasonic.de

Abstract. Elicitation of business process knowledge can be facilitated by visualization of conceptual process models. Models of collaborative business processes with actors participating in different roles are complex constructs with flows of individual activities that are coupled via acts of communication. The processes of elicitation in such cases can benefit from separating the modeling process for each role and let actors focus on their own contribution to work and their communication with other roles. This paper identifies concepts for model visualization and modeling support that enable a modeling process distributed across role while maintaining one consistent overall model representation. A prototypical implementation of these concepts using distributed tangible tabletop interfaces is presented and results of exploratory tests are discussed. Based on this results the introduced concepts are refined end extended together with an industry partner to create a table top device which can be used in real world model elicitation scenarios.

Keywords: Visualization Techniques for Collaboration and Distributed Processes, Elicitation of Process Knowledge, Tangible Tabletop Interfaces.

1 Introduction

Business Process Models are a recognized means for representation of knowledge about work in organizations [11][18]. They can be used for asynchronous communication of information about business processes [19] and also facilitate elicitation and alignment of business process knowledge [26].

Work is an inherently cooperative phenomenon [30] with activities distributed over different actors. These actors perform their contribution to the overall process in different roles and communicate with each other to pass on their work results [29]. Capturing information about work thus has to involve all relevant

C. Zehbold (Ed.): S-BPM ONE 2014, CCIS 422, pp. 3–20, 2014.

stakeholders to form a sound model of the work process as carried out in organizational reality [31][18]. The process of capturing knowledge about work in a business process model is a form of explicit Articulation Work [30]. It includes the externalization and alignment of different views on work processes from all involved actors [15] and is an collaborative activity itself.

Recent research in the area of collaborative business process modeling (cf. 2) focuses on means of support for collaboration and negotiation in physical or virtual shared spaces. The visualization of the model in general is shared among all participants and presents an overall view on the process. A shared overall view, however, might cause unnecessary cognitive load during elicitation of process knowledge [4]. Allowing actors to focus on their individual role in a process (i.e. their activities and communication with others) in contrast leads to more detailed and refined models that better reflect the actual perception of their work [5]. The objective of this work is to develop model visualizations and elicitation methods that enable capturing process knowledge separately for each involved role while maintaining one single overall model of the process.

The remainder of this paper is structured as follows: the next Section gives an overview about the current state of art in support for collaborative business process modeling. It describes how previous research has approached model visualization in spatially distributed settings and identifies modeling support relevant to the approach examined here. Section 3 elaborates in more detail on the notions of role and actor in the context of collaborative work and modeling processes and discussed requirements on suitable modeling languages. Based upon this conceptualization, different modes of model visualizations are proposed to support modeling of different interaction scenarios in collaborative processes.

Section 4 presents a prototypical implementation of the visualization concepts and describes a showcase to explore user interaction with respect to upon the developed visualizations. The Section closes with a description of the shortcomings that have been identified so far. Based on the identified shortcomings, possible solutions are discussed to enable an operation of the presented system under real world conditions. The paper closes with future directions of research.

2   Current Support for Collaborative Modeling Processes

Collaborative modeling of business processes is a field of research that has gained visibility in the last years. Several systems have been proposed to support collaborative modeling processes in different co-located and distributed settings. Model visualizations that separates a model into distinct parts along the involved roles inherently require a spatially distributed approach to modeling. In order to maintain a sound overall model, the distinct model parts should be created synchronously to allow for immediate interlinking and alignment of model parts. We therefore review the current state-of-the-art in cooperative business process modeling with a focus on solutions that target spatially distributed settings for synchronous modeling.

CEPE [28] was one of the first real-time cooperative modeling applications available and has been designed to support business process reengineering use-cases in distributed settings. All users share the same model visualization which is propagated synchronously to the attached modeling software.

Decker and Weske [6] present a tool to cooperatively manipulate BPMN models on a web-based platform, on which all participants share a common view on the process. SAP has presented similar functionality in their Gravity-system that is based upon Google Wave technology for synchronously propagating model changes [8]. Hahn et al. [14] have examined the effects of the same system on collaborative process modeling in distributed settings in an exploratory study and identified current shortcomings of the prototype. Those were mainly related to lacking means of communication and shared access to common information during the modeling process. Participants also requested clear guidelines on how to structure the process and use BPMN elements to model collaborative behavior. The shared modeling surface caused conflicts in concurrent modeling, which could not be resolved due to lacking modeling space.

Brown et al. [2] present a modeling approach for BPMN using virtual 3D-worlds. Collaboration support is not directly anchored on the model but shifted to the surrounding virtual environment that facilitates immediate interaction and communication even in distributed settings.

Dollmann et al. [7] have focused on transforming models on the fly to different semantically enriched representations, also including a transformation of the graphical notation. They present a procedural model to collaboratively develop cross-domain process models with a focus on semantic mapping and do not focus on collaboration support in their first prototype.

Riemer et al. [25] have examined a set of 12 commercially available business process modeling tools regarding their support for collaborative modeling. While they commonly found support for asynchronous modeling and concurrent modeling of independent models, none of the examined tools supported synchronous modeling of business processes in distributed settings.

Reviewing the current state-of-the-art, collaborative modeling of business processes so far has mainly been addressed in settings, where a model is manipulated concurrently by several users in spatially distributed editors. Approaches that explicitly support temporally asynchronous [9] or spatially co-located settings [24][16] have been omitted here, as their applicability for the use-case described here is limited. Although this work a different approach to visualization than all other approaches to collaborative process modeling, the requirements on support for the modeling process in general sustain. This work therefore draws from prior research mainly through adopting the following requirements:

- Provide means for communication about the modeling process, desirably not only via text but also using audio or video channels [14] or even non-verbal signals [2]. Directly anchoring communication on model elements allows for easier referencing of the points of discourse [6].
- Provide access to all information relevant for modeling all of the time [14]. In a setting, where model parts are created spatially distributed and no overall

view is available for all participants by default, this implies that the actors have to be provided at least with all model information that directly affects them (e.g. the behavior of other roles they are interacting with).

3   Role-Based Process Model Elicitation

Designing means of support for role-based elicitation of collaborative processes requires a detailed understanding of the entities involved in collaboration and their contributions to the overall process. In the first section of this paper, the phenomenon of collaborative work was described [30][29] and the notions of "actor", "role", "activity" and "communication" were introduced in this context. These notions are revisited here to more exactly specify the relevant concepts in the context of this work.

Actors are considered to be individuals active in an organization. Activities are carried out by an actor without immediate interaction with others. Activities of different actors happen in parallel and are coupled with each other via explicit acts of communication (i.e. transferring work results from one actor to another). Decisions on which activities are carried out from a number of options are made by the actor based upon the outcome of a prior activity or the content of incoming communication.

When designing support for eliciting knowledge about work processes, the different kinds of activities described above have to be considered as fundamental model elements. We distinguish the following types of activities:

- individual activities carried out by an actor (including decisions)
- communication acts to link individual activities of different actors
  - outgoing communication acts, i.e. actively sending work results
  - incoming communication acts, i.e. receiving work results

In general, (collaborative) business processes are not tailored towards one specific actor but are specified to be carried out by a set of interacting roles. A role is an area of responsibility in the business process at hand. Consequently, several actors are able to take a certain role in a business process. A role, per definition, can only be taken by one specific actor in a specific business process instance (i.e. there are no roles that involve several actors simultaneously). This does not prevent actors to be basically able to take different roles. Communication acts are carried out among roles and interlink the activities carried out by actors acting in a certain role.

Introducing roles in a business process as an abstraction from actual actors introduces another distinction relevant for supporting the elicitation process:

- roles that are represented by only one actor during elicitation
- roles that are represented by several actors during elicitation

Before elaborating on possibilities for visualization model information suitable for role-distributed elicitation, suitable modeling languages have to be identified. In order to allow for visualizing a model distributed along the roles involved in the process, the used modeling language has to provide modeling constructs that allow for structuring the model along these boundaries [1].

3.1   Suitable Modeling Languages

Languages for representation of business processes in general follow different approaches along which conceptual dimensions information is described. A modeling language, that provides constructs to use the "who"-Dimension [34] as the primary factor of structuring, enables to separate areas of concern in a model of a cooperative business process [12]. An overview about suitable modeling languages (without intending to be exhaustive) is given in the following:

Role-Activity-Diagrams (RAD) [23] are an early approach to structure business processes along roles in a business process. They provide "roles" as constructs for structuring activities along areas of responsibility and "interactions" to model communication among roles. Interactions, however, are always considered to be acts of synchronization and thus do not allow for sending messages asynchronously.

In UML Activity Diagrams [3], "partitions" can be used to distinguish roles (although they are semantically not restricted to represent roles). "Flows" are used to connect activities. The is no separate semantic construct to distinguish among flows within a partition and among partitions.

BPMN [33] provides "pools" and "lanes" to structure processes along areas of responsibility. "Message Flows" are a construct to explicitly model communication among pools - they cannot be used among lanes. For the use-case proposed here, mapping roles to BPMN-pools would be an appropriate decision. Message flows originate in sending message events and end in receiving message events. The necessary model elements specified above thus can be fully mapped to BPMN.

S-BPM [10] follows an approach very much in line with the concepts proposed above. Models consist of "subjects" that interact using "messages". Subjects basically maps to the concept of roles described above. Their behavior is modeled using "action states", "sending states" and "receiving states", where the latter two are used to send and receive messages respectively. S-BPM element thus also fully cover the necessary modeling elements described above.

Summarizing, BPMN and S-BPM are both suitable to implement the model visualization approach described in this paper. The concepts for visualization presented in the next section are language-independent and can be implemented using either BPMN or S-BPM (or any other language fulfilling the fundamental requirements).

3.2   Concepts for Role-Based Model Visualization and Modeling Support

Separating a process along the involved roles requires a number of support measures relevant for interlinking and aligning different views on a business process and ultimately deriving a commonly agreed upon model of the business process.

The role-based areas of concern are interconnected by communication processes. As described in Section 3.1, communication processes are generally represented by flows of discrete messages that are sent from one role to another to trigger certain behavior at the receiving end.

Modeling of Role Behavior. Each role's contribution to work is visualized as a separate part of the model. As noted above, one role can be taken by several actors in an organization. Different actors introduce different viewpoints about how one role's contribution should be implemented [15]. These different viewpoints require alignment in order to derive one single, commonly agreed upon view on a business process. Consequently, collaboration support for modeling role behavior has be provided. All participating actors in this case share the same view on the role's part of the model. Shared views during collaborative process modeling have already been addressed in literature (cf. Section 2). Solutions for both, distributed (such as as [8]) or co-located settings (such as [16]) are viable here.

Following the argumentation at the beginning of this section, modeling elements for activities, decisions and communication acts are required. All modeling languages mentioned above provide the required set of elements (e.g. tasks, gateways as well as sending and receiving message events in the case of BPMN). Elements to model communication require special treatment, as they conceptually span across roles and require visualization for both involved roles (cf. Figure 1).

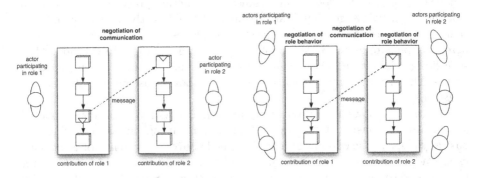

Fig. 1. Distributed manipulation of role-separated model with one actor per role (left) or multiple actors per role (right)

Modeling of Communication Acts. Communication among roles occurs whenever results of work (data and/or physical goods) have to be passed on from one role to another. In the following, the notion of "message" is used for these results of work. From a modeling process perspective, the following situations can occur:

- send a message to another role
- get notified that a message has been sent to one's own role
- request a message from another role to be able to proceed with one's own part of the process
- get notified that another role requests a message to be able to proceed with its part of the process

The first two situations occur regularly during the modeling process and would be sufficient to describe all communication situations if the business process was modeled in fully sequential manner across all involved roles. This would require the actors modeling a certain role to wait for another role to finish its work and send its result, before they can proceed modeling with their own process, if they are dependent on these result.

The third and fourth communication acts have been introduced to avoid those delays in modeling. Actors can specify messages they expect to arrive from another role and continue modeling as if this message already would have arrived. Aside from decoupling the roles' modeling processes the possibility to request messages also allows to uncover unclear communication flows or inconsistent expectations of who has to communicate which information to whom under which circumstances.

Whenever a message is created, either by sending a message to another role or requesting a message from another role (i.e. creating a local message proxy), its respective counterpart message has to show up at the communication partner's model side. Incoming messages or message requests however do not necessarily need to be processed immediately. For that reason, they are pooled in message trays that visualize all unprocessed messages separated by the according communication partners (for an example, see Figure 2).

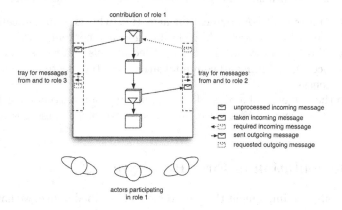

Fig. 2. Conceptual model visualization elements for one role

Communication about the Modeling Process. During the review of prior work in the area of collaborative business process modeling (cf. Section 2), providing means for communication about the modeling process has been identified as an important requirement for modeling support. Approaches to facilitate communication in all its aspects in distributed settings have been extensively reviewed in related work and are beyond of the scope of this paper. An important aspect to be considered when selecting means of communication support for the specific setting described in this paper is actors taking different roles by default do not see the same information and thus might have higher demand for communication about the modeling process and require more powerful tools for communication. This issue can be partially overcome with means to promote distributed model awareness as described in the next paragraph.

Distributed Model Awareness. The second requirement identified in Section 2 was to ensure availability of information about the process to be modeled and the current state of the model itself. Aside from measures like shared document repositories etc., the requirement needs to be considered more closely for the distributed model visualization used in this work. A view on the business process spanning across role boundaries is useful to develop an understanding about the overall structure of the process. Modeling is limited to the boundaries of a role in the approach presented here. While model visualization by default only contains a role's behavior and its direct communication with other roles, the model representation contains an overall model, thus allowing to visualize other model aspects.

However, which information is necessary about parts of processes affecting other roles, depends on the process to be modeled, i.e. is dependent on its complexity and potential restrictions due to confidentiality (especially relevant in cross-organizational settings, which are not explicitly excluded here). Following the modeling elements specified above and the partitioning approach, the following views can be identified (and be combined freely depending on the use-case):

- view on the overall communication acts (i.e. who is communication with whom about what), potentially including message content
- view on all role's behaviors (i.e. the detailed models of a role's contributions to the process), including all communication acts (i.e. flattened model of the overall process)
- view on the behavior of a role's direct communication partners (e.g. to follow up, how one' sent message are processed or received messages are being created)

4   Implementation of First Prototype

In a first attempt to implement the requirements described above, we have set up a role-based modeling environment based upon an existing interactive tabletop modeling system (cf. [21] for further details). The original system allows for synchronous co-located collaborative modeling and thus fits well the requirement to allow actors to collaboratively specify a role's behavior. The use of a physical tabletop setting for business process modeling is also in line with the positive experiences of Grosskopf et al. [13] in their pilot-study using non-electronically augmented tabletop business process modeling.

We here report on the system setup that has been developed to implement the distributed modeling environment and map its visualization approaches to the concepts described above. Additionally, we present our findings from a first round of exploratory tests that have been conducted to evaluate the applicability of the toolset for distributed collaborative modeling processes.

4.1 System Setup

The tabletop system has been used in a prototypical setting for modeling of business processes distributed across the involved roles. The result of the modeling process is a single process model representation containing the roles' contributions to the process interlinked via their communication acts. During the modeling process, however, the behavior of each involved role and its interaction with others has been modeled separately. A separate interactive table is used for the modeling process of each role.

In its recent iteration, the original system has been extended to support distributed modeling processes [32]. Multiple tables are used for synchronous modeling in a spatially distributed setting (cf. Figure 3). They are technically coupled using a message-based communication infrastructure (for details cf. [32]).

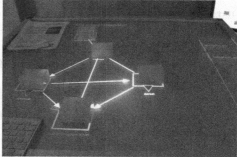

Fig. 3. Tabletop modeling system: two table setup with one table in the front and one in the back (left), model and communication tray of one table (right)

The table allows spatially distributed modeling of different parts of a business process model, which can be coupled via messages [20]. As for BPMN, each table represents one pool with its own sequence flow, while the interaction among pools is modeled by sending messages to represent the message flow. As for S-BPM, the tables map to subjects with the communication behavior being again represented by sent and received messages. In the following paragraphs, the mapping of concepts for role-based modeling support to actual features of the system is presented.

Modeling of role behavior is realized using one generic modeling element, that is used for representing activities, sending and receiving acts. Its semantics and the according visualization changes according to the use of the element in the model. Visualization is altered if an element is used to send or receive message (examples are visible on the right image in Figure 3) The advantages of using a generic modeling element during elicitation is discussed in [32].

Modeling of communication acts uses the communication trays proposed above. All tables are bidirectional interlinked using trays, that display unprocessed incoming messages and provide an area to send messages, that also contains visualizations of not yet processed requested messages. If a generic modeling element is placed in the sending area of the tray, its visualization and semantics are changed to become a sending message element and the name of the message can be specified. If placed next to a requested message element, the according message is sent. The same process is used to process incoming messages. A separate area in the incoming message tray allows to request messages from other roles. In this case, a message proxy is created and can be used for modeling. Modeling elements that are used for interaction with the trays do not affect the role behavior visualization, even if they already have been linked with other elements. The element temporarily removed from its position is replaced by a proxy visualization and allow for exact reconstruction of the actual model state.

Distributed Model Awareness is provided by different model visualization provided on the information display screen. By default, the messages exchanged with the immediate communication partners are graphically visualized. Actors can switch to a global communication view that visualizes all exchanged messages.

4.2   Exploratory Testing and Identified Shortcomings of the Prototype

Based upon findings from a first exploratory study [32] with a first prototype of the system, a second round of tests has been conducted in the course of a conference on subject-oriented business process management. Accordingly, the modeling approach used in the examination has been S-BPM. The aim of the test was to test the comprehensibility of the model visualization and identify areas for further improvement in terms of modeling support and model awareness.

The tables had been deployed in a co-located setting (cf. Figure 2, left). A scenario involving three roles had been prepared, where the behavior of one role was pre-scripted and simulated by a software component. The remaining two roles were assigned to one table each. The basic flow of activities as well as the necessary communication among the roles was provided textually separately for each role during the modeling sessions. Each role contained two to four activities, at least one act of sending and receiving messages and one decision. Prescribing the process to be modeled prevents examination of the systems effects on externalization and negotiation of meaning. A given modeling scenario, however, allows to focus on identifying issues in understanding the elements of the model visualization, their use and awareness about the model parts created on distant tables.

The system was deployed over a period of two days in an openly accessible area at the conference location. In total 42 people in 10 groups of 2 to 6 persons participated in the tests. All participants at least had fundamental knowledge in S-BPM. None of them had worked with the tabletop system earlier. They were briefly introduced to the system's features and modes of interaction and were asked to model the scenario afterwards. Data was collected via observation of the interaction with the system by a supervisor and qualitative feedback by the users after the modeling process.

Due to the co-located setting, support for communication about the modeling process has not been used. Additionally, message content negotiation has not been part of the modeling scenario and also was not used. The feature to request messages had not yet been implement at the time of the development, thus messages could only be used synchronously.

Initial Findings. The usefulness of the system for externalization and collaborative alignment of process knowledge in conceptual models has already been shown for co-located settings in earlier work [22]. The current prototype basically also met the expectations in terms of usability in the conceptually and spatially distributed setting presented here. In our tests, all groups except one were able to create a role-distributed model of the provided scenario after a brief introduction and occasional guidance in case of technical problems. There have been no observable or communicated misunderstandings in how to create models of role behavior or to send and receive messages. Some shortcomings of the current toolset, however, have been identified:

- **Asynchronous Request of Messages:** The need to wait for incoming messages in order to continue modeling has been experienced as a major obstacle in the modeling process.
- **View Overall Process:** An overall view of the complete process was hard to maintain but would have been helpful
- **Optimize Space Usage:** More complex models cannot be visualized at all due to space restrictions

5   Towards Deployment in Daily Business

The previous section identified shortcomings of the prototypical implementation based on an exploratory user study. This section presents possible solutions to create an enhanced system which can be examined under real-world settings together with the industry partner *Metasonic AG*. Therefore, practical issues such as logistics, maintainability and operability by business users had to be considered.

5.1   Adaptions for Business Use

Besides the conceptual issues, examined in Section 4.2, also some adaptions are necessary, to engage the industry partner in the research project.

The presented prototype needs to operate under controlled lightning conditions. In case of changing lightning conditions a correct detection of the graspable modeling elements could suffer. One additional issue was the assemble and disassemble of the tabletop interface itself. This was time-consuming, error prone and demands at least basic skills in craftsmanship. The solution to the mentioned hardware issues was to enable the software to operate also on professional hardware base from third party supplier which also support the TUIO protocol [17] for processing user interactions on the table top interface. Due to this, future research could consider user interaction concepts separately from hardware issues.

To enable the integration between the tabletop interface and the BPM-Suite from the industry partner, the communication server [32], which uses the Extensible Messaging and Presence Protocol (XMPP) [27], is replaced by the centralised model repository from the industry partner. As the centralised model repository stores an overall model representation and supports a concurrent modification of the same process by different users, concurrent process modeling on co-located and distributed table top interfaces is still supported. Additional the process modeling environment *Metasonic Build* can be used to visualise the evolution of role behaviour and acts of communications between roles. As the model repository stores the overall process it is possible to show and manipulate the behaviour of all roles on dislocated tables or with the modeling environment. Figure 4 shows different ways of model creation with a screen based modeling tool on a client pc, a co-located modelling session with two tables for elicitation of two roles and a further big screen to visualise communication acts and an other, dislocated table for elicitation of an additional role.

5.2   Resolution of Shortcomings of the Prototype

Additional to the practical changes, conceptional improvements to solve the issues in Section 4.2 were developed in workshops together with experts from the industry partner. The aim of the workshops was to improve the existing system and to be used for process model elicitation under real world conditions.

Asynchronous Request of Messages. As defined in Section 3.2 and as one of the findings in Section 4.2 the system has to be able to request messages in an asynchronous way without the need to wait until the message is created by the sending subject.This can be realised as user interaction pattern by putting a send or receive brick to the corresponding area on the tray. When the element is detected, a textbox opens, which allows to enter a name for the new message. After confirming the name with return, the new message is created and attached to the element for further use within the modeling process. Immediately after creation of the new message, the corresponding subject get aware of it as the new message is added to the tray representing the subject which created the message. Figure 5 shows a screenshot of the table representing *Subject 1*. The message tray on the left side represents the messages *Subject 1* exchanges with *Subject 2*. Additional the information that *Subject 1* sends *Message 1* to *Subject 2* and receives *Message 2* from *Subject 2* is visible for the user.

View Overall Process. The focus of the first prototype was to enable a distributed system where the different roles only exchange messages among each

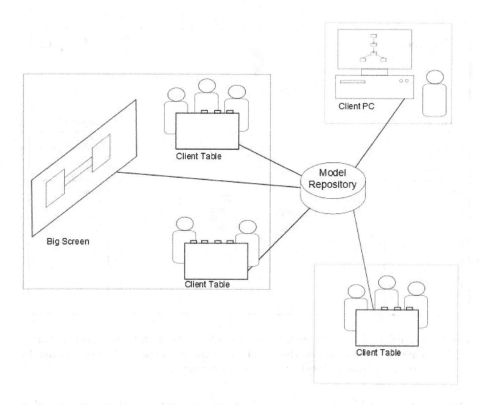

Fig. 4. Overview of possible distributions with a centralised model repository

other. Each modeling table therefore knew only its own internal behaviour. The interaction with other tables was managed and mapped via a centralised chat server where each process elicitation session was represented by a separated chatroom. Each role within the business process was represented by a user on the chat server and the messages, which are exchanged between the roles, have been mapped as chat messages between the users. This fits well to the Separation of Concerns approach, however it lacks in reality as it is not always clear if a certain task has been already performed by a different role during elicitation. Moreover, the experiment in Section 4.2 shows that users were missing an overall view of the process either to be able to identify all existing roles, or to have an overview which interactions happen between these or even to examine the behaviour of one special role. Therefore, it is necessary to be able to visualise, and eventually refine, the already modeled behaviour of other roles of the same process. This can be realised on the modeling table, with the need of removing all tangible elements to load an overview of the different roles and their interaction or to display the behaviour of one specific role. One other possibility would be to access the centralised model repository with an additional device to display the desired view on a extra screen (shown in Figure 4), a projector or even a tablet.

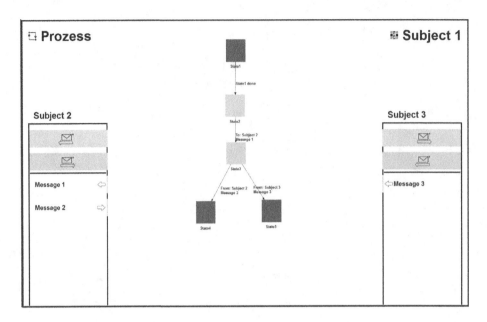

Fig. 5. Screenshot of the table surface with trays for each actor. By putting an element to the corresponding position on the top of each tray, new messages can be created. In the separated area below, already created messages are listed.

Optimize Space Usage. One lack of the existing system is that more complex models cannot be visualized at all due to space restrictions. This problem could be split into two dimensions, which have to be examined in two different ways.

One dimension of complexity covers the amount of different roles and the mapping of their interaction behaviour. Users which uses the examined prototype could only express acts of communication in maximum with two other subjects concurrently. This is due to the fact that the presented approach needs an own interaction tray for each role. Figure 5 shows that *Subject 1* interacts with the two roles *Subject 2* and *Subject 3*. If *Subject 1* also needs to interact with an additional role, *Subject 4* for instance, it has to disable one of the two currently displayed trays (exemplary *Subject 3*) to show a own tray for the additional role *Subject 4*. This has the negative side effect that if the prior disabled role *Subject 3* wants to interact with the role modeled on the tangible interface (*Subject 1*) will only get aware of this if it enables the tray for *Subject 3* again. With the result of having the same awareness problem with *Subject 4*.

A solution for this problem is to change the mapping of the trays itself from separated trays for each role to an own tray for incoming messages and one tray for outgoing messages. The corresponding role has to be shown next to the name of the message. With this approach only two different trays are sufficient to map the message interaction of one role. One for messages sent to the current modeled role and one for messages the current modeled role sends to other roles. Figure 6 illustrates the modeling surface of one table with only two trays. In difference to the Situation shown in Figure 5, the users also get aware that *Subject 4* needs an interaction. It sends *Message 5* to *Subject 1* and expects *Message 6* from *Subject 1*.

For sending a new message the user places a sending brick on the tray area for creating a new message. When the system detects a sending brick on the create message area, a selection menu with all available roles appears next to the brick. By rotating the brick the user has to choose the role which should receive the new message. Then the user has to name the new message. After the message is created it will appear in the tray for incoming messages of the receiving role, which can use it in the own internal behaviour.

It also can happen that a role did not know who is responsible for the message. Therefore it should also be possible that the creator of the new message could select *Unknown* as the receiver of the new message. If this happens, the new message appears in all input trays on the table until one role feels responsible for the new message and uses it in its own process behaviour.

The creation of a new incoming message can be modeled vice versa.

The second dimension covers the limited modeling space in terms of available spacial possibilities for placing elements on the table surface.Regarding this, first solutions such as hiding model complexity by embedding parts of the model in more generic elements or temporal removement of elements which are not relevant for the current elicitation act, have been discussed in [32]. One part of this problem was caused by recognition problems, which have been already mentioned in Section 5.1. The first tables forces users to place modeling bricks in a limited area near the center of the modeling surface to gain a stable marker recognition. Therefore, it was not possible to vacate the table center by putting currently non-essential bricks to the side (but still on the table) without loosing there already elicited, inherent information. As the new hardware base offers accurate element recognition over the whole modeling surface. This fact, in addition with slightly smaller modeling bricks has mitigated this problem.

6   Summary and Future Research

In this paper, we have presented an approach to role-based visualization of business process modeling that aids elicitation of work knowledge from actors involved in the process and facilitates alignment of their individual views on their work. We have derived concepts for model visualization and cooperative modeling support from both, earlier research on collaborative business process modeling and existing modeling languages that allow structuring the process along role boundaries. In a first attempt to implement the visualization concepts, we have created a distributed tangible tabletop interface. Initial results of the testing have been very promising, however, shortcomings have been identified in the examined implementation. Based on this, solutions and improvements to overcome the tracked shortcomings, that have been developed together with an industry partner, were presented. Future work will focus on the iterative refinement and extension of the system. Based upon such a fully usable version of the interactive

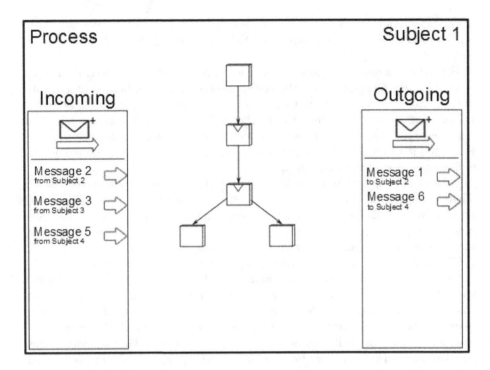

Fig. 6. Surface with separated trays for incoming and outgoing messages. On the top of each tray new messages can be created. In the separated area below, already existing messages are listed.

system, its usefulness in terms on supporting the distributed model elicitation and user interaction concepts can be evaluated. Ultimately, the suitability of the overall concept for process knowledge elicitation will be validated empirically in several case studies that will be conducted in the course of the academic-industry partnership IANES (http://www.ianes.eu).

Acknowledgements. The research leading to these results has received funding from the European Commission within the Marie Curie Industry and Academia Partnerships & Pathways (IAPP) programme under grant agreement n° 286083 (IANES).

References

1. Adamides, E., Karacapilidis, N.: A knowledge centred framework for collaborative business process modelling. Business Process Management Journal 12(5), 557–575 (2006)
2. Brown, R., Recker, J., West, S.: Using virtual worlds for collaborative business process modeling. Business Process Management Journal 17(3), 546–564 (2011)

3. de Cesare, S., Serrano, A.: Collaborative modeling using uml and business process simulation. In: Proceedings of HICSS 2006. IEEE Press (2006)
4. Crapo, A., Waisel, L., Wallace, W., Willemain, T.: Visualization and the process of modeling: a cognitive-theoretic view. In: Proceedings of the Sixth ACM SIGKDD International Conference on Knowledge Discovery and Data Mining, pp. 218–226. ACM Press, New York (2000)
5. Dann, H.D.: Variation von Lege-Strukturen zur Wissensrepräsentation. In: Scheele, B. (ed.) Struktur-Lege-Verfahren als Dialog-Konsens-Methodik., Arbeiten zur sozialwissenschaftlichen Psychologie, vol. 25, pp. 2–41. Aschendorff (1992)
6. Decker, G., Weske, M.: Towards collaborative business process modeling. Cutter IT Journal (2009)
7. Dollmann, T., Houy, C., Fettke, P., Loos, P.: Collaborative business process modeling with comomod-a toolkit for model integration in distributed cooperation environments. In: Proceedings of the WETICE 2011, pp. 217–222. IEEE Press (2011)
8. Dreiling, A.: Gravity – collaborative business process modelling within google wave (2009),
   http://scn.sap.com/people/alexander.dreiling/blog/2009/09/02/gravity-collaborative-business-process-modelling-within-google-wave
9. Erol, S., Mödritscher, F., Neumann, G.: A meta-design approach for collaborative process modeling. In: Proceedings of the 2nd International Workshop on Open Design Spaces (ODS 2010), pp. 46–62 (2010)
10. Fleischmann, A., Schmidt, W., Stary, C., Obermeier, S., Börger, E.: Subjektorientiertes Prozessmanagement. Hanser Verlag (2011)
11. Gasson, S.: The dynamics of sensemaking, knowledge, and expertise in collaborative, boundary-spanning design. Journal of Computer-Mediated Communication 10(4) (2005)
12. Giaglis, G.: A taxonomy of business process modeling and information systems modeling techniques. International Journal of Flexible Manufacturing Systems 13(2), 209–228 (2001)
13. Grosskopf, A., Edelman, J., Weske, M.: Tangible business process modeling – methodology and experiment design. In: Rinderle-Ma, S., Sadiq, S., Leymann, F. (eds.) BPM 2009. LNBIP, vol. 43, pp. 489–500. Springer, Heidelberg (2010)
14. Hahn, C., Recker, J., Mendling, J.: An exploratory study of IT-enabled collaborative process modeling. In: Muehlen, M.z., Su, J. (eds.) BPM 2010 Workshops. LNBIP, vol. 66, pp. 61–72. Springer, Heidelberg (2011)
15. Herrmann, T., Hoffmann, M., Kunau, G., Loser, K.: Modelling cooperative work: Chances and risks of structuring. In: Cooperative Systems Design, A Challenge of the Mobility Age. Proceedings of COOP 2002, pp. 53–70. IOS Press (2002)
16. Herrmann, T., Nolte, A.: The integration of collaborative process modeling and electronic brainstorming in co-located meetings. In: Kolfschoten, G., Herrmann, T., Lukosch, S. (eds.) CRIWG 2010. LNCS, vol. 6257, pp. 145–160. Springer, Heidelberg (2010), http://www.sociotech-lit.de/HeNo10-IoC.pdf
17. Kaltenbrunner, M., Bovermann, T., Bencina, R., Costanza, E.: TUIO: a protocol for table-top tangible user interfaces. In: Proc. of the 6th International Workshop on Gesture in Human-Computer Interaction and Simulation (2005),
   http://mtp.athlabs.com/export/90/docs/TUIO
18. Lewis, M., Young, B., Mathiassen, L., Rai, A., Welke, R.: Business process innovation based on stakeholder perceptions. Information, Knowledge, Systems Management 6(1), 7–27 (2007)
19. Niehaves, B., Plattfaut, R.: Collaborative business process management: status quo and quo vadis. Business Process Management Journal 17(3), 384–402 (2011)

20. Oppl, S.: Subject-Oriented Elicitation of Distributed Business Process Knowledge. In: Schmidt, W. (ed.) S-BPM ONE 2011. CCIS, vol. 213, pp. 16–33. Springer, Heidelberg (2011)

21. Oppl, S., Stary, C.: Tabletop concept mapping. In: Proceedings of the 3rd International Conference on Tangible and Embedded Interaction (TEI 2009). ACM Press (February 2009)

22. Oppl, S., Stary, C.: Effects of a Tabletop Interface on the Co-Construction of Concept Maps. In: Campos, P., Graham, N., Jorge, J., Nunes, N., Palanque, P., Winckler, M. (eds.) INTERACT 2011, Part III. LNCS, vol. 6948, pp. 443–460. Springer, Heidelberg (2011)

23. Ould, M.A.: Business Processes: Modelling and analysis for re-engineering and improvement. John Wiley and Sons (1995)

24. Renger, M., Kolfschoten, G., de Vreede, G.J.: Using interactive whiteboard technology to support collaborative modeling. In: Briggs, R.O., Antunes, P., de Vreede, G.-J., Read, A.S. (eds.) CRIWG 2008. LNCS, vol. 5411, pp. 356–363. Springer, Heidelberg (2008), http://dx.doi.org/10.1007/978-3-540-92831-7_29

25. Riemer, K., Holler, J., Indulska, M.: Collaborative process modelling-tool analysis and design implications. In: Proceedings of ECIS 2011, Association for Information Systems (2011)

26. Rittgen, P.: Negotiating models. In: Krogstie, J., Opdahl, A.L., Sindre, G. (eds.) CAiSE 2007 and WES 2007. LNCS, vol. 4495, pp. 561–573. Springer, Heidelberg (2007), http://dx.doi.org/10.1007/978-3-540-92831-7_29

27. Saint-Andre, P., et al.: Extensible messaging and presence protocol (XMPP): Core. RFC 3920, W3C (2004)

28. Santoro, F., Borges, M., Pino, J.: Cepe: cooperative editor for processes elicitation. In: Proceedings of the 33rd Annual Hawaii International Conference on System Sciences, 10 p. IEEE (2000)

29. Schmidt, K., Simone, C.: Coordination mechanisms: Towards a conceptual foundation of CSCW systems design. Computer Supported Cooperative Work 5(2/3), 155–200 (1996)

30. Strauss, A.: Continual Permutations of Action. Aldine de Gruyter, New York (1993)

31. Stuit, M., Wortmann, H., Szirbik, N., Roodenburg, J.: Multi-view interaction modelling of human collaboration processes: a business process study of head and neck cancer care in a dutch academic hospital. Journal of Biomedical Informatics (2011)

32. Wachholder, D., Oppl, S.: Stakeholder-Driven Collaborative Modeling of Subject-Oriented Business Processes. In: Stary, C. (ed.) S-BPM ONE 2012. LNBIP, vol. 104, pp. 145–162. Springer, Heidelberg (2012)

33. White, S.: Introduction to BPMN. BPTrends (2004)

34. Zachman, J.: A framework for information systems architecture. IBM Systems Journal 26(3), 276–292 (1987)

TicTacTuned – Subject-Oriented Business Process Model Elicitation

Boris Sobočan[1], Nils Meyer[1], and Christoph Fleischmann[2]

[1] Metasonic AG
{boris.sobocan,nils.meyer}@metasonic.de
[2] University of Technical Science, Vienna
chris.fleischmann@gmx.net

Abstract. In this paper we introduce the TicTacTuned method as S-BPM based objectives-driven, performance-oriented, way of building, validating and improving processes in organizations. The method is founded upon perpetual exchange of the context from process level to internal behavior level, and the working practice from collaborative to individual supported by automatic generation of executable process models out of internal behavior diagrams. The approach is focused on the employees with intent to raise their inspiration and motivation, to empower them to manage parts of the business processes on their own and to share the responsibility for process performance, to mitigate fear and reluctance towards change and to encourage creating and sharing of knowledge.

Keywords: Objectives, employees, roles, capabilities, empowerment, motivation, subject behavior perspective, automatic process model generation, automatic subject behavior data integration, process perspective, context awareness, aha moment, innovation.

1 Introduction

Processes are the most crucial part of an organization's value creation. This requires the company to execute its processes in the most effective and efficient way possible. Process Analysis is the initial point for the identification of weaknesses and possible improvements within a process. According to [1] a process analysis always begins with the process model which documents and describes the process itself.

Current literature is focusing how process-awareness can be introduced in a company, e.g. [2–4]. Process modeling meta-models, the models describing the processes for surveying and optimizing process models, e.g. [5], explain how interviews can be carried out. Typically the interviews and the modeling itself is carried out by business analysts and "end users are typically not participating in the modeling process" [6].

We argue that activating the business process participants for modeling and enacting business processes is possible with a subject oriented approach to business process management and can be beneficial for an organization for several reasons.

C. Zehbold (Ed.): S-BPM ONE 2014, CCIS 422, pp. 21–41, 2014.

1.1   Motivation for Stakeholder Involvement

First, process participants usually have strong process knowledge in terms of knowledge about other process participants, their communication and relations to those participants, and the flow of data. According to Mutschler [6], a direct access to this process knowledge can significantly reduce the cost of process modeling and implementation. As the main costs for BPM projects are personnel costs, reduced costs usually go along with less time needed. As a consequence there is a positive relationship between process participant involvement and the time needed for adapting business processes to changed requirements.

Second, accessing this process knowledge unlocks the potential for high-quality process improvements or even process innovations. The more dynamic an environment, the further away are central departments from the daily problems of the operational staff and potential solutions [7]. Empowering the operational staff to contribute directly to the adaption of business process models can leverage the value of the anticipated solutions for the organization.

Third, end-user fears as an important cost driver during process analysis and requirements definition [6] can be addressed by strong communication and involvement [8] of the process participants, being inherently given if they can directly adapt models of their own processes. Lowering those fears has positive effects on the time needed for process adaptions and thus for the implementation of inventions.

Forth, a stronger activation of the process participants can keep business process management departments from becoming a bottleneck with respect to business process adaption requests. Retained adaption requests have negative influence on the timely realization of inventions and therefore on innovations in agile organizations.

Fifth, the ability for process participants to contribute to the advancement of the organization and to take responsibility for their own way of working is positively correlated with their motivation [9]. Motivation has been identified as a major driver for innovation [10]. Or as [11] puts it "People tend to be supportive of the things they help create. Involving employees in developing SOPs can help assure the final product is more complete, useful and accepted."

Sixth, Stakeholder Input is a critical success factor for process modeling success [12]. Empowering process participants to model and enact business processes ensures their input without any additional endeavors.

1.2   Involving Process Participants during Model Elicitation

To involve business people in the modeling and enactment of business processes, process modeling meta-models need to describe their tasks explicitly. As current modeling meta-models do not focus the active involvement of business people in the modeling process we introduce our TicTacTuned method as meta-model tackling this shortcoming.

The rest of the paper is organized as follows: Section 2.1 shortly introduces S-BPM as process meta-model, the S-BPM framework as value delivery concept and a role concept as basic concepts needed to understand the approach presented in this paper. Section 2.2 describes our approach in detail with the necessary activities being carried out by the roles introduced in the section before. Section 2.3 sketches our approach as a subject-oriented process model. Section 3 concludes the paper with a summary of the sections before and an outlook on the further research we plan.

2   The TicTacTuned Method

"Standard BPM approaches have predefined control and information flow. They are often more a burden that an aid because they inappropriately restrict the control and information flow within the BPM cycle" [13].

Model-reality-divide and Lost innovation are two important problems of the standard BPM, "The roots of the model-reality-divide and lost innovation are manifold and interconnected" [14].

Most S-BPM process model elicitation methods start with creation of communication diagram, where messages and subjects coupled by sending/receiving these messages are defined. Then the internal behavior diagrams of coupled subjects are created.

Any predefined constrains of internal behavior logic create potential risk that the process participants will not relay on their own knowledge and experience and that decisions they make will not be autonomous, but influenced and narrowed without sound reason.

The TicTacTuned method is a S-BPM based, objectives-driven, performance-oriented way of building, validating and improving processes in organizations. It empowers process participants to negotiate and agree process objectives with other process participants, to take part of responsibility for the performance of the process and to manage the parts of the business processes that touch them directly on their own.

The elimination of pre-set constrains increases the inspiration, creativity and motivation of process participants to find optimal solutions for achieving their objectives. Representational change theory says that: "The problem solver initially has a low probability for success because they use inappropriate knowledge as they set unnecessary constraints on the problem. Once the person relaxes his or her constraints, they can bring previously unavailable knowledge into working memory to solve the problem." [15]

By perpetually exchanging the context from process level to internal behavior level and the working practice from collaborative to individual, by sharing and linking internal behavior diagrams process participants gain visibility and knowledge which enables them to understand how the entire process looks like and how their internal behavior fits in. This insight, i.e. understanding of a specific cause and effect relationship in a new context, enables them to figure out if, why and how it makes sense to change their internal behavior to improve overall process performance.

The TicTacTuned method enables the creation of internal behavior models with uncoupled messages. This feature enables the creation of a repository to provide storage, tag, retrieve, search and reuse of internal behavior models.

TicTacTuned activities are designed to achieve agreed objectives. Employees capable and willing to take responsibility are empowered to create, improve and innovate processes as a means of creating desired value.

Before explaining the method step by step in 2.2 we're briefly introducing some fundamental terms and ideas in 2.1.

2.1   S-BPM as a Basis

A subject oriented business process [16] is specified by the subjects being involved in the process, the messages they exchange and the internal behavior of the involved subjects. [17] gives a comprehensive overview of all different modeling construct. Below a high level overview being necessary to understand the following sections of the paper is given.

The communication between the process specific roles, the subjects, is described using a subject interaction diagram (SID). Fig. 1 shows a sample SID for a possible conference registration process inside of an organization. If an employee likes to attend a conference this attendance has to be approved by his supervisor before he triggers payment by the Accountant based on the Approved Conference Attendance.

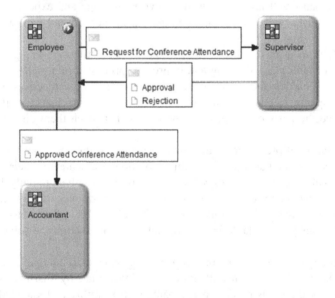

Fig. 1. Sample subject interaction diagram for a conference registration process

Each subject is further described by the subject behavior diagram (SBD). A subject behavior is described by send (red in the sample below), receive (green) and function (yellow) states and the transitions connecting these states. Fig. 2 shows the SBD for the subject Supervisor from the sample above.

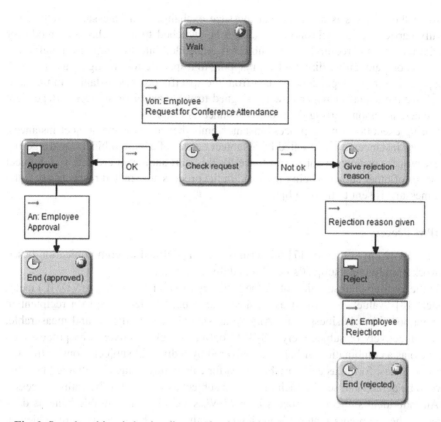

Fig. 2. Sample subject behavior diagram for the subject Supervisor from the sample above

Each SBD has one specific start state, marked with the Play symbol, and might have several end states. Subjects having a send or function state as start state are named start subjects as they can start a process instance. Transitions out of send and receive states reference communication partners and message types from the SID. Data is stored in so called business objects that can be provided by messages in receive states, that can be created, updated or read in internal functions and that can be send to other subjects in send states. All process steps can be carried out either manually or automated, while the majority of process steps especially for knowledge intensive processes are typically carried out by humans. If a process step is automated a refinement is called allowing arbitrary code execution for e.g. manipulating business objects or calling third-party systems. Inside one subject there are no parallel activities allow. Multiple outgoing transitions out of one state are implicitly XOR related. It is not necessary to ensure a block structure during modeling, that means loops and branching may overlap. Nevertheless the whole processes are executed highly parallel as each subject is running independently from other subjects and synchronization between the subjects is achieved via message exchange. This message exchange is usually carried out asynchronously but can be switched to a synchronous mode for special messages if required. Each subject is embedded into the organizational structure of a company either directly by a mapping to a specific role being connected with groups and users or dependent on data from the specific process instance. In the sample above the actual manager how is assigned to the Supervisor subject is dependent on the actual person starting the process instance as Employee.

During execution time a process instance embodies at least one subject instances. A process instance can be created by a subject carrier of a start subject. By triggering a new process instance a subject instance for this start subject is created, too. Subject instances of other subjects being involved in the process are created respectively if the first message is sent to those subjects.

S-BPM Process

In an S-BPM environment [17] the term process is defined as communication based network of individual subject's behaviors delivering value.

In the high-level abstraction of Value Delivery Modeling Language (VDML) meta-model [18] "value" is defined as "a measurable benefit delivered to a recipient in association with a business item. Any value should be identifiable and measurable, either objectively or subjectively". S-BPM defines benefits delivered by process (objectives) as a combination of benefits delivered by individual subjects constituting the process. Rules, formulas and variables used for calculating value of delivered benefits have to be agreed and set for each individual subject as well as for the entire process.

An individual subject or process is *in TUNE* state when measurable benefits delivered to the recipients match planned/agreed value, i.e. set objectives are achieved. Individual subjects or process is *NOT in TUNE* state when measurable delivered benefits are worse than planned, i.e. set objectives are not achieved.

in TUNE state indicator, showing achievement of defined objectives to process participants, is on Fig. 3 and Fig. 5 presented by crossed circles.

It is the objective of each organization to have all processes *in TUNE* state all the time. Processes being *in TUNE* state should stay in that state over the time and processes being *NOT in TUNE* should be brought to an *in TUNE* state as soon as possible Fig. 3). Processes *in TUNE* should not fall into *NOT in TUNE* state (left "X" on Fig. 3) and processes should not stay in *NOT in TUNE* state (lower "X" on Fig. 3).

[19] defines business process management as holistic management approach organizations use to achieve these objectives.

S-BPM Framework

The S-BPM framework (Fig. 4) is an interpretation of the Organizing Framework for Value driven BPM [20]. It consists of two value delivery concepts [18]: S-BPM roles and activities, both positioned in the framework context. The S-BPM context,

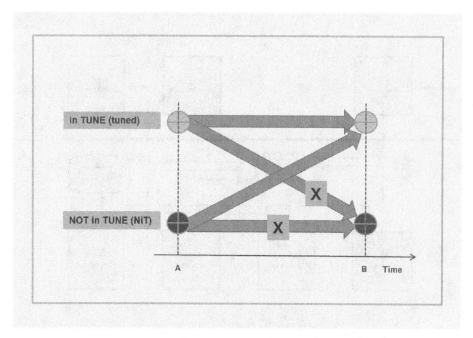

Fig. 3. In TUNE, NOT in TUNE state

depicted by Data symbol of Fig. 4, consists of attribute data and defines environment in which role holders (process participants) make decisions, select and execute activities based on their context awareness [13, 21, 22]. The *in TUNE* state indicator, showing achievement of set objectives, is the key S-BPM Framework context attribute.

The bold arrows represent S-BPM role holders executing activities while the thin arrows represent data flow during the execution of activities.

In the S-BPM framework activities are bundled into seven blocks:

- Build process block contains activities for collecting process related knowledge and activities for creating process model.
- Validate process block contains activities for validating process logic effectiveness and efficiency.
- Integrate process block contains activities for integrating process logic into organizations' infrastructure.
- Execute process block contains activities for executing, monitoring, evaluating and adapting process instances.
- Predict performance block contains activates for predicting/forecasting performance of running process instances.
- Analyze performance block contains activities for active and on demand analyzing process performance and achievement of strategic objectives.
- Manage strategy block contains activities for defining and adapting strategy, aligning strategic objectives with processes in organization, and for monitoring achievement of strategic objectives.

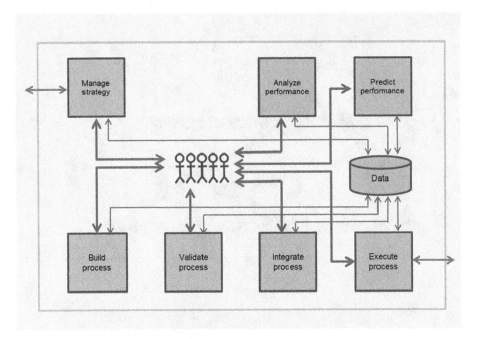

Fig. 4. S-BPM framework

Each block incorporates activities for identifying *NOT in TUNE* state. (Fig. 3, Fig. 5)

S-BPM Role Concept

The S-BPM role concept presented in Fig. 5 is an objectives-driven subject-oriented collaboration [23] structure. It defines rights, responsibilities and desirable capabilities for performing activities defined in the S-BPM framework (Fig. 4). Adequate level of desirable capabilities [18] is the key criteria for assigning role holders (process participants) to the S-BPM roles.

This role concept defines five S-BPM roles:

- Manager   (M)
- Process owner   (PO)
- Subject owner   (SO)
- Process instance owner   (PIO)
- Subject instance owner   (SIO)

These roles are positioned in three collaboration layers:

- strategy management layer
- process management layer
- process instance management layer

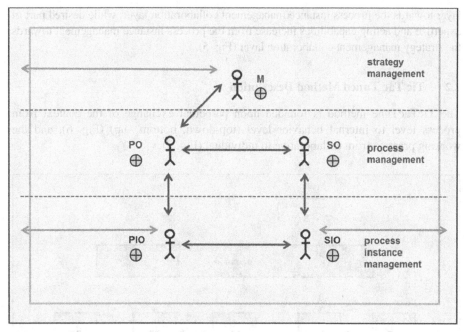

Fig. 5. S-BPM role concept

On the strategy management layer strategic objectives are defined and adapted. Processes to achieve these objectives are defined and aligned. For example: Managers collect and analyze environment data, identify strategic opportunities and threats, create strategy maps, relate strategic objectives to business processes and monitor the achievement of strategic objectives.

On the process management layer information about process performance is collected, and compared with agreed objectives/outcomes. On this layer process and internal behavior models are created, adapted, improved, and innovated. S-BPM Process elicitation methods fits to this layer. TicTacTuned activities performed by Process Owners and Subject Owners are described in section 2.2 of this paper.

On the process instance layer running process instances are managed. Execution of activities and instance rescue actions fits to this layer. For example: Subject Instance Owners have the right and responsibility to execute, skip, add or bypass internal behavior activities. Process Instance Owners have the right and responsibility to bypass or add subject instances and replace Subject Instance Owners.

S-BPM roles (Fig. 4, Fig. 5) are based on rights and responsibilities for performing activities defined in the S-BPM framework (Fig. 4). Roles: actor, facilitator, expert and governor presented in [17] are based on capabilities of process participants required for successful business process management. Each S-BPM role holder has to have acting, facilitating, expertize and governance capabilities to achieve set objectives (Fig. 5). Due to decreasing number of stakeholders and increasing concreteness of activities, the part of desired facilitation and governance capabilities decreases from the strategy management layer towards the process instance management collaboration layer, while desired part of expertize and acting capabilities increase from the process instance management towards the strategy management collaboration layer (Fig. 5).

2.2   Tic Tac Tuned Method Description

The TicTacTune method is founded upon perpetual exchange of the context from process level to internal behavior level (top-down, bottom –up) (Fig. 6), and the working practice from collaborative to individual (Fig. 7).

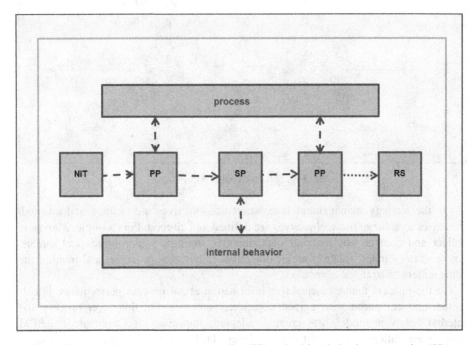

Fig. 6. Changing between process perspective (PP) and subject behavior perspective (SP)

TicTacTuned activities are triggered by process participants when *NOT in TUNE* status (NiT on Fig. 3, Fig. 6 and Fig. 7) is identified or predicted on any of collaboration layers (Fig. 5).

Process perspective activities are performed jointly (collaborative working practice) by Process Owner and Subject Owners. (Fig. 7)There process related knowledge is created and analyzed. Work to be done to achieve set objectives is split up to internal work items for each Subject Owner.

Subject behavior perspective activities are performed individually (Fig. 7) by Subject Owners. There internal behavior work items are handled.

The time window between the activities can range from few hours to few days (Fig. 6 and Fig. 7).

TicTacTuned activities are carried out until a satisfying solution for exiting or pre-venting *NOT in TUNE* state (Fig. 3) is found and released (RS of Fig. 6 and Fig. 7).

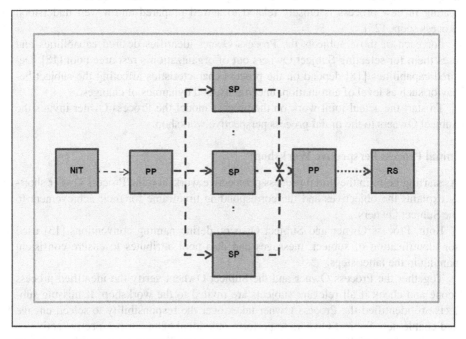

Fig. 7. From a NOT in TUNE (NiT) state to a Released Solution (RS)

Initializing

There are three possible reasons for *NOT in TUNE* (NiT) (Fig. 3) states in organiza-tions: one or more processes are obsolete, one or more processes are missing or one or more existing processes do not perform as planned, i.e. not achieving set objectives. If a process is obsolete there should be a clear process how this process is decommis-sioned [24]. We will not go into details regarding those procedures in this paper.

If a process is missing, the Manager identifies capabilities she/he expects from the owner of the new process. Desired capabilities depend on the anticipated characteris-tics of the process such as level of automation, uncertainty, and dynamics of changes. Then Manager selects the Process Owner out of the organization's resource pool [18]. Manager and Process Owner define the process scope, the expected measurable bene-fits delivered by the process, principles and policies which have to be applied during process building and execution.

If the existing process is not performing as planned the Process Owner is responsi-ble and authorized to push it back into an *In TUNE* state (Fig. 3). The Process Owner can engage Process Instance Owners to help him gathering relevant process related knowledge, mainly with respect to the weaknesses of the process and proposals how to handle them.

As preparation for the first joint work on the process perspective the Process Owner identifies subjects [13] whose internal behavior will have to be captured, improved, adapted or changed to achieve the set objectives. The identification of subjects participating in new process is closely related to a well prepared and a well understood process scope [25].

For each of those subjects the Process Owner identifies desired capabilities and uses them for selecting Subject Owners out of organization's resource pool [18]. Desired capabilities [18] depend on the process characteristics affecting the subject behavior such as level of automation, uncertainty, and dynamics of changes.

To start the actual joint work on the process model the Process Owner invites the Subject Owners to the initial process perspective workshop.

Initial Process Perspective Workshop

As starting point in the Initial process perspective workshop the Process Owner shortly explains the objectives and the corresponding timeframe for their achievement to the Subject Owners.

Both, Process Owner and Subject Owners, define naming conventions [13] used for identification of subject, messages and data-pool attributes to ensure consistent naming in the latter steps.

Together the Process Owner and the Subject Owners verify the identified process scope and check if all relevant subjects are invited to the workshop. If missing subjects are identified the Process Owner takes over the responsibility to select, engage and enable new Subject Owners to perform individual behavior perspective activities following the Initial process perspective workshop simultaneously with workshop participants [13].

The Process Owner and Subject Owners prepare a list with the names of all engaged subjects and Subject Owners.

This list is used by the Subject Owners for the identification of subjects from whom they expect or to whom they send message while creating or adjusting subject behavior diagrams.

Then the current situation is analyzed. The result is a common understanding of the gap between the set objectives and achieved results. Based on these findings each Subject Owner identifies possibilities and necessities for improvements in his subject behavior area, identifies elements being difficult to change or adapt [26] and prepares a rough estimation of the time needed for the accomplishment of these activities.

The Process Owner makes sure that the entire process is covered.

The Process Owner and Subject Owners compare, align, evaluate and synchronize prepared proposals and create a list of activities and objectives for each Subject Owner. Each Subject Owner commits to delivering agreed outcome on time.

The Process Owner can replace a Subject Owner if the agreed objectives of the workshop were not achieved. The replacement procedure is the same as the one if a missing subject is identified.

The following workshop is scheduled jointly at the end of workshop.

The Process Owner sends report to the Manager.

The Manager can replace the Process Owner if agreed objectives were not achieved.

Initial Subject Behavior Perspective Modeling

Subject behavior perspective activities are performed by Subject Owners, individually by each Subject Owner and simultaneously in terms of independent from other Subject Owners, not necessarily at the same point in time but during the same period of time, between the two workshops (Fig. 4). Subject Owners can invite Subject Instance Owners to join them at subject behavior perspective modeling meeting if their knowledge and experience is of relevance in particular case. These activities have to be finished before next process perspective workshop.

Each Subject Owner creates or adjusts his subject behavior diagram. The subject behavior diagram consists of do, send and receive actions. [27] (Fig. 8).

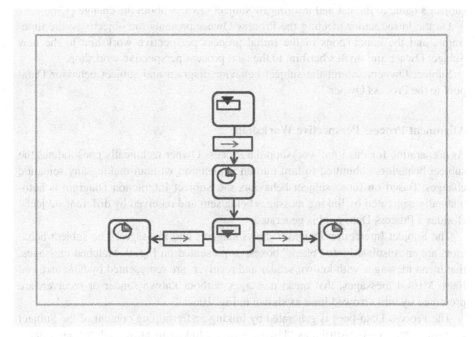

Fig. 8. Example subject behavior diagram

Actions defined in the subject behavior diagram are automatically stored into the Subject Behavior Data-pool. During the creation of the subject behavior diagram the Subject Owners collect, create and save additional subject behavior related data (attributes) such as:

- Used data
- Created data
- Used equipment (e.g. IT systems, machines, sensors, ...)

- Used knowledge
- Created knowledge
- Performance indicators (basis for identification and prediction of *NOT in TUNE* status)
- Governance requirements
- Lessons learned
- Proposals for improvements

Attributes can be related to an action or to the entire subject behavior.

If during the work on the work items a Subject Owner identifies subjects which are not on the list created on the Initial process perspective workshop she/he informs the Process Owner. Missing subjects are closely related to an imprecise definition of the process scope on Initial process perspective workshop. The Process Owner decides if the new Subject Owner will be added to the list. In the case off a positive decision the Process Owner invites the new Subject Owner to an introductory meeting, adds the subject's name to the list and informs all Subject Owners about the change [13].

On the introductory meeting the Process Owner presents the objectives, the time-frame, and the conclusions of the Initial process perspective workshop to the new Subject Owner and invites her/him to the next process perspective workshop.

Subject Owners submit the subject behavior diagram and subject behavior Data-pool to the Process Owner.

Alignment Process Perspective Workshop

As preparation for this joint workshop the Process Owner technically consolidates the subject behaviors submitted to him into an application without making any semantic changes. Based on those subject behaviors the Subject Interaction Diagram is auto-matically generated by linking messages being sent and received by different subjects. Besides a Process Data-pool is generated.

The Subject Interaction Diagram shows subjects and messages. The subject beha-viors are encapsulated into "black" boxes, as presented on Fig. 9. Matched messages, that mean messages with known sender and receiver, are represented by *bold* arrowed lines. Missed messages, that mean messages without known sender or receiver, are presented by thin arrowed lines as shown in Fig. 10.

The Process Data-pool is generated by linking and grouping content of the Subject Behavior Data-pools. Attributes "Used data" are linked to attributed "Created data" (data flow), "Used knowledge" to "Created knowledge" (knowledge flow). Subjects using the same equipment, having the same governance requirements or the same performance indicators are grouped. Proposals for improvements and lessons learned are aligned.

The Process Owner presents the Subject Interaction Diagram and the Process Data-pool to the workshop participants.

At his point in time all Subject Owners are able for the first time to see the process logic "ground truth" created out of their subject behaviors. Result might differ sub-stantially from their expectations.

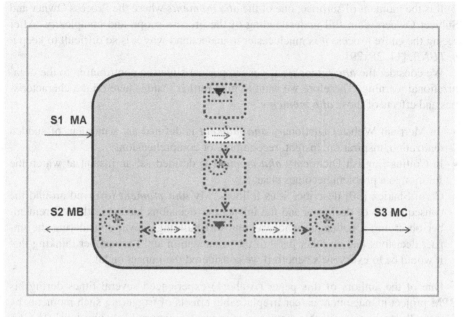

Fig. 9. Encapsulation principle (S = subject, M = message)

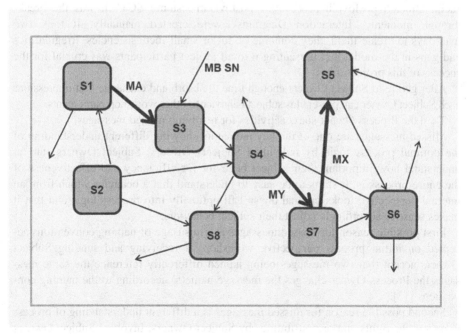

Fig. 10. Subject Interaction Diagram (incomplete)

It is the moment of surprise, one of the *aha moments* where the Process Owner and Subject Owners gain full understanding of the process scope and complexity. After seeing the entire process it is much easier to understand why it is so difficult to keep it *in TUNE*. [11, 28, 29]

We consider the *aha moments* as very important situation contributing to the organizational learning. Therefore we want to give further insides here on the characteristics and effects of those *aha moments*.

- In Merriam Webster Dictionary *aha moment* is defined as; a moment of sudden realization, inspiration, insight, recognition, or comprehension.
- In Collins English Dictionary *aha moment* is defined as; an instant at which the solution to a problem becomes clear.
- Carol Sharicz [30] describes it as follows "My *aha moment* revolved around the consequences of decisions and the impact our decisions have on others. I remember observing a colleague who was into turf-building...never considering the impact decisions had on other parts of the organization and I remember thinking that it would be to everyone's benefit if we considered the impact on all."

One of the authors of this paper (Author1) experienced several times during his BPM project management career irreplaceable effects of triggering such moments by perpetually exchanging of the context from process to internal behavior level (Fig. 6), and the working practice from collaborative to individual (Fig. 7) which are two key features of the TicTacTuned method. In the BPM project "Racionalizacija in optimizacija ključnih poslovnih procesov v poslovnem sistemu SCT" it was the breakthrough moment. "Interaction Diagrams" were created manually. It took two man-days to create them, they contained a lot of small inconsistencies, irregularities and gaps in the model, but presenting it to all project participants was crucial for the success of this project.

After giving to Subject Owners enough time to absorb and exchange first impressions each Subject Owner can present his subject behavior to other workshop participants.

Then the Process Owner starts activities for resolving missed messages.

Missed messages are one of the key indicators showing different understanding of the optimal process logic by individual Subjects Owners. Subject Owners start to understand how important their subject behavior for efficiency and effectiveness of the entire process is. It starts to be easy to understand that a behavior which from an internal perspective looks optimal doesn't fit optimally into process logic and that it makes sense to accordingly adjust their subject behaviors.

First possible reason for missed messages is a misusage of naming conventions accepted on initial process perspective workshop. If receiving and sending Subject Owners accept that two messages being named differently reference the same messages the Process Owner changes the message name(s) according to the naming conventions [13].

Second possible reason for missed messages is a different understanding of process logic and the rights and responsibilities by Subject Owners. Involved Subject Owners analyze the reasons for mismatch and try to find a solution. If the sending Subject Owner agrees not to send the message and accordingly adapt his subject behavior or the receiving Subject Owner agrees to accept message and accordingly adapt his subject behavior, the Process Owner keeps hold of this agreement in the workshop minutes.

If the missed message receiving and sending Subject Owners can't agree how to solve the problem, the Process Owner has the authority to impose solution: the sending subject will not send the message or that the receiving subject has to accept it. The Process Owner keeps hold of this decision in the workshop minutes,

Despite of eventual missed messages the Subject Interaction Diagram and Process Data-pool enable apprehensive analysis of the soundness and completeness of process logic. Special attention is given to identification, overlaps of actions, grey zones, loops and bottlenecks. Subject Owners analyze data flows and efficiency and effectiveness with respect to the usage of equipment, fulfillment of governance requirements, relationships between performance indicators, proposed improvements and lessons learned.

Each Subject Owner has to present to the other workshop participants his evaluation of process logic and has to create proposals for improvements.

The Process Owner makes sure that all proposals are consolidated and aligned.

The following workshop is scheduled jointly at the end of this first workshop.

The Process Owner sends the report to the Manager.

Subject Behavior Perspective Adjustments

Based on the outcome of the Alignment process perspective workshop Subject Owners adjusts their subject behavior diagram and Subject Behavior Data-pool. They reevaluate the effects of changes they make and document findings and proposals into Subject Behavior Data-pool. Subject Owners can invite Subject Instance Owners to join them at subject behavior perspective adjustment meeting if their knowledge and experience is of relevance in particular case. Subject behavior adjustment activities have to be finished before next process perspective workshop.

Subject Owners submit the subject behavior diagram and Subject Behavior Data-pool to the Process Owner.

Release Process Perspective Workshop

As preparation for this workshop the Process Owner again technically consolidates the received inputs from the Subject Owners into an application and generates a Subject Interaction Diagram and Process Data-pools.

The Process Owner and the Subject Owners see and evaluate improved process logic created out of their inputs. Result still might differ from their or Process Manager's expectations and agreements, but not substantially. There should not be any missed messages left, as shown in Fig. 11. There should not be any overlaps of actions, grey zones, unnecessary loops and bottlenecks. There should not be any breaks in data and knowledge flow. Equipment should be used efficiently, performance indicators should be aligned, governance requirements and proposals for improvements should be implemented.

The Process Owner decides if proposed solution is good enough to be releases (RS on Fig. 6 and Fig. 7).

If yes, process is officially released and ready for implementation. Process Owner and Subject Owners prepare lesson learned report.

If not, the work is further carried out as an alignment process perspective work-shop.

The Process Owner sends the report to the Manager.

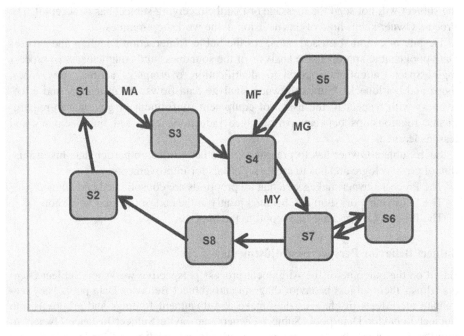

Fig. 11. Final Subject Interaction Diagram without missed messages

Options

In certain situations subject behavior activities can be supported by collaborative modeling features, that means Subject Owners can exchange info and messages while modeling. In this case the effect of *aha moment* is substantially reduced. Too early disclosure of partitioned expectations and requirements of other subjects in different stages of development of their subject behavior diagrams raises the risk that the Subject Owners will not have enough time to relay on their own knowledge and experience and that decisions they will make will not be autonomous but will be too soon influenced by other Subject Owners, without sound reason.

2.3   Process Model

The necessary activities described in the earlier parts of this section can of course be represented as a S-BPM model, too. Fig. 12 gives a first impression of a possible subject interaction diagram for three involved subjects. Further details are omitted here for space reasons.

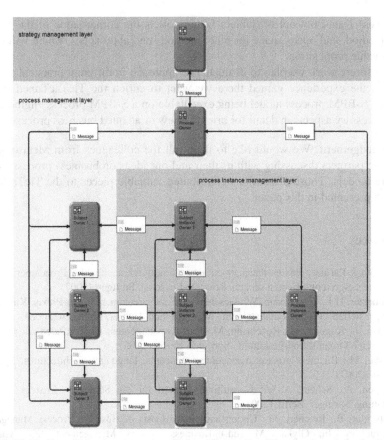

Fig. 12. TicTacTuned based meta-process Subject Interaction Diagram (example: 3 subjects)

3   Conclusion and Outlook

In this paper we have introduced the TicTacTuned method as S-BPM based, objectives-driven, performance-oriented way of building, validating and improving processes in organization. The method is focused on the employees with the intention to raise their inspiration and motivation, to empower them to manage parts of the business processes on their own and to share the responsibility for process performance, to mitigate fear and reluctance towards change and to encourage creation and sharing of knowledge.

In this paper we're y focusing on the activities that need to be carried out by BPM role holders, their collaboration and key features of BPM suite supporting TicTac-Tuned method. Main matters under consideration are objectives, subjects, employees, roles, subject behavior, automatic generation of process model, automatic subject behavior data integration, and process logic optimization. The handling of necessary data structures and IT systems is only touched but not fully elaborated. The automatic generation of the Subject Interaction Diagram out of the subject behavior diagrams and Process Data-Pool out of Subject Data-pools is the corner stone of the TicTac-Tuned method, and opens space for other methods and approaches, which will enrich S-BPM value proposition.

In our future work we plan to evaluate our approach in different practical settings. Based on the experience gained there we want to enrich the TicTacTuned method towards a S-BPM process model being executable on a S-BPM process engine covering all necessary aspects in detail for bringing new or adapted business processes live.

Acknowledgement. We would like to thank all the colleagues from Metasonic and Metasonic partners discussing with us their and our ideas on business process modeling meta-models. Those discussions contributed valuable pieces to the TicTacTuned approach presented in this paper.

References

1. Horváth & Partner.: Prozessmanagement umsetzen: durch nachhaltige Prozessperformance Umsatz steigern und Kosten senken. Schäffer-Poeschel, Stuttgart (2007)
2. Schmelzer, H.J., Sesselmann, W.: Geschäftsprozessmanagement in der Praxis: Kunden zufrieden stellen - Produktivität steigern - Wert erhöhen. Hanser, München (2008)
3. Becker, J., Kugeler, M., Rosemann, M.: Prozessmanagement ein Leitfaden zur prozessorientierten Organisationsgestaltung. Springer, Berlin (2005)
4. Weske, M.: Business process management concepts, languages, architectures. Springer, Berlin (2007)
5. Köppen, A., Scheer, A.-W.: Consulting: Wissen für die Strategie-, Prozess- und IT-Beratung. Springer, Berlin (2001)
6. Mutschler, B., Reichert, M.: Understanding the Costs of Business Process Management Technology. In: Glykas, M. (ed.) Business Process Management. SCI, vol. 444, pp. 157–194. Springer, Heidelberg (2013)
7. Wohland, G., Wiemeyer, M.: Denkwerkzeuge der Höchstleister wie dynamikrobuste Unternehmen Marktdruck erzeugen. Murmann, Hamburg (2007)
8. Mutschler, B.: Modeling and Simulating Causal Dependencies on Process-aware Information Systems from a Cost Perspective (2008), http://dbis.eprints.uni-ulm.de/684/
9. Herzberg, F.: One more time: How do you motivate employees. Harvard Business Review (1968)
10. Mohr, L.B.: Determinants of Innovation in Organizations. Am. Polit. Sci. Rev. 63, 111–126 (1969)
11. Grusenmeyer, D.: Developing Effective Standard Operating Procedures, http://www.ansci.cornell.edu/pdfs/sopsdir.pdf
12. Bandara, W., Gable, G.G., Rosemann, M.: Critical success factors of business process modeling (2007)
13. Bruno, G., Dengler, F., Jennings, B., Khalaf, R., Nurcan, S., Prilla, M., Sarini, M., Schmidt, R., Silva, R.: Key challenges for enabling agile BPM with social software. J. Softw. Maint. Evol. Res. Pr. 23, 297–326 (2011)
14. Erol, S., Granitzer, M., Happ, S., Jantunen, S., Jennings, B., Johannesson, P., Koschmider, A., Nurcan, S., Rossi, D., Schmidt, R.: Combining BPM and social software: contradiction or chance? J. Softw. Maint. Evol. Res. Pr. 22, 449–476 (2010)

15. Jones, G.: Testing two cognitive theories of insight. J. Exp. Psychol. Learn. Mem. Cogn. 29, 1017–1027 (2003)
16. Fleischmann, A., Schmidt, W., Stary, C., Obermeier, S., Börger, E.: Subjektorientiertes Prozessmanagement: Mitarbeiter einbinden, Motivation und Prozessakzeptanz steigern. Carl Hanser Verlag GmbH & CO., KG (2011)
17. Fleischmann, A., Schmidt, W., Stary, C., Obermeier, S., Börger, E.: Subject-Oriented Business Process Management - an Open Access book (2012)
18. Cummins, F., De Man, H., Allee, V., Berre, A.J.: Value Delivery Modeling Language, VDML (2012)
19. vom Brocke, J., Rosemann, M.: Handbook on Business Process Management 2 - Strategic Alignment, Governance, People and Culture. Springer, Heidelberg (2010)
20. Franz, P., Kirchmer, M.: Value-Driven Business Process Management. Mcgraw-Hill Professional, New York (2012)
21. Bucur, O., Beaune, P., Boissier, O.: Knowledge Sharing on How to Recognize and Use Context to Make Decisions. In: International Workshop on Context Modeling for Decision Support Context 2005. CEUR-WS. Alexandre Gachet, Paris (2005)
22. Turban, E., Aronson, J.E.: Decision Support Systems and Intelligent Systems. Prentice Hall (2000)
23. Salonen, E.: A designer's guide to collaboration (2013), http://www.designingcollaboration.com/
24. Palachuk, K.W.: SOP Friday: When Policies and Procedures Become Obsolete (2013), http://blog.smallbizthoughts.com/2013/02/sop-friday-when-policies-and-procedures.html
25. Helm, F.: Participants and processes. University of Padova (2012)
26. Gall, N.: Best Practices for Business Process Modeling: Model for Change. Gartner Inc. (2013)
27. Fleischmann, A., Schmidt, W., Stary, C., Obermeier, S., Börger, E.: Modeling Processes in a Subject-Oriented Way. In: Subject-Oriented Business Process Management, pp. 63–127. Springer, Heidelberg (2012)
28. Maroney, J.: Employee Motivation - The 5 Master Keys for Success (2004), http://www.jpmaroney.com/Free-Articles/employee-motivation.htm
29. Kotelnikov, V.: Resistance to Change - Understanding and Overcoming Human and Organizational Barriers, http://www.1000ventures.com/business_guide/crosscuttings/change_resistance.html
30. Sharicz, C.: Systems Thinking Aha Moments, http://www.systemswiki.org/index.php?title=Systems_Thinking_Aha_Moments#Carol_Sharicz

An Interactional View of Context in Business Processes

Udo Kannengiesser[1], Alexandra Totter[2], and David Bonaldi[2]

[1] Metasonic AG
Münchner Straße 29 – Hettenshausen, 85276 Pfaffenhofen, Germany
Udo.Kannengiesser@metasonic.de
[2] ByElement GmbH
Chaltenbodenstraße 4, 8834 Schindellegi, Switzerland
{totter,bonaldi}@byelement.com

Abstract. Incorporating context in business process descriptions has found increasing interest in the business process management (BPM) community. Most approaches are based on a notion of context as a static representation of relevant aspects of a process. This paper proposes that an understanding of context as a process that generates subjective views of context is more beneficial for business process applications. The paper develops a subject-oriented model for the alignment of the individual contextual views of workers and business process experts, as the basis of a framework for developing methods and tools for interactional context.

Keywords: Context, Business Process Management.

1 Introduction

Business process modelling is concerned with generating abstract representations of planned or existing operations within a business domain. The resulting process models typically include descriptions of tasks, the sequencing of tasks, the resources required, and the data objects created and consumed [1]. They allow performing most activities in the life cycle of business processes, such as design, analysis and optimisation. The abstract nature of process models assists many business process analysts in developing a clear view of the essential properties of a process without being obstructed by specific details. On the other hand, the applicability of process models to specific organisations, users or business situations requires additional information that is often referred to as context. Context can be described generally as "the circumstances that form the setting for an event, statement, or idea, and in terms of which it can be fully understood" (*Oxford Dictionaries Online*). In business process management (BPM), the notion of context has been defined and categorised in several ways [2-4]. Most approaches argue that context is the driver for changes in the design and execution of business processes and that the arising need for process flexibility must be addressed by making business processes context-aware [2]. The motivation underpinning the existing body of research is the goal to manage business processes more effectively and efficiently.

C. Zehbold (Ed.): S-BPM ONE 2014, CCIS 422, pp. 42–54, 2014.

This paper aims to augment the business perspective of context with a people-centred one. It is based on the recognition that a necessary factor for realising any business process, including business process changes, is the human being involved in executing the process. Any model constructed of a particular context, even if it includes detailed characteristics of the process participant, must be consistent with the subjective view of the context that the individual participant interacts with. Questions relating to the ways in which subjective context models can be captured and aligned with objective models of processes (and context) form a research agenda that will be discussed in this paper. Section 2 presents an overview of related work in context-aware business processes and explores the different notions and classifications of context developed to date. Section 3 introduces subject-oriented modelling as a basis for an interactional view of context that is presented in Section 4. Section 4 formulates an initial framework for studying interactional context Section 5 concludes the paper with short discussion.

2   Views of Context

The notion of context has been the object of scientific investigation both in terms of its basic nature and in terms of its application to a multitude of domains. In the last few years the notion of context has slowly become an important source of information in the computing environment [5], for ubiquitous computing [6] as well as for business processes [4, 7, 8]. On the other hand, there is still a lot of controversy based on the heterogeneous nature of context and the context-dependence of the concept itself [9-12], making it almost impossible for the scientific community to agree on a single definition or a unanimously accepted theoretical perspective. Frequently, only few aspects of context are described, modelled or formalized. To get a better understanding of the different views of context for business processes, we conducted a literature review to summarize the accumulated state of knowledge concerning the topic and to highlight important issues that research has left unresolved.

Most research in introducing context into business processes is driven by the need to make business processes more flexible, agile and adaptable [2, 3, 7, 8, 13, 14] and to improve real time handling of process-related issues [14] in the physical world [7]. Specifically, context (and knowledge about the context) is used for achieving a number of goals:

- to identify extrinsic drivers for process flexibility [2, 8],
- to control the flow between activities [7],
- to adapt the execution of the instances to the change and to the stakeholders' requirements . The notion of context covers any circumstances that impacts assignment relations [3],
- to dynamically integrate knowledge and workflow processes by supporting the real-time handling of both the current context of a process and its execution path for knowledge intensive tasks [14],
- to facilitate dealing with contingencies in the business environment and to continuously improve process performance.

With respect to the definition of context, most authors refer to the ones proposed by Dey [5] and Roseman and Recker [2]. Dey [5] introduces a definition for application developers to specify the context for a given application: *"Context is any information that can be used to characterize the situation of an entity. An entity is a person, place, or object that is considered relevant to the interaction between a user and an application, including the user and applications themselves."* Furthermore, he provides a definition of context-aware computing: *"A system is context-aware if it uses context to provide relevant information and/or services to the user, where relevancy depends on the user's task"* (p. 5). Rosemann and Recker [2] apply Dey's view of context to the domain of business processes, defining it as *"the minimum set of variables containing all relevant information that impact the design and execution of a business process"* (p. 154). Saidani & Nurcan [3] provide a further definition of context as *"... the collection of implicit assumptions that is required to activate accurate assignments in the BP model at the process instance level"*.

A summary of existing approaches and methods for identifying, analysing and modelling context in business processes as well as dimensions of context is shown in Table 1. It indicates that most approaches are based on the notion of context as a representational problem [12, 15, 16] that can be characterised using the following statements [12]:

- Context is a form of information that can be encoded and represented.
- Context is delineable, as it can be pre-defined for specific applications.
- Context is stable. The variables that represent the context do not change across different instances of activities or events.
- Context is separable from activity. Information about the context can be captured independently of the action that generated it.

In addition to the understanding of *context-as-representation* (or context as state), Dourish and others [6, 9, 12, 14-16] propose the notion of context as an interactional problem (*context-as-interaction* or context as process) with the following characteristics:

- Context is a relational property that holds between objects or activities. Something may or may not be contextually relevant to a particular activity at a given time.
- Context cannot be delineated and defined in advance. The scope of contextual features is constantly (re-)defined dynamically.
- Context is an occasioned property. It is relevant to particular settings, instances of action and parties involved in that action.
- Context arises from the activity. It is actively produced, maintained and enacted. Context is a process and has a history.

Table 1. Approaches for identifying and analysing context, and dimensions of context in business processes

Authors and approaches	Dimensions of context
Rosemann & Recker [2] Context-aware process design approach 1) Context description 2) Design for context 3) Process adaptation	Time; location; legislation; culture; performance requirements
Wieland, et al. [7] *Context data* sensed via RFID tags mounted to tools, Ubisense tags carried by transport carts / workers. *Context event* defined by event description language, registered at context management platform for observation. *Context query* used to get position of worker, spare part, state of machine. Objects of interest are queried at context management platform, injected into internal workflow data. *Context decision* allows process to route process control flow based on context data using context-aware operators.	*Geographical* context (map data); dynamic context (sensor data); *information* context (documents and virtual information); *technical* context (sensors, networks, devices, etc.)
Saidani & Nurcan [3] Context model uses i) Three-dimensional space to describe context related knowledge: S = <ASPECTS, FACETS, ATTRIBUTES> CONTEXT is captured using ASPECTS which are non-functional features; each of them is addressed by some FACETS. FACETS are described by ATTRIBUTES. ATTRIBUTES have features that are directly measurable. ii) Context tree is a three-level tree which root represents global context, nodes at first level refer to ASPECTS, nodes at second level refer to FACETS, leaves at third level refer to ATTRIBUTES.	*Time* (performing time, urgency, frequency, saving of time); location (physical location); *resources* (material & human resource properties, some in relation with work); *organisation* (workplace characteristics)
Heravizadeh & Edmond [14] Context relevance space 1) Identifying issues 2) Identifying context attributes for an issue 3) Defining context attributes 4) Establish conditions over context attributes 5) Reasoning with respect to an issue 6) A set of possible solutions (that is, ways of rectifying the issue).	*Resource-oriented context* (whatever resource are involved); *method-oriented context* (way a task is being executed & time taken to perform task); *environment-oriented context* (conditions applied outside process at the time a task was being carried out)
Rosemann, et al. [8] Procedure for context identification 1) Identify Process goals (hard & soft-goals related to given process & their appropriate measures) 2) Decompose process 3) Determine relevance of context (goal-relevant, extrinsic information on achievement of goal) 4) Identify contextual elements and their interrelations 5) Type context (with the help of the onion model)	Immediate context; internal context, external context; environmental context
Ploesser, et al. [13] Context-aware process management cycle 1) Context mining & learning 2) Context modelling 3) Context taxonomies for industries 4) Context-aware process operations	Variables driving *context-dependent process change* (weather, time, location, resource prices, business partners, strategies, macroeconomic factors); *case context* (properties of customer, asset, purchase order, location)
de la Vara, et al. [4] Context analysis 1) Modelling of initial business process 2) Analysis of business process context 3) Analysis of context variants 4) Modelling of contextualised business process	Context specified as formula of *world predicates*, which can be combined conjunctively & disjunctively; world predicates can be *facts* (verified by a process participant) or *statements* (cannot be verified).

Applying this *context-as-interaction* perspective to business processes would allow making them more adaptive compared to approaches based on static, pre-defined context representations. Such an interaction-based context would directly emerge from the real-time environment in which a process takes place and consider the local interactions and experiences of individual actors within the process. This would enhance the acceptance of business processes among business actors as the processes can be tailored to their individual needs and subjective perceptions of the current process environment. On the long run it would allow contextual business process modelling as a task that can only be achieved when business process experts work together with employees or workers on creating processes and process environments.

Based on the *context-as-interaction* perspective, we define *interactional context* as a process that generates subjective views of a workplace. The workplace is the environment with which a process participant interacts; it can include the techno-physical environment (tools, business objects, physical layout, etc.) and the socio-cultural environment (values, norms, organisational structures, etc.).

Business process "experts" have their own subjective views of what constitutes the context of a particular process, work environment and workplace. However, as they are not personally immersed in business processes and thus do not have first-hand knowledge of the intricacies of daily work routines; their view of a human actor's (i.e.; worker's) context is typically limited. These limitations do not so much concern the major categories or dimensions of context (according to Johns [11] major categories can also be understood as "omnibus context", or representational context); they are more related to the coverage and granularity of contextual parameters within every dimension (with reference to Johns [11] these can be named as "discrete context" or interactional context). The divergence between the process expert's and the worker's views of the business process context is shown conceptually in Fig. 1.

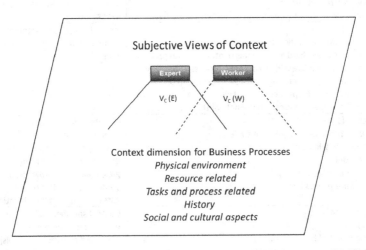

Fig. 1. Different views of context: contextual view constructed by the expert ($V_C(E)$) and contextual view constructed by the worker ($V_C(W)$)

The overlap (or intersection) of the two views in Fig. 1 represents an inter-subjective agreement on the context relevant for both experts and workers, which is the precondition for any representation of context to be applicable in the real world. Inconsistencies of the contextual views with business goals or people-centred goals require their alignment through direct communication between business process experts and workers, and/or through changing the process. This mechanism for contextual view alignment forms the basis of a framework of interactional context that can be represented using subject-oriented modelling.

3   Subject-Oriented Modelling

Subject-oriented business process management (S-BPM) [17] is based on a view of business processes as emerging from the interactions and local behaviours of human actors (i.e. process participants). S-BPM provides a small set of simple building blocks for modelling processes, derived from natural language. The building blocks include subjects (denoting actors), predicates (denoting activities including sending and receiving messages, and performing local tasks), and objects (denoting messages and business objects). The notational simplicity and the natural-language structure of S-BPM afford easy modelling of processes from a first-person view, one that can be easily understood and generated by the process participants themselves.

Figure 2 shows a meta-model consisting of the basic modelling constructs of S-BPM and their connection with actors [18]. A set of subjects compose a business process. They execute actions, captured as predicates, operating on objects. Subjects can execute three different types of actions: Sending messages to other subjects, receiving messages from other subjects and performing local actions on business objects. Business objects can be transported via messages from the sending subject to the receiving subject. Subjects are connected to actors via their roles within an organization or group.

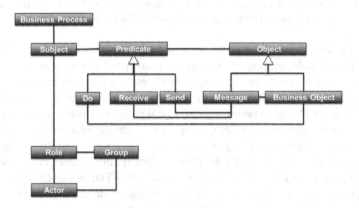

Fig. 2. Meta-model of S-BPM (adapted from Fleischmann, et al. [18])

S-BPM models use two types of diagrams: Subject Interaction Diagrams (SID) specifying the messages exchanged between subjects, and Subject Behaviour Diagrams (SBD) specifying the behaviours of subjects including "receive" and "send" actions operating on messages, and "do" actions operating on business objects. Examples of a SID and a SBD are shown in Fig. 3 and Fig. 4, respectively. Details of the notational elements used can be found in Fleischmann et al. [17].

Fig. 3. Subject Interaction Diagram (SID) showing the communication between subjects

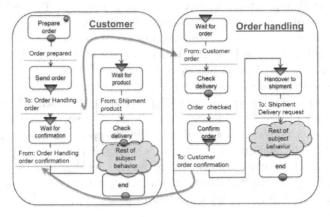

Fig. 4. Subject Behaviour Diagram (SBD) showing the individual behaviours of the "Customer" subject and the "Order handling" subject. Pairs of corresponding "send" and "receive" actions are highlighted using double-headed arrows (not part of the S-BPM notation)

One of the key features of S-BPM is the separation between subjects and roles, as shown in Fig. 2. Roles correspond to organisational positions such as workers, managers, administrative staff, and external consultants. Subjects, in contrast, represent process-specific functionalities that are conceptually independent of the organisational resources deployed to perform them. The separation between subjects and roles allows varying the particular implementation and execution of a process using different roles (and different actors or groups of actors associated with these roles). Take the example of the subject "Order handling": Usually, this subject may be executed by an employee having an "administrative staff" role. Yet, in the case that none of these employees is available (due to holidays, illness or strike), a "worker" or "manager" role may temporarily be assigned to this subject.

4   A Subject-Oriented Model of Interactional Context in Business Processes

Using the S-BPM modelling approach, we can describe the alignment of contextual views with a Subject Interaction Diagram as shown in the SID in Fig. 5. It includes three subjects:

Workplace Designer: develops and introduces formal changes to a workplace to achieve a set of process goals.

Workplace Adopter: uses the designed workplace to perform the work to be done.

Workplace: makes a set of physical and conceptual entities available for interpretation and interaction.

In this process, the subject "Workplace Designer" performs design actions (i.e., actions oriented to designing a workplace) to change the work environment encapsulated in the subject "Workplace". For example, a production manager may rearrange shopfloor operations to include a new production process with a new set of tools, machines, work instructions etc. The current state of this environment is made available to the subjects "Workplace Designer" and "Workplace Adopter". The Workplace Adopter uses this information to construct a subjective view of the workplace, which, in turn, informs further interactions with the workplace by means of use actions (i.e., actions oriented to using a designed workplace). In the production example, the workers construct their individual views and understanding of the changed production process. They interact with the process by executing the process steps, using the tools and machines provided. Feedback regarding the workplace design can be communicated to the Workplace Designer, who, in turn, notifies the Workplace Adopter of workplace design decisions.

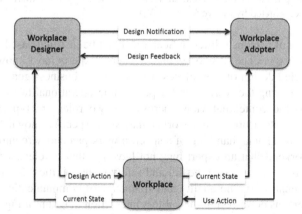

Fig. 5. The process of aligning different views of a workplace represented using a Subject Interaction Diagram (SID)

Different roles may be associated with the subjects in this process. Specifically, two distinct roles are commonly associated with the subjects "Workplace Designer" and "Workplace Adopter":

Expert: is a role that subsumes a set of activities related to specifying business processes. The expert role may be played by managers within an organisation or by external consultants.

Worker: is a role that subsumes a set of activities related to executing business processes. The worker role is played by people directly performing the operations within the business process.

Most organisations use experts as workplace designers and workers as workplace adopters, as illustrated in the production example above. This assignment of roles to subjects is shown as "Scenario 1" on the left-hand side of Fig. 6.

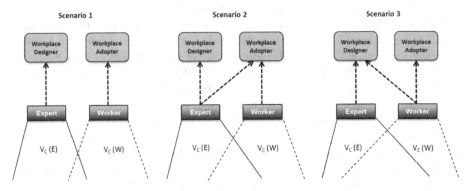

Fig. 6. Three scenarios based on assigning different roles to subjects, with different consequences for the alignment of the contextual view constructed by the expert ($V_C(E)$) and the contextual view constructed by the worker ($V_C(W)$)

The separation of responsibilities in Scenario 1 can be justified based on the different training and experience of experts and workers. Experts have knowledge in the formal analysis and design of workplaces with respect to business goals, while workers are trained in using the workplace for performing operational tasks. However, in such a scenario the contextual views across the two roles are typically not well aligned. For example, a production worker may have specific knowledge about the workplace (e.g. the manual handling of a specific work piece may require high physical effort by workers) that an expert may not have but that is relevant for achieving certain process requirements (e.g. health and safety goals). Critical for aiding context alignment in Scenario 1 is the quality and frequency of communication between experts and workers, as described in the subject interaction diagram in Fig. 5. Establishing a systematic information exchange between them, in regular intervals, may lead to a more people-centred process of workplace design and an increased contextual view alignment.

Another scenario, labelled "Scenario 2" in Fig. 6, can be seen as an extension of "Scenario 1" in that the Workplace Adopter is now associated not only with the worker but also with the expert. Here, experts *"put themselves in the shoes"* of workers, e.g. by following the workers going about their work or even by executing some of the workers' tasks. Immersing themselves in the same work environment as the workers allows the experts to gain direct experience of the effects of different workplace designs (e.g. the high physical effort involved in handling a work piece) and thus to enhance contextual view alignment with the workers for improved workplace design (e.g. automated handling of work pieces). This technique is more generally known as empathic design [19].

A third scenario, labelled "Scenario 3" in Fig. 6, expands the responsibility of workers to include not just workplace adoption but also workplace design. While there may still be an expert assigned to the Workplace Designer to assist in developing finer-grained details of design decisions, workers can autonomously change workplace designs to better suit their individual needs. This is similar to approaches such as mass customisation that defer some design decisions to the user of a design [20]. The contextual views tend to be well aligned in this scenario based on the close fit between the designed workplace and its adopter. In the production example, the worker may develop own ideas to improve work piece handling, such as modifying the order of assembling the work piece to produce sub-assemblies with reduced physical weight.

We believe that empowering workers to take an active role in workplace design is a first step towards integrating *context-as-interaction* into business processes (see also Section 2). Empowerment refers to a form of employee involvement initiative focussing on task-based involvement and attitudinal change [21, 22]. Workers have the first-hand knowledge necessary to decide which contextual aspects are relevant to a particular activity at a given time. They know about the setting, instances of actions and parties involved in a particular activity.

Experts in their role as workplace designers can provide a frame of reference in terms of representational context. They may suggest which information might count as context based on their own contextual views and provide a system for encoding and representing this information. But for context to have a real impact on making business processes more flexible and efficient, this information must be confirmed in an interactional way based on the real-life experience of the workers. Traditional approaches of business process modelling support the separation of responsibilities according to "Scenario 1". To enable "Scenario 2" and "Scenario 3" one has to enter new territory. Our proposed framework can be seen as a set of practices to support structural as well as psychological empowerment at work [22]. With its subject-oriented model of interactional context in business processes, it is a first step into this direction as outlined in this Section. It supports structural empowerment at work enabling participative decision making with respect to changes in the work process. Furthermore it opens the upward flow of information for improvement ideas as well as enables employees to build knowledge, skills and abilities. Giving employees the possibility to take initiative empowers them also in terms of competence to perform work activities using their skills. Additionally workers can improve their self-determination in initiating and regulating their actions and impact, being able to influence e.g. operating outcomes at work, which also addresses dimensions of psychological empowerment.

5   Discussion

Developing a common understanding of what is and what constitutes context has been a difficult endeavour for researchers across various IT domains. The brief overview of related work in this paper indicates that differences in understanding and representing context also prevail within the business process management community. Yet, what most current approaches have in common is the *context-as-representation* perspective: Context is viewed as a static, pre-definable set of aspects that can be represented independently of its use. This understanding of context has only limited potential to be useful for process applications beyond standardised and highly automated operations. When human workers are involved having their own views of context, discrepancies with the process expert may occur that can undermine the acceptance of processes and lead to decreased motivation and work performance. The idea of *context-as-interaction* as proposed by Dourish [12] and others can augment current approaches by providing a process through which both process experts and workers can align their individual views of context.

This paper proposes a framework for this idea, formalised using a subject-oriented model. It allows describing different scenarios based on assigning experts and workers to either workplace designers or workplace adopters. Each of these scenarios has different effects on the expected alignment of individual contextual views. Of particular interest are the scenarios in which experts are assigned to workplace adoption and workers are assigned to workplace design, as they depart from the traditional, isolated role assignments and can strongly enhance contextual view alignment. Theoretical groundwork for these scenarios is provided by existing work in design science (such as empathic design [19] and user innovation [20]), organisational behaviour, and job design. These approaches may be used as conceptual input for developing new techniques supporting the alignment of context in business processes. Our preliminary investigations in this area concentrate on tools supporting the workers to act as workplace designers. These tools

- increase the awareness and reflection of workers on their workplace through using sensor technology and psychological methods of job design,
- raise issues concerning different workplace designs through the use of contextual design tools to capture interactional context information and providing a platform for real-time postings, and
- facilitate the empowerment of workers as workplace designers based on S-BPM as a simple and intuitive modelling notation.

The development of these tools and two case studies for the implementation and evaluation are part of an on-going European research project on people-centred production workplaces (www.so-pc-pro.eu).

Acknowledgments. The research leading to these results has received funding from the European Union Seventh Framework Programme FP7-2013-NMP-ICT-FOF(RTD) under grant agreement n° 609190.

References

1. Curtis, B., Kellner, M.I., Over, J.: Process Modeling. Communications of the ACM 35, 75–90 (1992)
2. Rosemann, M., Recker, J.: Context-aware Process Design: Exploring the Extrinsic Drivers for Process Flexibility. In: 18th International Conference on Advanced Information Systems Enginnering, Proceedings of Workshops and Doctoral Consortium (2006)
3. Saidani, O., Nurcan, S.: Towards context aware business process modelling. In: 8th Workshop on Business Process Modeling, Development, and Support (BPMDS 2007), Electronic Ressource (2007)
4. de la Vara, J.L., Ali, R., Dalpiaz, F., Sánchez, J., Giorgini, P.: Business Process Contextualisation via Context Analysis. In: Parsons, J., Saeki, M., Shoval, P., Woo, C., Wand, Y. (eds.) ER 2010. LNCS, vol. 6412, pp. 471–476. Springer, Heidelberg (2010)
5. Dey, A.K.: Understanding and Using Context. Personal Ubiquitous Computing 5(1), 4–7 (2001)
6. Coutaz, J., et al.: Context is key. Communications of the ACM 48(3), 49–53 (2005)
7. Wieland, M., et al.: Towards context-aware workflows. In: CAiSE (2007)
8. Rosemann, M., Recker, J.C., Flender, C.: Contextualisation of business processes. International Journal of Business Process Integration and Management 3(1), 47–60 (2008)
9. Chalmers, M.: A historical view of context. Computer Supported Cooperative Work (CSCW) 13(3-4), 223–247 (2004)
10. Fetzer, A. (ed.): Context and appropriateness: micro meets macro. Pragmatics & Beyond New Series. John Benjamins, Amsterdam (2007); Jucker, A.H. (ed.)
11. Johns, G.: The Essential Impact of Context on Organizational Behavior. Academy of Managment Review 31(2), 386–408 (2006)
12. Dourish, P.: What we talk about when we talk about context. Personal Ubiquitous Comput. 8(1), 19–30 (2004)
13. Ploesser, K., et al.: Learning from Context to Improve Business Processes. BP Trends 6(1), 1–7 (2009)
14. Heravizadeh, M., Edmond, D.: Making workflows context-aware: a way to support knowledge-intensive tasks. In: Proceedings of the Fifth Asia-Pacific Conference on Conceptual Modelling, vol. 79, pp. 79–88. Australian Computer Society, Inc., Wollongong (2008)
15. Pérez, E., Fortier, A., Rossi, G., Gordillo, S.: Rethinking context models. In: Meersman, R., Herrero, P., Dillon, T. (eds.) OTM 2009 Workshops. LNCS, vol. 5872, pp. 78–87. Springer, Heidelberg (2009)
16. Oulasvirta, A., Tamminen, S., Höök, K.: Comparing two approaches to context: realism and constructivism. In: Proceedings of the 4th Decennial Conference on Critical Computing: Between Sense and Sensibility. ACM (2005)
17. Fleischmann, A., et al.: Subject-Oriented Business Process Management. Springer, Berlin (2012)

18. Fleischmann, A., et al.: Subject-Oriented Modeling and Execution of Multi-Agent Business Processes. In: International Conference on Intelligent Agent Technology, Atlanta, GA (in press)
19. Kouprie, M., Visser, F.S.: A Framework for Empathy in Design: Stepping into and out of the User's Life. Journal of Engineering Design 20(5), 437–448 (2009)
20. Von Hippel, E., Katz, R.: Shifting Innovation to Users via Toolkits. Management Science 48, 821–833 (2002)
21. Wilkinson, A.: Empowerment: theory and practice. Personnel Review 27(1), 40–56 (1998)
22. Spreitzer, G.: Toward the integration of two perspectives: A review of social-structural and psychological empowerment at work. In: Cooper, C., Barling, J. (eds.) The Handbook of Organizational Behavior. Sage Publications, Thousand Oaks (2007)

Exploration of a Method for COSMIC Size Estimation from S-BPM

Murat Salmanoğlu[1], Onur Demirörs[1], and Oktay Türetken[2]

[1] Informatics Institute, Middle East Technical University, Ankara, Turkey
{musalman,demirors}@metu.edu.tr
[2] Industrial Engineering & Innovation Sciences, Technische Universiteit Eindhoven
o.turetken@tue.nl

Abstract. Effort is the main cost in software development projects, and software size is the main input for effort estimation. Project managers need to have sound size estimations to estimate required software effort. The inputs for size estimation models are generally software artifacts that are produced later in software development life cycle; however project managers need the estimations prior to the project start date. In this research we explore a method to estimate COSMIC functional size by using S-BPM diagrams that may be created before the project's start date. We tested our method with a case study and observed a 5% estimation error with respect to COSMIC size measurements.

Keywords: Software size estimation, software size estimation, COSMIC, S-BPM, Software project management.

1 Introduction

Effort is the main cost item for software development projects and for good management practices effort estimation is one of the main activities of software project manager. To make realistic effort estimations, managers need to assess the size of the software, however measuring software size accurately at the beginning of the project, when the artifacts like requirements documents or use cases are not ready, is not possible. There are methods to estimate (instead of measure) the size of the software to be developed to give project manager the opportunity to use and make effort estimations, but they also require some project artifacts to be ready.

In this research we propose and explore a method to estimate functional software size at the beginning of the software development lifecycle by using Subject Behavior Diagrams (SBD) of Subject-Oriented Business Process Management (S-BPM), a recent approach in the business process management field.

Functional size measurement is one of the most used approaches for measuring software size. It is introduced to software world by Albrecht [1]. It aims to measure the functionality of the software using different artifacts produced in the software life cycle. There are several methods to measure functional size, the most commonly used methods are IFPUG [2], MkII [3], COMIC [4], NESMA [5], FISMA [6]. These functional size measurement methods are accepted by ISO and are widely used throughout the world

C. Zehbold (Ed.): S-BPM ONE 2014, CCIS 422, pp. 55–66, 2014.
© Springer International Publishing Switzerland 2014

by software practitioners. In this study, we used COSMIC functional size measurement method to estimate the functional size from subject behavior diagrams. COSMIC is the most commonly used method after IFPUG [7] and better suited for automated measurement as it has been shown in previous works [8].

COSMIC measures the functionality of the software by counting data movements in and out of the software boundaries [9]. There are four types of data movements defined in COSMIC: Entry (E), eXit (X), Read(R), and Write (W) (Fig. 1). Entry is a data movement from the user to the functional process in the software, eXit is a data movement from the functional process to the user, Read is a data movement from persistent storage to the functional process, and Write is a data movement from the functional process to the persistent storage. Before starting measurement, measurer should first define Functional User Requirements (FUR), than Functional Processes (FP) of these requirements. Functional Processes includes Object of Interests (OOI) and Data Groups (DG), DG is a distinct, non-empty, non-ordered and non-redundant group of attributes related with one OOI and they represent the data that move with the Data Movements (DM).

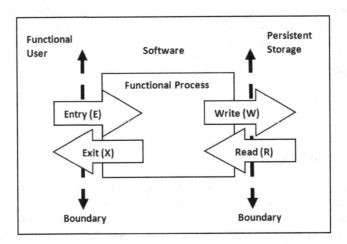

Fig. 1. Data movements in COSMIC Functional Size Measurement Method

COSMIC measurement can be conducted in different phases of development by using different types of artifacts like requirement specification, design documents, user manuals, and graphical user interface. There are some methods suggested for early size estimation in COSMIC [10] and in IFPUG [11], however these early estimation methods are usually criticized of being subjective. Buglione et. al. [12] introduced a method to estimate functional size from Project Size Unit (PSU) at the beginning of the project. PSU can be calculated at the beginning stages of the project and functional size can be estimated from PSU by using historical data of the organization. There are other successful methods suggested to measure functional size by using UML [13],[14] and xUML [15]. These methods use UML to calculate functional size. These available methods help to measure of estimate software size early in the lifecycle, however, we want to build a model which will help us to estimate software size accurately and objectively even before the development project starts. Process models are ideal to use for our purposes as they are constructed usually during organizational process improvement activities and are readily available before software development project begins.

There are studies focusing on size estimation from process models; Kaya suggested a model to estimate software functional size from eEPC diagrams [16], Monsalve *et. al.* [17], [18] used Qualigram and BPMN for functional size estimation and reached promising results. The research of Aysolmaz *et. al.* [19] suggested a method to make effort estimation directly from BPM measures with statistical methods skipping the size estimation phase All these research show that functional size can be estimated from process models before starting a development projects. The improvement we want to introduce with our study is subject perspective. We want to focus on the users of the processes in our process models and estimate functional size from subjects' view points. To reach this goal we will use S-BPM.

We want to build a model specifically for S-BPM, because we predict that S-BPM has significant potential for size estimation as it focuses on users of the processes as a modeling approach. Our hypothesis is that we may easily isolate the target software system and its users from other participants of the business processes by using subject behavior diagrams of S-BPM and this approach may result accurate size estimation. In this study we want to explore and test the possibility of this hypothesis.

We will give the details of our proposed method in section 2 and after that in section 3 we will explain and discuss our case study that we conducted to test the accuracy of suggested method. Finally, section 4 will summarize our findings and provide a roadmap for future studies.

2   Proposed Method

With our method we aim to estimate functional size of the software according to COSMIC by using SBDs of a business process. Usually process models are available as a part of analysis activities in organizations before software development projects start. In this study our first assumption is that the project team has Subject Behavior Diagrams of all subjects related with the software that they want to develop.

In COSMIC, software size may vary according to the definition of the boundaries of the software to be measured. While measuring software size by using S-BPM we should start with defining the boundaries of the software. In our method, we defined the boundary of the software as SBD of the software subject and messages interacting with this software. We make two main assumptions:

- All subjects interacting with software have available SBD's
- All users of the software are represented as subjects in S-BPM diagrams

In S-BPM the perspectives of all subjects in the process should be considered and Subject Behavior Diagrams for each subjects participating in the process should be drawn. The definition of subjects in S-BPM does not include the computer systems, however; for our exploratory study we included the software that we will measure as a subject in the process and created SBD's for it. As explained in the last section we plan to exclude software subject from our future work and improve our model accordingly. In this study we use behavior diagrams of software subject and other subjects who send message to or receive message from it without using the Business Objects. Even though S-BPM has the capability to represent OOI's with the help of Business Objects, for simplicity purposes we didn't represent them. In next phases we will integrate business objects into the model, and with the help of Business Objects we can identify Objects of Interests and Data Groups.

To estimate the functional size, we need to identify the number of data movements in the software. There are four types of movements defined in COSMIC, if we can estimate the numbers of each movement realistically, we can estimate total size of the software. For Enter data movements, we should count the number of data movements from the user of the software to the software. We can find these movements by counting the number of sent message states In SBD's of the users of the software. Similarly, eXit movements are represented by the receive message states of the user subjects from software subject.

We also need to count Write and Read movements. These movements represent data read from and written into persistent storage by the software. As the movements are initiated by the software subject we should find some representatives for them in software SBD. The problem is; in software SBD send and receive states are dealing with message relations between software users and software, not between software and persistent storage. To solve this problem we define two new function states; read and write. We propose to define every functions of the software with one of these two keywords and then count reads and writes to find the number of Read and Write data movements.

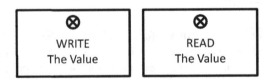

Fig. 2. Read and Write function states for software SBD

After finding estimated sizes of four DM types, we need to sum them up to reach the estimated functional size of the software.

We structured the model based on counting data movements from SBD's. The model needs to be tested to observe its effectiveness in real life situations. To validate our model we conducted a case study by using a real life case study. In the next section the detail of the case study and the discussions of the results are explained.

3 Case Study

3.1 Case Study Design

After we defined the structure of the model to estimate functional size by using SBD's of S-BPM, we designed a case study to test our initial idea. The purpose of this case study was to evaluate the potential of proposed methodology for real life application. We plan to improve our method using findings from this case study and conduct follow up case studies until reaching satisfactory results.

In this study we used a real business process from the "Ministry of Development", former Development Agency, of Turkey that involves the activities to extend the auditor pool that the agency is using to assign auditors to different projects for independent evaluation ('extending independent auditor pool'). The process is simple enough to evaluate the improvement opportunities in our model and complex enough to test the model with different possible actions and movements. The same process is also used by Kaya [20] to test e-COSMIC method which aims to derive COSMIC size estimation from eEPC notation, and the details of the process can be found in [20]. Using same case study gave us the opportunity to compare effectiveness of these two approaches in future studies. Moreover, we already have the COSMIC size measurement of the software system proposed in this process model as a part of a project conducted with Ministry of Development, which helps us to compare the estimated size from the proposed method with the functional size of the software which is measured from use cases designed specifically for the software.

The steps we took during the case study were as follows:

- Derive SBD's of the subjects in the process
- Apply proposed measurement method to find estimated COSMIC functional size
- Compare findings with the already measured size of the final product.
- Evaluate the results

The business process, expanding auditor pool, consists of 13 functional user requirements (FUR). The names of the FUR's are given in Table 1 with their respective measurement results. We started by modeling the FUR's using S-BPM subject behavior diagrams , because of the space limitations only the diagrams of the first FUR is given in this paper. The first FUR, "Create IA selection criteria" includes two users; Project Management Unit (PMU) Expert and software system. There are three functional processes in this FUR, which are; create selection criteria, delete selection criteria, and update selection criteria.

The diagrams for the first functional user requirement are as follows: for Program Management Unit (PMU) Expert; "Create Independent Auditor (IA) selection criteria" is given in Fig. 3, "Delete and update selection criteria" is presented in Fig. 4.The diagrams for software system subject are as follows: "Create Independent Auditor (IA) selection criteria" is given in Fig. 5 and "Delete and update selection criteria" is given in Fig. 6.

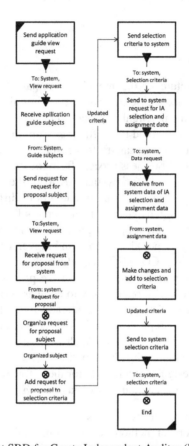

Fig. 3. PMU Expert SBD for Create Independent Auditor (IA) selection criteria

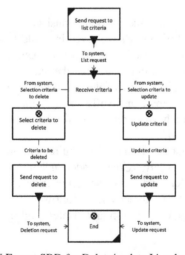

Fig. 4. PMU Expert SBD for Delete/update IA selection criteria

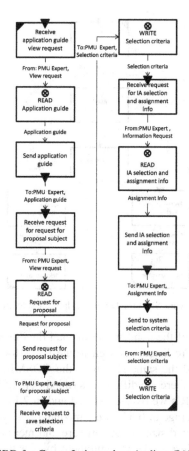

Fig. 5. Software SBD for Create Independent Auditor (IA) selection criteria

After we derived SBD's for all 13 functional user requirements, we applied our proposed estimation method to all of them. For the first functional user requirement, given in detail in this paper, we first examined the diagram of the PMU expert to find Enter and eXit data movements by the messages sent to and received from the software. There are six messages sent and three messages received (create, update, and delete combined). This makes six Enter and three eXit data movements. Then we examined the SBD of the software for Read and Write data movements. As mentioned before, we used keywords of READ and WRITE during modeling in the functional states of the software, and in SBD we observed that there are three READ and six WRITE function states, that makes three Read, six Write data movements.

After we completed the examination of SBD's for all functional user requirements and for all subjects, we compared the resulting COSMIC estimations with the measured functional sizes of the functional user requirements. (The detailed use cases and COSMIC measurements of all functional user requirements can be found in [20])

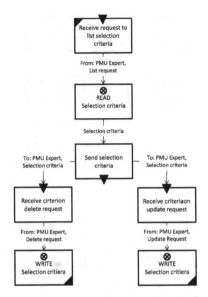

Fig. 6. Software SBD for Delete/update IA selection criteria

In Table 1, the results of the comparison of total data movements for all 13 functional user requirements are listed. As seen in the table, for the first functional user requirement, we estimated the same size with the COSMIC measurement, however for all of the other FUR's there are differences (maximum of 11 and minimum of 1 in absolute values). In 5 FUR's we over-estimated and in 7 FUR's we under-estimated, the differences has the average of 0,54 with a median of -1. When we look at the total difference between estimated size of the software and measured size of the software, we can see that we are close to the measurement by 7 data movements, considering that the total size is 137 COSMIC Function Points (CFP) our error is 5%.

After comparing the total sizes of the FUR's, we also compared the differences between numbers data movement types. The results are listed in Table 2. As seen in the table errors are distributed across all data movement types.

3.2   Discussions, Results, and Threats

After comparing the results of the estimation model with the COSMIC measurements, we observed that even though the total difference in the size is 7 CFP, for individual FUR's the estimations are not as accurate as we anticipated. The differences vary from 1 CFP to 11 CFP. To find out the reason of this variance we examined in detail the FUR's with largest estimation differences.

Largest difference is in FUR 7, which is "Update outputs". When we look at this FUR we realized that the reason of the difference is the concept of Data Group. In FUR 7 there is a message from the user to the software which requests retrieval of application documents, hire plan, announcement text, selection criteria, and approval status. For this message in the SBD of the software we draw one read function state to

Table 1. Comparison of S-BPM estimation and COSMIC measurement for 13 FUR's

FUR#	(A) S-BPM Estimation	(B) COSMIC Measurement	B-A Difference
1- Create IA selection criteria	17	17	0
2- Create IA announcement	18	14	-4
3- Create IA application documents	17	12	-5
4- Plan IA announcement time, media, and duration	15	9	-6
5- Send outputs to approval	7	5	-2
6- Review the outputs	10	14	4
7- Update outputs	8	19	11
8- Preparations for announcement tools	5	3	-2
9- Publish announcement on web page	5	11	6
10- Receive applications	5	4	-1
11- Decide selection commission	6	5	-1
12- Evaluate applications	9	13	4
13- Approve selected applications and save into database	8	11	3
Total	**130**	**137**	**7**
		Average	0,54
		Median	-1

read all of these data and counted as one read data movement. Whereas in COSMIC we need to count 5 different reads for 5 different data groups. Particularly for FUR 7 this situation appears 4 times, resulting 14 under-estimated data movements.

Another problem is related with the reuse of functional processes. In the SBD's we draw every functional processes in every FUR, independent from each other. If there a functional process, like listing all applicants, is included in several FUR's, we should represent this functional process in all of SBD's related with the FUR's. Than in each SBD, we will count same data movements related with this functional process repeatedly. However, in COSMIC we should count the movements in a functional process only once regardless of its repetition in different functional user requirements. Because of this conflict we have over-estimated data movements in some FUR's. For example there are 3 over-estimated data movements in FUR7 in the case study.

Our observations about the results of the comparison gave us two main reasons for the difference between estimated size and measured size:

- Data groups wasn't considered in the model,
- Reused functional processes duplicated whenever used.

Table 2. Difference between data movements types for 13 FUR's

Difference (Measurement-Estimation)					
FUR#	E	X	R	W	Total
1- Create IA selection criteria	0	1	0	-1	0
2- Create IA announcement	-1	-1	-2	0	-4
3- Create IA application documents	-1	-2	-2	0	-5
4- Plan IA announcement time, media, and duration	-2	-2	-2	0	-6
5- Send outputs to approval	0	-1	-1	0	-2
6- Review the outputs	-3	4	4	-1	4
7- Update outputs	2	3	3	3	11
8- Preparations for announcement tools	-1	0	0	-1	-2
9- Publish announcement on web page	-1	4	4	-1	6
10- Receive applications	0	-1	0	0	-1
11- Decide selection commission	0	-1	0	0	-1
12- Evaluate applications	3	-1	0	2	4
13- Approve selected applications and save into database	1	1	1	0	3
Total	-3	4	5	1	7

In the next phases of the research our goal will be to resolve these two issues to improve the model and then test it with another case study.

Even though we estimated the size of the software with 5% error rate, it is important to stress that this case study was for exploratory purposes and not mean to yield statistically significant results.

4   Conclusion and Future Work

In this study we proposed a method to make early COSMIC size estimations by using S-BPM diagrams and we test the estimation model in a case study. Results of the case study showed that the method has potential; however it needs to be improved to cover the excluded aspects.

In the case study, we estimated the size of the software with 5% error. 5% should be considered as a promising result for an exploratory study of a newly proposed method. During detailed examination of the case study results, we observed that the model has over-estimations and under-estimations for some functional processes. We identified two main reasons for these under- and over-estimations; first one is related with the lack of data group concept in the model. Data groups are the smallest data items in COSMIC that are moved by the data movements. In our method the diagrams weren't designed to carry enough detail to let us count individual data groups. As listed as a future work, we plan to overcome this issue by using Business Objects to carry information about the Data Groups. The second point is related with the reuse of the functional processes; in COSMIC, regardless of its reuse, one functional process should be counted only once. Our method wasn't designed according to this rule; in our diagrams, reused functional processes are represented in every diagram and as a result they are counted more than once.

The first issue results over-estimation of software size, and the second one results under-estimation. When combined they neutralized each other and give us an under-estimation with only 7 CFP in a 137 CFP functional user requirement.

To conclude, we think this method has potential to be used as an early size estimation method, we plan to improve the model to include precautions to cover these missing points and test with additional real life use cases to find statistically significant results. Also the future work related with this study can be listed as follows:

- Improving the model to use without the SBD for software system
- Carrying information about Data Groups by using Business Objects
- Implementing reuse of functional processes
- Designing a tool for automatic size estimation from S-BPM
- Conducting case studies with different contexts and level of detail

References

1. Albrecht, A.J.: Measuring Application Development Productivity. In: Proceedings of IBM Application Development Symposium, pp. 83–92 (1979)
2. ISO/IEC, 20926: Software and systems engineering – Software measurement – IFPUG functional size measurement method (2009)
3. ISO/IEC, 20968: Software engineering – Mk II Function Point Analysis – Counting Practices Manual (2002)
4. ISO/IEC, 19761: Software engineering – COSMIC: a functional size measurement method (2011)
5. ISO/IEC, 24570: Software engineering – NESMA functional size measurement method version 2.1 – Definitions and counting guidelines for the application of Function Point Analysis (2005)
6. ISO/IEC, 29881: Information technology – Systems and software engineering – FiSMA 1.1 functional size measurement method (2010)
7. OVERVIEW of Function Points, Total Metrics, http://www.totalmetrics.com/function-point-resources/what-are-function-points
8. Abran, A.: Automating Functional Size Measurement – a Survey. In: UKSMA/COSMIC Conference 2011- 22nd Annual Conference on Metrics and Estimating: Hosted in Collaboration with COSMIC (2011)
9. Abran, A., Desharnais, J.-M., Oligny, S., St-Pierre, D., Symons, C.: COSMIC Method Measurement Manual Version 3.0.1 (COSMIC) The Common Software Measurement International Consortium (2009)
10. Conte, M., Iorio, T., Meli, R., Santillo, L.: E&Q: An Early & Quick Approach to Functional Size Measurement Methods. In: Software Measurement European Forum, SMEF (2004)
11. Meli, R.: Early and Extended Function Point: A New Method for Function Points Estimation. In: IFPUG-Fall Conference, pp. 15–19 (1997)
12. Buglione, L., Ormandjieva, O., Daneva, M.: Using PSU for early prediction of COSMIC size of functional and non-functional requirements. In: Dumke, R.R., Braungarten, R., Büren, G., Abran, A., Cuadrado-Gallego, J.J. (eds.) IWSM/MetriKon/Mensura 2008. LNCS, vol. 5338, pp. 352–361. Springer, Heidelberg (2008)

13. Lavazza, L., Del Bianco, V.: A case study in COSMIC functional size measurement: The rice cooker revisited. In: Abran, A., Braungarten, R., Dumke, R.R., Cuadrado-Gallego, J.J., Brunekreef, J. (eds.) IWSM/Mensura 2009. LNCS, vol. 5891, pp. 101–121. Springer, Heidelberg (2009)

14. Azzouz, S., Abran, A.: A proposed measurement role in the Rational Unified Process (RUP) and its implementation with ISO 19761: COSMIC FFP. In: Software Measurement European Forum (2004)

15. Nagano, S., Ajisaka, T.: Functional metrics using COSMIC-FFP for object-oriented real-time systems. In: 13th International Workshop on Software Measurement (2003)

16. Kaya, M., Demirors, O.: E-Cosmic: A Business Process Model Based Functional Size Estimation Approach. In: 2011 37th EUROMICRO Conf. Softw. Eng. Adv. Appl., pp. 404–410 (August 2011)

17. Monsalve, C., Abran, A., April, A.: Functional Size Measurement with Business Process Models: The Business Application Domain. In: International Conferences on Software Measurement (IWSM/MetriKon/Mensura 2010) (2010)

18. Monsalve, C., Abran, A., April, A.: Measuring Software Functional Size From Business Process Models. Int. J. Softw. Eng. Knowl. Eng. 21(03), 311–338 (2011)

19. Aysolmaz, B., İren, D., Demirörs, O.: An Effort Prediction Model Based on BPM Measures for Process Automation. In: Nurcan, S., Proper, H.A., Soffer, P., Krogstie, J., Schmidt, R., Halpin, T., Bider, I. (eds.) BPMDS 2013 and EMMSAD 2013. LNBIP, vol. 147, pp. 154–167. Springer, Heidelberg (2013)

20. Kaya, M.: E-COSMIC: A Business Process Model Based Functional Size Estimation Approach. In: METU (2010)

Applying the Strategy-Oriented
Business Process Modeling to S-BPM

Matthias Lederer[1], Matthias Kurz[2], and Ulrike Lembcke[1]

[1] University of Erlangen-Nuremberg, Chair for Information Systems
(Services-Processes-Intelligence),
Lange Gasse 20, 90403 Nuremberg, Germany
matthias.lederer@fau.de
[2] DATEV eG, Enterprise Solutions,
Paumgartnerstr. 6-14, 90429 Nuremberg
matthias.kurz@datev.de

Abstract. Business processes should be aligned to the corporate strategy. However, implementing such a strategy in the day-to-day operations of a company is
a challenging task as there is little support for holistically deriving actionable
changes to business processes from a company's strategy. This contribution
proposes linking strategy maps with process models in order to close this gap.
The resulting Strategy Process Map approach has been successfully applied in a
case study at a large German automotive supplier.

Keywords: Business Process Strategy, Strategy Process Matrix, Strategy
Alignment.

1   Introduction

The implementation of a corporate strategy on the level of business processes is considered as an important factor for the success of companies in theory and practice
[1;2;3]. The strategy development and the optimization of strategically relevant
processes should therefore not be addressed separately but with a holistic approach
[4;1]. Nevertheless, [5] point out that the implementation of the strategy in the corporate practice is still often lacking. Therefore many companies and particularly the
middle management are facing the challenge of translating a long-term strategy in
operational business processes actions [3;6]. Recent studies on the current state of
business process management confirm the existence of this challenge: The operational
implementation of a business strategy is a key challenge for process owners as holistic
approaches to solve this challenge are still missing [2;7;8;9]. Therefore, necessary
strategic measures often cannot be implemented in operational business.

2   Challenges in Strategy Implementation

Middle managers find it particularly difficult to align and justify their operational
management of business processes as well as their leadership style with the long-term

C. Zehbold (Ed.): S-BPM ONE 2014, CCIS 422, pp. 67–84, 2014.

corporate strategy [10]. They perform management tasks such as planning, organizing, decision-making, and controlling. In order to fulfill this function, they and are located in the organizational structure between the top management (e.g., management board) and the process teams (e.g., workers, clerks) [11;12]. According to a study of [13], middle managers use strategy-oriented methods for operational process planning (e.g., the Balanced Scorecard) for three main reasons: (1) Decisions, process resources, and actions of the manager need to be justified. (2) A process team needs to be coordinated efficiently. (3) Middle managers themselves use methods for the purpose of self-controlling (e.g., documenting a rational plan for emotional or ad hoc instructions).

While it is up to the top management to design a business policy and strategic decisions autonomously [14], middle managers have a transfer function [15] in two directions of communication and are stuck in a so called *double membership conflict* [16]:

On the one hand, middle managers are responsible for an adequate interpretation and *cascading* of a long-term and sometimes abstract corporate strategy (e.g., increasing productivity) for their area of responsibility (e.g., customer order process). Moreover, middle managers have to lead workers and clerks, in order to ensure the daily implementation of the strategy in manual operational processes (*instructions*). *Requirements* document changes to IT applications supporting the respective process.

On the other hand, middle managers have to justify their taken decisions to the top management (*strategic reporting*). This is why managers need profound support how to explain operational tasks as well as necessary process resources (e.g., staff). *Operational reports* from the process team or from BPM software can be used to generate and aggregate the necessary data

The tasks arising from the organizational position of middle process managers are summarized in figure 1.

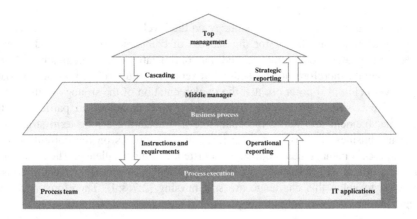

Fig. 1. Tasks of middle managers in an organizational context

3   Research Question

In summary, both in business science and corporate practice a need is recognized, to plan and execute business process management based on strategic goals. However, so far there are no notations which integrate business goals with strategic aspects in a process model. Middle managers may use such a notation for communicating instructions and requirements to their process team as well as reporting the achievement of strategic objectives to the top management.

Several studies were conducted [e.g. 17] and some solutions are presented in literature [e.g. 18] to overcome the separation of business objectives and business process models. Textual as well as specific graphical approaches try to integrate strategy in process and workflow models. Nevertheless, available comprehensive approaches have the major disadvantage that they introduce another specific process notation [e.g. 19], which cannot be used for middle managers provided with limited decision-making-power. Other present frameworks are too general [e.g. 18] and are not able to offer an actual decision support which results in actionable measures to increase strategy implementation. To summarize, there is still no accepted standard approach available how the separation can be solved in different cases and different domains.

However, some BPM software solutions offer features to comprehensively plan and measure strategy-relevant information, but middle process managers are often facing highly heterogeneous organizational and technical infrastructures and have no decision-making authority or skills to implement an integrated software solution [20]. Therefore they require appropriate communication approaches to meet their expected transfer function instead of implementing a holistic BPM tool which bridges interfaces.

In order to address this gap, this contribution addresses the following research question:

How can strategic objectives be integrated into business process models as communication tool for middle managers?

The following section 4 introduces an approach which has been developed to specifically address this research question. The approach has been successfully applied in three case studies at large German companies from automotive, energy and building industry. Section 5 reports about one of these case studies which has been conducted at a large automotive supplier. This case study has been selected for this contribution, as it had been the most comprehensive of the three case studies. As the original approach described in section 4 relies on BPMN process notation, section 6 adapts the approach for S-BPM and thereby contributes to extending S-BPM to the field of strategy-oriented business process modeling.

4   Strategy-Oriented Business Process Modeling

The strategy-oriented business process modeling approach provides both a method and a notation for linking process models with strategy [21]. Creating such a refined process model comprises the following components:

1. First, the strategy should be documented in the semi-formal notation of a *strategy map* (see section 4.1).
2. In the next step, the *process model* is refined utilizing an extension of BPMN (see section 4.2).
3. Finally, the proposed *Strategy Process Matrix* combines both the process model with the strategy map (see section 4.3).

4.1   Strategy Map

To make use of business strategy for the proposed approach, a mostly informal and abstract documented strategy (e.g., by using values cards or corporate policies) needs to be transferred into a semi-formal form, in which explicit individual strategic objectives of the same granularity can be identified.

In order to select a semi-formal way for representing strategies, a systematic literature review has been conducted. The review yielded different methods for the systematic documentation of strategic objectives. Among the found approaches (including Hoshin planning and program-based planning), the strategy map [22] is most appropriate form for this approach: The four perspectives of the Balanced Scorecard (BSc) describe a set of focused and balanced strategic objectives. A strategy map (see figure 2) visualizes these objectives using causal chains [23;24]. This way of strategy documentation offers many advantages: The strategy map by [12] is often described as a superior approach to present a strategy, because using different perspectives assists in establishing a holistic view on objectives [3;24]. Furthermore, the arrangement of targets in causal chains supports interpreting the dependencies between objectives. In addition, the BSc is a widely used [25] standard tool in business practice [26]. Since a strategy map can be easily derived from a BSc, the strategy map is one of the most simple and quick ways but also provides a sufficient form of formalization. The BSc paradigm of a general framework translating long-term objectives into short-term action can be used in this approach by linking it to business processes and workflows. This approach can therefore also be seen as extension and specialization of the BSc procedure for middle managers in the field of BPM.

Two adjustments to the original concept of [22;23] are proposed in order to be able to use the strategy map for creating the Strategy Process Matrix in the third step:

- *Stakeholder perspective*: The strategy map originally considers objectives in four perspectives, namely the financial, customer, business process and development perspective [22;23]. The strategy map, however, was constantly developed in scientific research and allows a flexible adaptation of new or changed perspectives [1;27]. This adaptability is used by this approach as well. The perspectives and their hierarchy remain unchanged with one exception: The customer perspective is generalized into the *stakeholder perspective*. By doing so, objectives can be assigned to all internal and external stakeholders of a business process (e.g., internal customers as well as external organizations).

- *Vertical uniqueness of entries*: For the later assignment in the matrix it is necessary that entries in the strategy map need to be modeled on unique vertical levels. This means that each row of the strategy map frames only one objective (see figure 2).

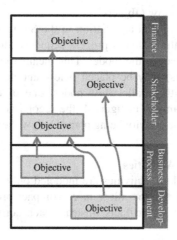

Fig. 2. Structure of a strategy map

Depending on the application by the responsible middle manager, the entries of the strategy map can present objectives for the entire company, certain business processes, or departments. However, the case studies show that the strategic goals for certain process domains (e.g., objectives for PLM) provide a particularly suitable input.

4.2   Business Process Model

There are numerous possibilities for the formal as well as semi-formal documentation of business processes. Control flow-oriented notations such as event-driven process chains and BPMN diagrams are quite popular for middle process managers [28;29;30]. Data and object-oriented notations do not exactly fit with the strategy-oriented approach because they aim mainly on the downstream programming and are therefore not suitable to make organizational processes explicit [30;31].

Since BPMN is one of the most known and widely used notation forms for business practice and offers a huge range of organizational elements [28;31;32], BPMN 2.0 is used as the modeling notation for this approach. Section 6 demonstrates how the strategy-oriented business process modeling approach works with the communications-based subject-oriented business process management (S-BPM) notation from [33]. Compared to other solutions (see above), this proposed general approach of a Strategy Process Matrix can be used even for other modeling notations than BPMN and S-BPM, as long as the described following fundamental principles can be guaranteed.

In order to use BPMN 2.0 for the approach, three adjustments to the original specification [34] are necessary:

Uniqueness of Horizontal Flow Objects
To later ensure a unique graphical association in the Strategy Process Matrix in step three, each flow object in the business process sequence flow needs to be designed horizontally on a unique level in the model. This means that no flow node (e.g., activities, gateways, or events) may be placed below another flow node. If there are parallel sequence flows with parallel flow nodes, one of the flow nodes must be moved to the right. For example, in figure 4, the second activity has been moved to the right in order to avoid the activity being placed below the decision gateway.

Expanded Information in Activities
According the BPMN standard, activities are modeled only using a describing name. In order to save space and thereby allow more compact process models, additional information is not added using artifacts. Instead, each activity is divided into four parts (see figure 3):

- *Activity Name*: Just like standard BPMN activities, the extended activities have a name as well.
- *Number*: Each activity has a unique number in this proposed approach. This extension has the advantage that users can describe all additional information relevant for middle managers in a referenced process description. The actual numbering (e.g., consecutive numbering) is up to the user.
- *Method and/or IT support*: Each activity may contain the methods or supporting IT tools used during executing a task. This allows models showing for example which tools (e.g., checklists) are used for an activity or which applications are used (e.g., SAP mask names). When connecting the process activities with strategic objectives in the third step, it will become more transparent, which tools, methods, and IT-enabled services are relevant for achieving strategic objectives in heterogeneous environments.
- *Role*: With an assignment of a role for each activity, it becomes transparent for middle managers, who is in charge of the implementation of an activity and thus of a strategic objective. This combination can later be used for incentive systems and a strategy-oriented variable income to foster extrinsic motivation.

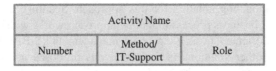

Fig. 3. Extended activities

Pools and Swimlanes According to the Company's Organization and Cooperation

By documenting roles as the smallest unit of the human hierarchy of an organization, lanes and pools can be used to map the formal organizational structure of a company. Furthermore, pools can be used to design company areas or independent companies, which participate in a common business process. This extension supports especially cross-company collaborations and process networks. In many cases (e.g., in the case study of section 5), strategies and processes are designed and modeled beyond the formal boundaries of a company. By capturing the actors of process networks in the pools, common strategies and networks can be controlled effectively.

All other graphic elements like *connecting objects* (e.g., sequence flows) and *data objects* (e.g., documents) can be used according to the BPMN standard. However, the conducted case studies suggest that only simple standard elements should be used in order to not exceed the complexity of the models. For example, a generic data object is preferred to differentiating between input and output documents. The communication approach of the Strategy Process Matrix focusses on a graphical combination of strategic objectives with process and workflow models instead of an exact mapping of all process details.

4.3   Strategy Process Matrix

A graphical connection between strategic objectives and the process flow can be realized in two basic approaches.

First, it is possible to *visually complement* strategic objectives into existing process models. The BPMN standard already provides the opportunity to enrich models by artifacts like annotations (e.g., comments) data objects (e.g., documents), and groups (e.g., graphical framing of elements). This way of adding strategic information, however, has some essential drawbacks: Already complex process models become increasingly difficult to understand when adding more and unfamiliar elements. This makes it difficult to use the complemented process models as a communication tool for middle managers. Furthermore, strategic objectives can address multiple process elements, which can be graphically widely separated. Hence, groups are not a feasible solution and artifacts tend to contain redundant strategy information in several places in the model.

Second, it is possible to arrange the components *graphically diagonally*. The resulting *Strategy Process Matrix* (see figure 4) combines each objective of the strategy map (lines) with flow objects of the BPMN process flow (rows). This approach usually needs much space, but its benefits could be confirmed in the conducted case studies: The individual components, that is, the process and the strategy, can be developed independently in teams and then brought together in workshops. Likewise, both inputs can still be used separately and can also individually be adjusted if changes are needed (e.g., removing process steps or adding strategic objectives).

The Strategy Process Matrix is divided into individual strategy process fields. Each flow object (perhaps enriched by modeling elements like databases or documents) may be assigned to one or more objectives. If multiple flow objects support the achievement of an objective, several fields of the matrix may contain information in the same row.

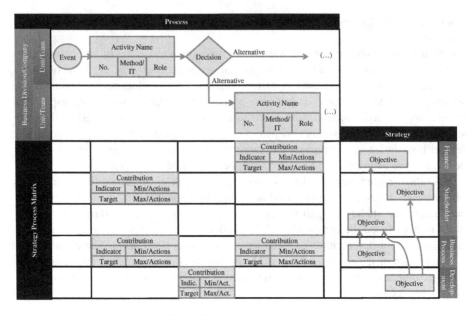

Fig. 4. Structure of the matrix

Within each matrix field, the following information is proposed to be documented:

- *Contribution*: The contribution describes how a flow object can support strategy achievement. If, for example, the assigned objective to an approval activity is to "decrease time to market", the contribution may explain that the flow objects should guarantee a "quick pass".

- *Performance indicator:* The indicator represents the quantitative measure of the contribution by using a key figure. For the example, the "throughput time in hours" can be measured. The overall achievement of a strategic objective in a certain process can be assessed by the aggregation of all key figures in a row. Following the basic idea of traceable and strategy-oriented key performance indicators by [22;23], the identified indicators on the one hand need to actually represent the achievement or non-achievement of the contribution. On the other hand assigned actions should have the potential to directly influence the value of the indicator. These requirements imply that indicators can be generic as well as very specific dependent on the hierarchical level of the process (e.g. first pass yield on the top level, failure rates of specific process steps on lower levels).

- *Target:* The target value for the performance indicator will be recorded together with acceptable deviations (e.g., a "maximum of 4 days").
  Min/Max and actions: If a target value cannot be achieved, specific actions can be documented (e.g., using a numerical reference to a document or process model) depending on the direction of the deviation. These measures are expected to increase the achievement of objectives. An example action may be a team leader "sending an urgent mail to the process team pointing out an unacceptable delay".

The graphical matrix representation can be used for planning and controlling processes which are performed in a heterogeneous IT infrastructure where a middle manager is not in the position to implement a holistic BPM software solution.

5   Case Study

The Strategy Process Matrix has been successfully implemented in three large-sized German companies to measure the actual achievement of the overall process strategy in different process groups. BPMN 2.0 was used to create the process models. Chapter 6 will present possibilities how to transfer the approach to S-BPM. The following case study describes an application in the quality assurance of a German automotive supplier[1].

5.1   Scenario

During an internal management review, the quality control board of a car supplier identified various potential improvements in the process documentation. In particular, the degree of strategy achievement of the processes was considered to be insufficiently measured.

In the production line of the supplier, all relevant data for car components was documented in a digital file folder. The processes for this data documentation, the data transfer to external partners in case of warranty claims as well as the change management processes were designed to secure compliance with EU directives, national legal requirements as well as relevant internal standards (e.g., data protection). For each manufactured car part and especially for those with a necessary rework, with customer-specific adaptations and with special events in the production process, data was collected to later proof a correct production process in case of damages or complaints in the final product.

Although in large manufacturing companies in the automotive industry such documentation processes are typically standardized, in this case the documentation and data management process were neither completely documented nor communicated to the process team. In particular, it remained unclear whether the processes really supported the set strategic goals (e.g., "increase profitability" and "improve partner relationships") sufficiently.

In the case study, the responsible process owner from middle management needed a communication tool with which she can plan, measure, and report impacts to strategic objectives to the top management. Moreover she needed an overview over the relevant tasks and their degree of strategic objective achievement in order to motivate and teach a process team to act in a strategic sense.

---

[1] On request of the organization, the name of the well-known large company cannot be mentioned. For confidentiality reasons, parts of the case study were modified.

5.2   Application

In this case study, the Strategy Process Matrix was amongst others utilized for the process of transferring recorded data to internal (e.g., legal department) and external (e.g., car manufacturer as partner) stakeholders. Figure 5 shows the Strategy Process Matrix that was developed during the case study.

The start event of the process depicted in figure 5 is a request from such a stakeholder. In the first step, it is necessary to examine whether the particular request asks for data regarding product liability issues. If so, a team leader has to confirm this data transfer by using a checklist. Requests from internal stakeholders can directly be submitted to the clerks of the data teams without an approval by the head of the team, because in this case the "need to know" principle is valid. If approved, the team translates the request into internal naming and follows limitations which may be given by the team lead. Then, the team searches the requested data from the internal production database and reports the information back to the requestor (feedback steps are not included in figure 5).

In the Strategy Process Matrix it became transparent for the responsible middle manager that many flow objects made valuable contributions to the achievement of strategic objectives which were communicated from the top management. For example, the activities of the formal examination and the granting of permits makes a special contribution to the operationalization of the strategic objectives and in particular to the compliance with external laws and internal process standards. Complementary process descriptions with details of measuring the strategy's contribution could be found behind the numbering of individual activities. Table 1 shows an extract of this additional process documentation.

5.3   Evaluation

In addition to the collection of qualitative assessments this case study also contained a structured survey to check whether the developed graphical approach satisfies the typical requirements for strategy-oriented business process modeling.

[35] proposes five quality aspects, a new modeling language has to follow: New notations need to be (1) easy to understand, (2) accurate and complete, (3) verifiable, (4) quick and easy to model as well as (5) traceable .

Control questions were asked about all developed components in the case study models in five structured interviews to examine these requirements. The control questions were structured so that each component of the approach (strategy map, process model, strategy process matrix) was addressed by three questions covering the five quality aspects (e.g., "Do workshops with data teams of other lines help to increase the compliance with external regulations in the case targets are not reached?"). All questions could only be accepted or denied by the interviewee. At least one question per quality aspect had to be answered in the negative way by the respondents. The test of the time required for creating the matrix and its components, could not be checked with binary questions. Instead, the evaluation was done by using key statements and concrete drawing of model components in the interviews.

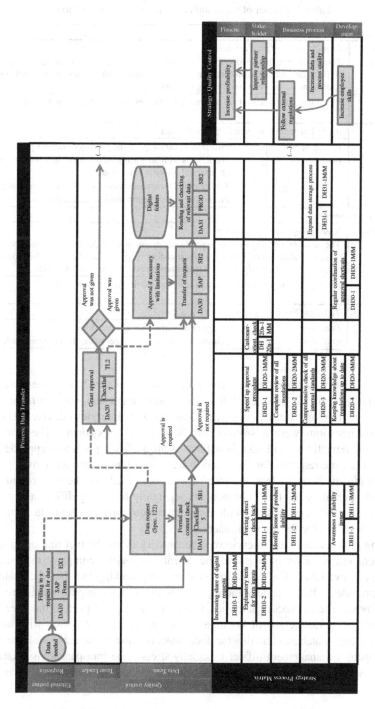

Fig. 5. Extract of the matrix for the data transfer process

Table 1. Extract of the complementary process description

DA11: Formal and content check		
Contribution (DH11-2)	*Identify issues of product liability* The distinction between critical and non-critical data is essential for any potential claim. The process team has to recognize at least weak signals for product liability-related incidents when interpreting the data request.	
Performance indicator	Percentage of queries where relevant aspects were not detected (annual review)	
Target	0,5%; Exceeding of up to 0.25% is allowed	
Actions	*In case of exceeding*	• Information exchange in the protected intranet portal • Workshops with data teams of other product lines to foster an informal information sharing • Add of typical sentences and examples into checklist 5 • Promotion of building individual decision rules
DA20: Grant approval		
Contribution (DH20-1)	*Speed up approval procedure* The rapid processing of data requests can ensure a good partnership with internal and external stakeholders. Delays in data transfer process in the past were often the subject of criticism and usually the team leader represents the bottleneck resource.	
Performance indicator	Average waiting and processing time of the activity (quarterly review)	
Target	72 hours; Exceeding of up to 33% is allowed	
Actions	*In case of exceeding*	• Usage of a shorter checklist version • Automatic forwarding trigger to the deputy team leader

The five interviews were conducted with various stakeholders of the case study: One craftsman from the production line, two middle managers, one top manager and one manager from an external cooperation partner were interviewed. Overall, 90% of the control questions were answered correctly by the respondents. The few wrong answers and deviations were distributed across all quality aspects and approach components. The time required for the creation was judged as significantly over previous modeling efforts. Nevertheless, the interviewees described that the time requirements are less than creating the three components separately following different approaches and the trying to integrate them with each other. Summing up, the time requirement seems to be justifiable for the respondents.

During the execution the interviewees became aware of the fact that up to now no transparent visualization of the strategic orientation of the company in operational processes is available. The practitioners especially highlighted that the matrix approach provides a better understanding of how long-term company goals are implemented by short-term process activities. Out of the user's perspective the exceedingly heterogeneous infrastructure of documentation and release processes with an ERP-system, different databases and diverse documents became manageable with the matrix. The company's management officer especially stresses the transparent visualization of the process and strategy view that is often neglected in companies. The single components could be used for coordination meetings, whereas the responsible process manager could use the matrix for the coordination of tasks.

According to the interviewees, the matrix could especially help managers of support processes to justify resources, because these processes were often facing hard cost pressure from the top management. The approach is suitable in particular to provide actual evidences by using key figures to point out and visualize the value of the process within the long-term company strategy.

One expert doubted that the pure combination of the single components could lead to a more effective control of strategy achievement, as long as the approach is not yet realized with IT support. An IT application can for example provide features such as a strategy controlling cockpit or reporting functions. Hence, the supplier is currently specifying an IT-based solution for the Strategy Process Matrix.

6   Transfer to S-BPM

The approach was originally developed by using BPMN but was then transferred to S-BPM. Main reason for this further development was to foster the subject orientation for the approach by following [33]. Since humans are predominantly involved in most of the corporate processes and thus are primarily responsible for the implementation of strategies, an approach with S-BPM can help to focus more on the human aspects of strategy achievement.

6.1   Subject Behavior Matrix

As already described for BPMN, each process model node which potentially can represent the implementation of the strategy is horizontally modeled in a unique column. In the case of subject behavior diagrams (SBD), all states (action/function, sending and receiving states) of the process model are assigned to a unique horizontal place. Since transitions present only the change of states, they are not modeled in unique columns. Figure 6 shows an excerpt of the matrix for the described data transfer process from the team view using the SBD for the process component.

If a process model is transferred from BPMN to S-BPM, activities sometimes need to be modeled in more than one status. In this case, most of the contributions to the strategy will probably be assigned to action states. Nevertheless, it is possible to enrich the states by new and more specific strategy contributions. In figure 6, for example, two more contributions for the reception status "receive approval" were added. With the fine-grained representation of process steps from the actor's point of view, more contributions can be identified (even implicit contributions can be made explicit). These can be recorded either from the middle managers as a guide for his/her team or the subject is instructed to think himself/herself about how to promote the strategy with all states.

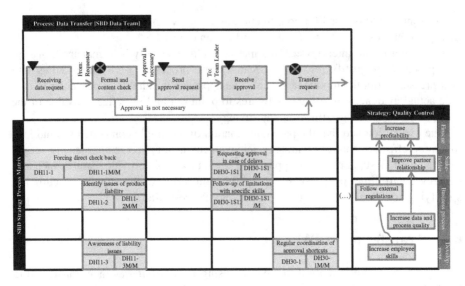

Fig. 6. Extract of the subject behavior matrix for the data team

If process managers use SBD for the communication, they can profit from the following advantages compared to models based on BPMN:

- *Reduced complexity:* The main task of the middle manager is to motivate the process team in terms of strategy implementation. The overall process information (see figure 5), however, may seem to be too complex. Figure 6, however, can be used for possibly unskilled employees as a reasonable process description.
- *Comprehensibility:* Oftentimes, only one actor needs to be addressed in a process model in the manager's communication. Instead of explaining the entire process, the contributions of one single subject can be used to show strategy-relevant actions. This idea is also supported by the fact that the matrix is not overloaded with entries. Whereas in BPMN representations the process manager could think about removing process steps, which have no contributions to strategy, the representation with SBD can subdivide a business process. Necessary steps, which are perhaps only indirectly involved in the strategy implementation (e.g. receiving the data request to later check it in a formal way), are included in the model. This idea is shown for the first two states in figure 6: The receiving as well as the formal and content check of a request can both contribute to a better partner relationship. In these cases, matrix fields can be extended over one single column.
- *Empowerment:* By having more empty matrix fields, actors are encouraged proactively to make themself think about further contributions. Instead of cementing a top-down communication, the S-BPM variant promotes the empowerment of subjects with bottom-up proposals.

6.2 Interaction Matrix

In the Interaction Diagram (ID), each message needs also to be arranged on a unique horizontal level. Since the behaviors of the actors mentioned are described in the SBD, only the messages are mapped in the matrix fields.

Figure 7 shows the case of interactions between the external partner (data requestor, e.g., a car manufacturer) and the internal quality control. The data team receives the data requests and answers it if necessary with an adequate data response. Since messages per se are not able to contribute to the strategic objectives given in the strategy map, the matrix fields document only two entries:

- *Relevancy:* With the description of the relevance, a process manager can get an overview over interactions contributing to the achievement of strategic objectives. For example, a competent and fast response to the requestor is particularly relevant to improve partner relationships in the case study.
- *Contribution references:* The references can indicate which contributions, indicators and measures from other diagrams are especially important in the interaction between the actors mentioned in order to focus on strategic objectives.

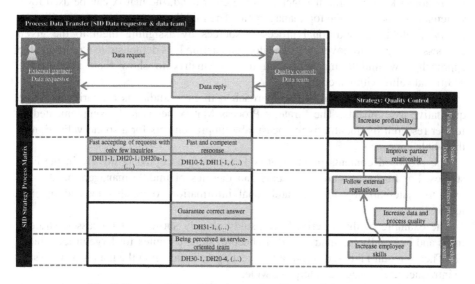

Fig. 7. Extract of the subject interaction diagram for two actors

The chosen example presents the consideration of messages to an external actor and can therefore also show how this message-centric view can enrich the strategy-oriented approach by an adequate support for process networks: Strategic objectives, like in the case study, can also include objectives for processes which range beyond the formal boundaries of an organization. The new stakeholder perspective of the strategy map makes it possible, for example, to outline which messages are important to focus on in order to strategically manage partnership relations.

For middle managers this approach using SIDs has the advantage that the strategy contribution of internal and external messages is transparently documented. Overall, the existing approach can be enriched by a communication-oriented view. By linking and referencing additional information, the process manager can work and guide process teams according to strategic objectives in his/her area of responsibility.

7   Summary

The motivation for the proposed Strategy Process Matrix is to develop a graphical approach to integrate strategic objectives with business process models. The approach contributes to sustainably aligning business processes with corporate strategy by outlining, measuring, and controlling particularly critical activities for strategy implementation. Associating flow objects, strategic objectives and roles supports middle managers in motivating a process team to work in line with the strategy. On the one hand, the approach seems to be suitable to strategically manage a process team, which is a major task for middle managers. On the other hand, the matrix can be used for a systematic reporting to the top management. The middle manager is in the position to justify available or additional process resources by assigning them to the given business strategy. Moreover, the indicators and action lists demonstrate a reproducible approach how middle managers can use the matrix to show their measureable additional value within a company.

However, the evaluation of the approach with case studies is primarily based on qualitative assessments. The Strategy Process Matrix needs to be supplemented in further research by quantitatively measurable improvements for a sound validation of the whole approach.

The proposed contents of the matrix fields were accepted positively in the case studies. For further research, concepts and theories of middle managers need to be used to systematically identify additional information to be documented in each matrix field.

The example of the described case study already shows that processes, strategy maps and especially the matrix tends to become quite complex for large process models. Therefore, an IT-based solution for creating and managing the matrix is necessary to introduce the procedure enterprise-wide.

By examining how the Strategy Process Matrix can be used in concert with S-BPM, this contribution not only demonstrates the Strategy Process Matrix is to a large extent notation agnostic, but also contributes to extending the methodical set of frameworks surrounding S-BPM. As a matter of fact, using the S-BPM notation for documenting processes promises to substantially simplify communication by using multiple smaller subject behavior diagrams instead of a single large BPMN.

References

1. Kaplan, R.S., Norton, D.P.: The Execution Premium: Linking Strategy to Operations for Competitive Advantage. Harvard Business Press, Boston (2008)
2. Lederer, M.: Business Process Transparency Management: An Approach to Aligning Business Processes and Corporate Strategy. In: Nunes, M.B., Peng, G.C., Roth, J. (eds.) Proceedings of the International Conference Information Systems Post-Implementation and Change Management 2013, pp. 55–58. IADIS Press, Prague (2013)
3. Wolf, C., Harmon, P.: The State of Business Process Management 2012. BPTrend (2012)
4. Gaitanides, M.: Prozessorganisation. 2. Auflage. Vahlen, München (2007)
5. Kaplan, R.S., Norton, D.P.: The Strategy-Focused Organization: How Balanced Scorecard Companies Thrive in the New Business Environment. Harvard Business Press, Boston (2001)
6. Saaksvuori, A., Immonen, A.: Product Lifecycle Management. Springer, Berlin (2004)
7. Minonne, C., Turner, G.: Business Process Management – Are you ready for the future? Knowledge and Process Management 19(3), 111–120 (2012)
8. Müller, T.: Zukunftsthema Geschäftsprozessmanagement. Eine Studie zum Status Quo des Geschäftsprozessmanagements in deutschen und österreichischen Unternehmen. PricewaterhouseCoopers, Wien (2011)
9. Sidorova, A., Isik, O.: Business Process Research: A Cross-Disciplinary Review. Business Process Management Journal 16, 566–597 (2010)
10. Heracleous, L.: Strategy and Organization: Realizing Strategic Management. Cambridge University Press, Cambridge (2003)
11. Staehle, W.: Management. Vahlen, München (1990)
12. Wooldridge, B., Floyd, S.W.: The strategy process, middle management involvement, and organizational performance. Strategic Management Journal 11(3), 231–241 (1990)
13. Wiersma, E.: For which purposes do managers use balanced scorecards? An empirical study. Management Accounting Research 20(4), 239–251 (2009)
14. Gutenberg, E.: Unternehmensführung. Organisation und Entscheidungen. Gabler, Wiesbaden (1962)
15. Leisgang, W.: Soziale Praxis und soziale Kompetenzen des mittleren Managements. Eine qualitativ-empirische Analyse von Hospitationen in der Sozialen Arbeit. Hampp, München (2011)
16. Weyerer, M.: Ändert sich das mittlere Management? Hernsteiner 11, 6–9 (1998)
17. Galliers, R.D.: Towards a flexible information architecture: integrating business strategies, information systems strategies and business process redesign. Information Systems Journal 3(10), 199–213 (1993)
18. Melchert, F., Winter, R., Klesse, M.: Aligning Process Automation and Business Intelligence to Support Corporate Performance Management. Association for Information Systems (2004)
19. Bleistein, S.J., Cox, K., Verner, J., Phalp, K.T.: B-SCP: A requirements analysis framework for validating strategic alignment of organizational IT based on strategy, context, and process. Information and Software Technology 48, 846–868 (2005)
20. Menz, M., Schmid, T., Müller-Stewens, G., Lechner, C.: Strategische Initiativen und Programme. Gabler, Wiesbaden (2011)
21. Lederer, M., Lembcke, U.: Business Process Transparency Management Modeling Notation. Working Paper 02/2013, Chair for Information Systems (Services-Processes-Intelligence), Friedrich-Alexander-University Erlangen-Nuremberg, Nuremberg

22. Kaplan, R.S., Norton, D.P.: Linking the Balanced Scorecard to Strategy. California Management Review 39(1), 53–79 (1996)
23. William, B.T.: The Balanced Scorecard as a Strategy-Evaluation Tool: The Effects of Implementation Involvement and a Causal-Chain Focus. The Accounting Review 85(3), 1095–1117 (2010)
24. Quezada, L.E., Cordova, F.M., Palominos, P., Godoy, K., Ross, J.: Method for identifying strategic objectives in strategy maps. International Journal of Production Economics 122(1), 492–500 (2009)
25. Chen, C.C., Jones, K.: Are Employees Buying the Balanced Scorecard? Management Accounting Quarterly 11(1), 36–44 (2009)
26. Chavan, M.: The balanced scorecard: a new challenge. Journal of Management Development 28(5), 393–406 (2009)
27. Crespo, I., Bergmann, L., Portmann, S., Lacker, T., Lacker, M., Fleischmann, J., Kozó, H.: Umsetzung der Unternehmensstrategie mit der Balanced Scorecard. In: Dombrowski, U., Herrmann, C., Lacker, T., Sonnentag, S. (eds.) Modernisierung kleiner und mittlerer Unternehmen. Ein ganzheitliches Konzept. Springer, Berlin (2009)
28. Recker, J.: BPMN Modeling – Who, Where, How and Why. BPTrends 5(3), 1–8 (2008)
29. Gadatsch, A., Alpar, P.: Grundkurs Geschäftsprozess-Management. Vieweg+Teubner, Wiesbaden (2005)
30. Meyer, A., Smirnov, S., Weske, M.: Data in Business Processes. EMISA-Forum 2011 3(5), 5–29 (2011)
31. Recker, J.C., Indulska, M., Rosemann, M., Green, P.: How Good is BPMN Really? Insights from Theory and Practice. In: Ljungberg, J., Andersson, M. (eds.) 14th European Conference on Information Systems, Goeteborg (2006)
32. Kocian, C.: Geschäftsprozessmodellierung mit BPMN 2.0. Business Process Model and Notation im Methodenvergleich. Working Paper Hochschule Neu-Ulm, Neu-Ulm (2011)
33. Fleischmann, A., Schmidt, W., Stary, C., Obermeier, S., Börger, E.: Subject-oriented business process management. Springer, Heidelberg (2012)
34. Object Management Group: Business Process Model and Notation, http://www.omg.org/spec/BPMN/2.0/PDF/ (accessed August 25, 2013)
35. Hogrebe, F., Nüttgens, M.: Rahmenkonzept zur Messung und Bewertung der Gebrauchstauglichkeit von Modellierungssprachen: Literaturauswertung und Untersuchungsrahmen für Usability-Eyetracking-Studien. In: Nüttgens, M. (ed.) Arbeitsberichte zur Wirtschaftsinformatik der Universität Hamburg Nr. 7, Hamburg (2009)

Using Meta Processes for the Structured Discovery and Self-learning Improvement of S-BPM Processes

Christoph Fleischmann[1] and Gerhard Stein[2]

[1] University of Technology, Vienna, Austria
chris.fleischmann@gmx.net
[2] Metasonic AG, Münchner Straße 29, Hettenshausen, 85276 Pfaffenhofen, Germany
Gerhard.stein@metasonic.de

Abstract. The Neural Approach is a Methodology for structured discovery of S-BPM processes based on the Open Control Cycle. It is realized as an S-BPM Meta Process which creates operative S-BPM processes in a structured and controlled manner and enables the users to improve those processes dynamically during execution. The Neural Approach enables self-learning processes which improve their subjects, their interactions, their behavior and message content.

1 Introduction and Objectives

The purpose of this framework is **agile development** and **quality assurance** of S-BPM process models. It increases the ability to react to unexpected incidents and **ensures the continuous quality** of the process model by precisely defining and automating an agile, **self-improving lifecycle** for **S-BPM processes**.

One of the advantages of S-BPM modeling is its intuitiveness and simplicity[1].

By using Subjects in a professional environment it will become obvious quite soon that modeling a common understanding of the business logic is only part of the story. There are commercial goals, financial and timing constraints, laws and compliance rules which have to be followed. Business users are rarely familiar with the modeling tools in use in the organization. Often overwhelmed by the complexity of the modeling process, they may be tempted to give the responsibility for the development of a process back to business process analysts.

This paper proposes the Open Control Cycle to guide the inexperienced business user in small, simple steps through the creation of a complete process, without the constraints of a narrow corset, without being disappointed by insurmountable obstacles or punished by merciless failure messages. Every step in the Open Control Cycle gives these users a clear feeling of progressing towards the development goal. More experienced users, on the other hand, are provided with all the information they need without restricting their preferred way of modeling.

Neural Approach and Open Control Cycle

The **Neural Approach** describes how to develop an S-BPM process in an agile way. It provides the business user with the freedom to define her/his individual working

C. Zehbold (Ed.): S-BPM ONE 2014, CCIS 422, pp. 85–106, 2014.

place. This agility makes it necessary to guide the business user to focus onto the objectives and to assure that compliance rules are observed without limiting the agility of the process evolvement. This guidance and continuous control of the progress of an emerging process by agile software quality assurance methods is done by the **Open Control Cycle**.

Once the process is running, the same support assists both kinds of users in using the experiences of daily business to continually improve and adapt the running process and all further processes in a controlled manner. The defined goals and rules set by the meta-process serve as a control mechanism and prevent users from forgetting necessary steps.

This self-improving process method is accomplished by meta-processes based on the Open Control Cycle thus ensuring that the process is always in accordance with its goals and compliance rules.

Outline

This document starts after the introduction to explain the basics: *Meta Processes*.

Based on Meta-processes is the *Open Control Cycle* which is described next. The following chapter describes the vision: The *Neural Approach* which leads to chapter 5: the *Realization* of the Neural Approach, which itself is divided into two main parts. The first describing what is already realized and the second one describing what could be realized to implement the neural approach in a very user friendly way. The *Conclusion* combines the four parts to show the possibilities offered by using the neural approach.

2   Meta Processes

Colette Rolland (1999) [2] defines a "Meta-Process" in the paper "Multi-model view" which was applied to the CREWS-L'Ecritoire method. The CREWS-L'Ecritoire method represents a methodical approach for Requirements Engineering, "the part of the IS development that involves investigating problems and requirements of the users community and developing a specification of the future system, the so-called conceptual schema."

For reusing processes a meta-process model identifies "the common, generic features of process models and represents them in a system of concepts. Such a representation has the potential to 'generate' all process models that share these features. This potential is realized when a generation technique is defined whose application results in the desired process model."[3]

With this concept of meta-levels the S-BPM method can be divided into three layers: the *meta-process*, the *process model* and the *process instance*.

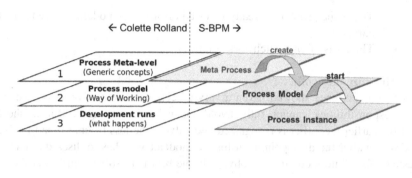

Fig. 1. Process Levels

The *process model* describes how the process shall be executed and the *process instance* is started every time the *process model* is executed. Unlike the *process model* the *process instance* has an editor, has data, such as start data, number of orders etc.

The *meta-process* is one level above and creates a *process model* when executed.

3   The Neural Approach – Establishing Connections

S-BPM enables distributed modeling where each modeler defines her/his individual subject behavior, which has numerous advantages (see: [1], [4] pp. 43-51).But applying such a bottom-up approach bears the risk that messages are not consistent, which may result in uncoordinated activities.

An Example: A simple ordering process with the subjects requestor, manager and purchasing. Every subject behavior is modeled independently on its own. The requestor requests an item at the manager and assumes to receive an approval from the manager. So he models the purchasing of the requested item after having received the approval. But the manager sends the approval instead to the subject purchasing, which orders the requested item.

The manager obviously has a different view on that process than the requestor which leads into a wrong subject behavior based on a wrong assumption. To handle such conflict situations there are three possibilities:

1.   Avoid the conflict
This can be done by a clear definition of objectives and responsibilities. But to avoid any possible conflict the effort for such an absolute precise definition rises dramatically. A complete avoidance is probably never possible.

2.   Manage the conflict
A conflict management is established. The drawback of conflict management is that:
  • The conflict is often not recognized before it starts to be a serious issue
  • Participants are already frustrated. Engagement is lost

- To fix the problem, already invested efforts into modeling have to be discarded
- The fix is often a patchwork solution

3. Minimize the conflict

Practical experience showed: Even a very precise definition of process objectives and responsibilities cannot fully avoid inconsistent messages. But it showed that the earlier a conflict is recognized and solved, the less troublesome to solve it and the smaller the disappointment for the modeler who has to discard already invested efforts into modeling. So obviously the best is to solve conflicts at the very beginning.

Where does a potential conflict start? Probably not inside the subject. It starts when a subject interfaces with another subject. That's when the message is created. So, the two involved participants (sender and receiver subject) have to make a clear defined agreement about that message, called *service level agreement*(SLA). Only if that message is clearly defined between the two subjects than both subjects can define their subject behavior independently without the risk of investing efforts into modeling which has to be discarded.

Message Service Level Agreement (SLA)

SLAs create clarity about the activities to be done and help reduce the coordination effort between customer and supplier. Failures due to missing or wrong information are avoided by SLAs. This saves time and costs by reducing the number of improvements [5].

Only if both parties are committed to fulfill the SLA, both parties can rely on receiving the required messages and information. The SLA also ensures that a subject is not allowed to simplify its subject behavior by removing all send states and the corresponding function states.

3.1   The Neural Approach

For the approach of a self-governing process the metaphor of neural structures is used for modeling dynamic and flexible communication structures. Neural networks cannot do anything that cannot be done using traditional computing techniques, but they can do some things which would otherwise be very difficult. In particular, they can form a model from their training data (or possibly input data) alone[6].

This neural structure is similar to the communication structure of subjects within a process. All interactions between subjects are handled through messages which the subjects send between each other. The subjects follow existing communication paths to process information and complete their given tasks. If required the subjects establish new communication paths to complete their task.

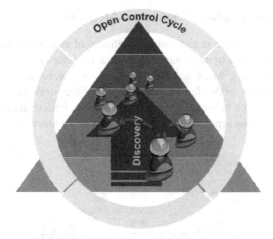

Fig. 2. The Neural Approach

An Example: The HR-Manager starts to implement a new on-boarding process. He needs an e-mail account for the new colleague. So he sends a request for this e-mail account to IT department. They in turn need the first name, last name and the location for activating the requested e-mail account at their service provider.

3.2   Implementation of the Neural Approach

The concept of neural structures has to be implemented across all three levels of the meta-process. To avoid confusion we want to distinguish clearly between the meta-process which is generating a process model and the process model which is generated, called *"Operative-process"*.

The *Meta-process*, which is executed by the responsible *subject owners*, is represented using green figures, text and lines. The *Operative-process*, executed by the *operative users*, is represented using blue figures, text and lines. These figures execute the previously described example of the HR manager and the employee [Chapter 3.1]

Fig. 3. Green: Meta Process   **Fig. 4.** Blue: Process Level

3.3   Establishment of a New Connection – Meta Level

Establishing a new message is not just the decision of one individual subject owner but has to be agreed upon by both participants: the initiator of a message and the corresponding subject. Only when having agreed on the exchange of a message, both subject owners can rely on the delivery and content of the message.

In the example shown below, the subject *HR-Manager* needs an *e-mail address for the new employee* and so sends a message request to the subject *IT*.

Fig. 5. Create Message Request (Meta Level)

The subject *IT* now has four possibilities from which to choose accordingly:
- It can accept the message request
- It can reject the message request
- It can forward the message request to another subject
- It can accept the message request conditionally

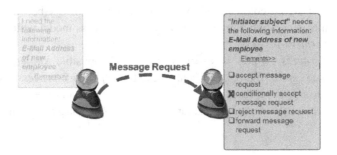

Fig. 6. Conditional Acceptance (Meta Level)

In the example the *IT* subject needs the *first name*, the *last name* and the *location* of the new employee to be able to fulfill the message request. The *IT* subject accepts the request if certain conditions are met: the *HR-Manager* subject has to provide the requested *Employee Details*. The message *Conditional Acceptance* in turn is accepted by the subject *HR-Manager*.

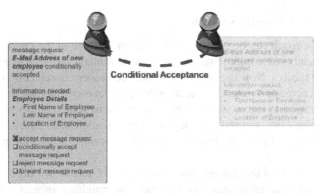

Fig. 7. Message Request Acceptance (Meta Level)

3.4   Establishment of a New Connection – Operative Level

The Meta-Process defines the abstract structure of the process which is then executed on the Operative Level where the subjects and messages receive concrete identifiers. In the example shown in Fig.8Fig.8 - Established Connection (Operative Level) the subject *HR-Manager* sends the message *Employee Details* to the subject *IT* and receives the message *E-Mail of new Employee* from the subject *IT*.

Fig. 8. Established Connection (Operative Level)

Dynamic Improvement of a Process

With the neural approach the border between creation of a process and the improvement of a process disappears. In the extreme case, the first state of a process may be already the first executable version of a process which is then continuously improved. This is a radical change from existing modeling techniques, where only processes could be deployed that are completely modeled, making process improvements difficult and time-consuming. The neural approach allows to start with an incomplete process and to improve it dynamically. In practice, however, at least the "sunshine path" should be modeled more or less completely. The dynamic improvement allows the users of the process to improve it as required.

Improvement of Message Content

The neural approach can be used also for the improvement of the content. So if a subject owner needs some additional information he sends a message change request to the neighbor subject. Now the neighbor subject can accept it, reject it or conditionally accept it. Acceptance means, that the neighbor subject now commits to send this additional information to the requestor. This may result in some additional modifications of its behavior. For example it may require an additional function state which enters manually or by integration the additional information into the requested business object.

It also may happen that the neighbor subject is not able or willing to fulfill that request for additional information. In that case the neighbor subject can forward the message request (*"I know somebody who knows what you want"*) to another subject, which in turn can now accept the message request, reject or forward it.

Improvement by Additional Subjects

If a message request is forwarded to a "new" subject and this new subject accepts the message request, the process has been expanded by that subject.

Now the question may arise: How can a new subject be addressed which is not already a member in the process? This subject is not a subject in the operative process level. Instead it is a subject of the meta-process, the Open Control Cycle process. There all modeling subjects are modeled as a so called multi-subject. All instances of such a multi-subject have the same behavior. In this case they model one subject behavior. Multi-subject instances can be added at execution time.

4   Open Control Cycle

Subject-oriented Business Process Management (S-BPM) [1] uses an Open Control Cycle to accumulate information about processes and process design. The gathered information is then documented as a process model which then serves as a starting point for further process analysis and improvement. The S-BPM Open Control Cycle describes different phases, or activity bundles, to accumulate the process information. They include definition, modeling, validation, optimization, organization-specific implementation, IT implementation, operation and monitoring. These activities are not performed in a strict sequence; activities may be skipped or redone. As a result, the execution of the meta-process is not over-constrained. The various tasks of process management are not always executed in a strict order; employees jump back and forth between tasks or even skip them entirely, depending on the situation at hand.

Taking the concept of non-sequential activities we defined a modified set of activity bundles to create a new Open Control Cycle which is oriented on agile software development. This new control cycle represents the framework for the meta-process and self-improving processes. The modified activity bundles are definition, business logic, data structure, integration & automation, role assignment, and execution.

In addition, validation has been divided into small, understandable and controllable checkpoints, which validates every activity bundle according to the goals and compliance rules defined for the specific process.

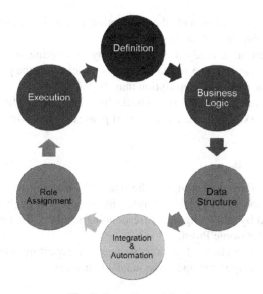

Fig. 9. Open Control Cycle

4.1   The Validation Cycle

In order not to limit the outstanding agility of the neural approach, agile test methods in software engineering[6]are used, where testing is done continuously. This reduces feedback latency whereas long gaps between implementing and testing increase risk and waste [6]. After each phase it must be proved that all the defined goals and compliance rules are reached. Those tests, often called "Quality Gates", are called "Checkpoint" in this paper. The checkpoints have to be defined in a structured way during the definition phase, the first phase of the Open Control Cycle.

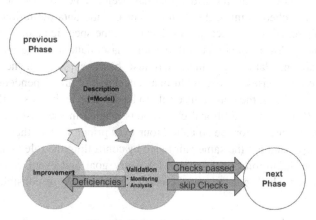

Fig. 10. Validation Cycle

The validation cycle starts with the description phase. Each phase uses different methods for describing its part of the process.

Once the description is ready it is validated by monitoring or visualizing the description and analyzing it. If the validation shows deficiencies the process model must be improved and the improved description must be validated.

The validation cycle can be left if all checks have been successfully passed or if the validator decides to skip a check. Then the next phase can be started.

Monitoring

Also Monitoring differs depending on the phase. Monitoring the business logic requires a visualization of the path generated by stepping through the branches and decision points and by activating the corresponding subjects. This monitoring is provided by the tool Metasonic Proof.

Monitoring the execution of a process needs a reporting tool visualizing the process KPIs in a configurable and understandable manner.

Analysis

Also the analysis differs from phase to phase. For the analysis of the business logic it must be checked that all branches are verified, all subjects are activated, that there are no deadlocks and forbidden combinations are impossible.

In contrast, if you want to analyze the execution phase you may prefer trend lines, thresholds, totals, extrapolations and other functions of modern Business Intelligence (BI) tools.

It is not necessary to have one checkpoint for every goal and compliance rule in every phase. But every goal has to be defined in terms of a way of measuring, the so-called KPI, and a threshold which determines if the goal has been reached or not. At execution it must be measured if the goal has been reached or not. So for every goal there must be a checkpoint at the definition phase, the data definition phase and the execution phase. All other checkpoints depend on the specific goal. For the validation of compliance rules checkpoints at definition phase, data structure phase and execution phase are mandatory. But there may also be checkpoints in the business logic phase and other phases. Those additional checkpoints are dependent on the compliance rule. So if e.g. the compliance rule to be fulfilled is the Basel III rule for money transfer[7], there are additional checkpoints needed in the business logic and the role assignment phases for the so-called four-eyes principle: that there are two different pairs of eyes and not the same pair twice by controlling the role assignment.

During the definition phase it must for every goal and every compliance rule it must be defined which phases must be checked and who is responsible for doing the validation.

Combination of Open Process Cycle and Validation Cycle

If Open Control Cycle and Validation Cycle are combined into one diagram then it looks as follows:

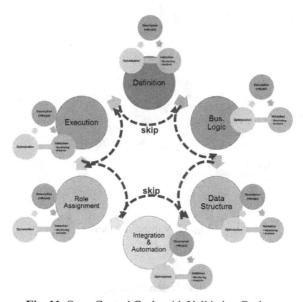

Fig. 11. Open Control Cycle with Validation Cycles

This diagram shows all the possibilities to enter the next phase by validating or skipping it.

Validation Protocol

The **validation protocol** records the validation status of each checkpoint after completion of a validation cycle. A checkpoint can be either:

- Not done (white)
- Successfully passed (green)
- Skipped (yellow)
- Failed (red)
- Not applicable (x)

The **validation status** shows the actual situation and can be regarded as a snapshot of the validation protocol.

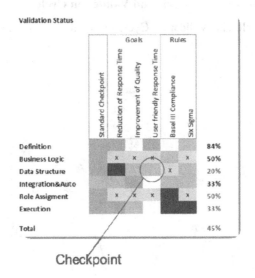

Fig. 12. Validation Status

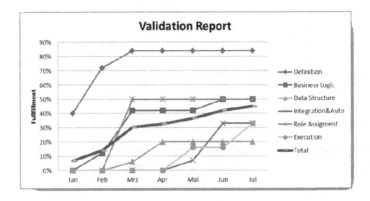

Fig. 13. Validation Report

The validation report is the graphical representation of the whole validation protocol. It gives a good idea how far the process has been developed and how much is still missing. Extrapolating the "Total" line gives a good idea about when the process is expected to be ready. If the Open Process Cycle is viewed as an operative process then goals and rules are nothing but the KPIs of the Open Process Cycle process.

4.2   Phase Framework Definition

The business strategy is the basis for the process strategy and a crucial factor in identifying and defining processes [5]. Based on the company strategy precise targets can now be defined [4] which support the achievement of the strategy. Extensive targets can now be divided into single, detailed targets. This allows establishing a comprehensive target system for the whole company. [4]Before any actions are taken the goals for the planned actions and the organization have to be defined. This includes the definition of guidelines and compliance rules towards which every involved subject orients its actions [8]. In addition, it is important to define key performance indicators (KPIs) to measure the process goals accordingly. This procedure is overseen and steered by a previously defined steering committee and potential process owners.

The introduction of compliance rules serves the purpose to guide process development towards the defined goal and to simultaneously set restrictions. Compliance rules include

- vertical (industry sector) compliance rules (e.g. Basel III),
- governmental laws,
- company rules,
- customer agreements, and
- constraints regarding time, budget, or personal.

Compliance Management is using three approaches:
- Design Time Compliance Checking (DTCC) (see: [9])
- Run Time Compliance Checking (RTCC) (see: [10])
- Backward Compliance Checking

During Framework Definition DTCC is used to define which rules have to be followed, where the compliance of the model has to be validated and who is responsible for the validation of the rule at the corresponding phase.

Run Time Compliance Checking (RTCC) ensures the measurement and enforcement of the previously set compliance rules during execution of the correct modeled process.

Accordingly for each goal appropriate indicators or KPIs have to be defined to check if the goal has been reached [4]. Also it has to be defined in which phase of the Open Control Cycle those KPIs have to be validated and who is responsible for the validation of the goal. KPIs are used to show the effectivity and efficiency of the business process and to visualize the effect of process modifications for commercial results. [5]

4.3   Phase Business Logic

The task of the „Business Logic"-phase is to create a model and an accompanying logic of the desired process by defining prerequisites for the various activities. Although there is no sequential order for the Open Control Cycle the execution of the phases is not entirely arbitrary.

This phase also includes the creation of the Communication Diagram which describes all the subjects involved in the process, their interactions and the subject behaviors which reflects the S-BPM method to create process models. Such a model creation can be done, for example, with the MetasonicSuite [11] or MetasonicTouch [12].

4.4   Phase Data Structure

In this phase it has to be defined which data the subjects require to complete the tasks of the process.

- This includes data needed to
  - enable all decisions
  - enable all KPI measuring
  - enable all SLAs
  - enable all reports

Often integrated IT-systems or business rules need certain restrictions for the process data. So if you want to calculate the number of days between a start day and an end day of a vacation request in order to check if the applicant has enough vacation days available, the start and end date must be in a certain format, the end date must be later than the start date and both must be within the current or next year.

- Data Restrictions
  - mainly based on limitations of integrated systems
  - KPIs, SLAs and reports may require specific data types
  - User may be guided by choices
  - Automated calculations may limit parameter to specific types and ranges

There is the possibility to provide different views of the same data structure, called *business object*, for different subjects and tasks.

- Visibility and Access Rights
  - Views for different subjects
  - Views for specific tasks

These rights and different views serve as a control mechanism for the metaprocess. Each subject may only see and change data in accordance to its respective tasks.

4.5   Phase Integration and Automation

Integration and Automation are so closely connected that it makes no sense to separate them into different phases. In reality it is almost never possible to automate something without integration. So e.g. if you want to set the full name of the editor automatically, you need to integrate the user database and if you want to enter automatically the amount of available articles you have to somehow integrate the article database.

You can start to implement a process without any integration or/and automation. But to make the process more comfortable or more secure in terms of typing errors, a process has to be integrated into the existing IT-environment.

Also, to fulfill compliance rules, data has to be taken from existing IT thus preventing the user from entering invalid data and also decisions have to be automated in order to force the process following certain branches according to the actual process instance data.

Once a process has been completely integrated there is no more manual data entry because all information is taken automatically from the IT-environment. Then the user is required only for control and management of the process.

4.6   Phase Role Assignment

The efficiency of business process management relies significantly on how the processes are embedded into the organizational structure of the company [5].

In greater organizations exists the process organization, which defines which tasks have to be done by whom and in which sequence has to be defined as well as the organizational structure[4]. Kosiol[13] splits business operations into the smallest possible basic tasks and bundles them to organizational units, which are then assigned to resources, which themselves are assigned to employees. This is exactly how S-BPM works. Process organization roles, as defined by the S-BPM method [1], are assigned to the subjects. The process organization roles themselves are mapped to the real persons who will take the role of the subject at process instantiation in a very flexible way. This flexibility allows the same process to be executed in different organizations just by mapping the subjects in a different way according to the different organization charts.

The role assignment ensures that the right persons act as the right subject at execution time. Because a subject defines precisely what can and has to be done by the persons who take the role of this subject, the security manager can define precisely who is allowed to take that role. This definition is called role assignment.

Every subject has to be assigned to at least one role but it is not restricted to just one. A process actor, for instance, may not only execute the role of an actor, because an actor is directly involved in executing the process he also provides specific knowledge in a certain field. This means that a subject can additionally incorporate the role of an expert regarding its specific processes (see [1]).

4.7   Phase Execution of Modeled Process

The task of this phase is to execute the modeled process; either in a real life environment after the integration of the process or in a test environment to validate the internal process logic and process consistency. A possible evaluation environment to test the process can be Metasonic Build/Proof.

4.8   Skipping

Each phase may be skipped taking into account of the prerequisites. E.g. phase *Execution* requires phase *Business Logic* and phase *Role Assignment*.

This allows stepping through the Open Control Cycle in nearly **any sequence**.

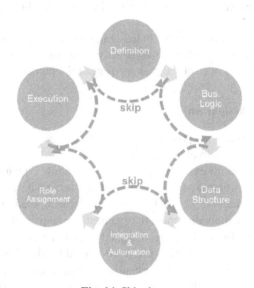

Fig. 14. Skipping

But there are some restrictions. So for defining the business logic the definition has to be done at least partially. Also the business logic is required for the execution of a process. The validation protocol shows which checkpoints have been passed, failed or skipped. The complete process model is validated if all checkpoints have been passed (successfully validated) or if the process owner decides to go live despite known deficiencies (validated with deficiencies).

4.9   Process Creation versus Process Improvement

The Open Control Cycles combines process creation and process improvement. If the Open Control Cycle is followed in a very strict manner, a phase is only started after the preceding phase has been successfully validated. The first cycle is the process creation and all consecutive phases are process improvements. Once you start to skip cycles, the borderline between creation and improvement fades. But as long as there is a checkpoint which has not been passed successfully the process is still in the creation phase. Once the goals of a process have been changed, the process is in the improvement phase. So there may be a process which is not yet complete but already improved.

This possibility is one of the greatest advantages of S-BPM and the Neural Approach. You can start with the execution of a very basic process and improve the process at execution time by implementing the goals of the definition phase and feedback from real experience step by step as necessary.

4.10   Roles and Responsibilities

Every phase has a role assigned which is responsible that all necessary tasks and goals are accomplished according to the defined goals, compliance rules and company rules. Roles are independent from specific persons. These roles are Management, Citizen Developer, IT Appl. Developer, IT Security and User.

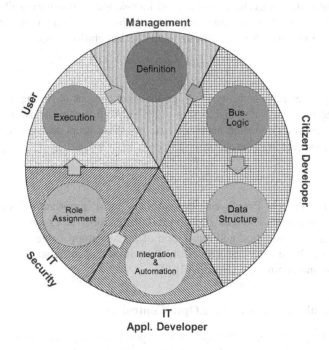

Fig. 15. Roles

Management

The task of the management team is to solve cross-cutting process questions and problems. It is the link between executive board, functional units and business processes [5].

The "Management" is not a single role but does consist of various roles which bundle specific tasks, competences, and responsibilities. These roles are the "Sponsor", the "Steering Committee", the "Process Owner", the CIO, the Security Manager and the QA Manager. They are responsible to define all the deliverables of the definition phase.

Citizen Developer

Gartner defines a **citizen developer** as a user who creates new business applications for consumption by others using development and runtime environments sanctioned by corporate IT. In the past, end-user application development has typically been limited to single-user or workgroup solutions built with tools such as Microsoft Excel and Access. However, today, end users can build departmental, enterprise and even public applications using shared services, fourth-generation language (4GL)-style development platforms and cloud computing services. [14]

IT – Application Developer

The IT-Application Developer has a good knowledge of integrating IT-Services and systems. He typically is familiar with Java, Web-Services and Web-Applications as well as with Enterprise Service Bus and other IT-Integration tools.

IT – Security

IT-Security takes responsibility to assign the right persons to the right roles by using the existing user and role databases in order to avoid malicious use of processes by granting roles in a controlled manner to exactly those users who are necessary at the appropriate subject in the process.

User

The user, or "Process Employee", is one of the most important roles in the area of process management. The user's responsibilities include the execution of the process activities and the initiation and realization of process improvements. To achieve this goal the users have a certain freedom to act within a specific scope of preset guidelines, rules, and control mechanism. [5][4]

4.11   Neural Approach and the Open Control Cycle

The Neural Approach is a very agile way of generating a process model by providing maximum parallelism of development with a minimum of interface definition effort. This outstanding agility and distribution of activities would bear the risk to lose the focus onto the objectives of the process or to violate compliance policies without the Open Control Cycle. The Open Control Cycle assures by using highly agile quality assurance methods that the business users who generates the process are guided toward the objectives of the process. Also it controls continuously that the process complies to compliance rules process achieves the process and company goals and is compliant with existing rules and restrictions.

The Open Control Cycle guides the business users generating the process toward the process objectives and continuously controls that the process follows the compliance rules, without limiting the agility of the process evolvement. This guidance and continuous control of the progress of an emerging process by agile SW quality assurance methods is done by the **Open Control Cycle.**

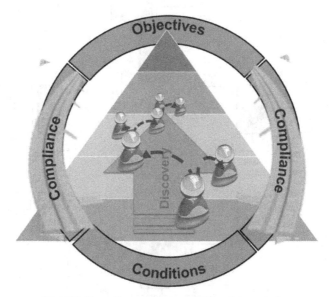

Fig. 16. Open Control Cycle and Neural Approach

5   Implementation of the Open Control Cycle Process

If this sounds complicated and if you want to be sure that no step is forgotten then developing a model of the meta-process is likely to be useful. This meta-process guide you through all the process phases and validation cycles, showing which steps are done and which steps are still missing. It also provides you with reports and analysis functions. Which process could do that better than an S-BPM process?

The Metasonic Suite and its multi-subject functionality offer a possible solution for the realization of that process.

The validation process consists of two processes: The „*Open Control Cycle*" and the „*Validation Cycle*". The resulting communication view is shown below:

The "*Open Control Cycle*" is started once for every process that is created, and the "*Validation Cycle*" is started for each individual checkpoint.

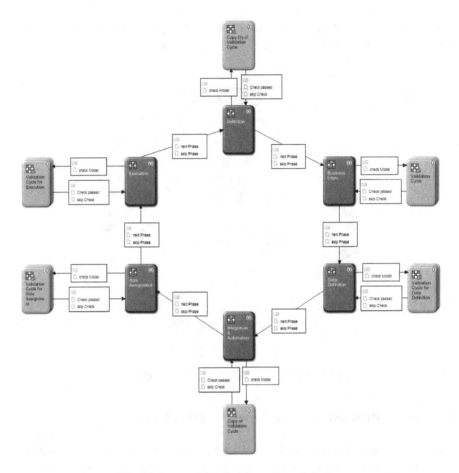

Fig. 17. Process Model of Open Control Cycle

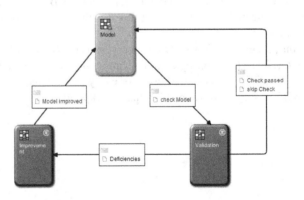

Fig. 18. Process Model of Validation Cycle

The subjects of the *"Open Control Cycle"* are assigned to the roles *"Management"*, *"Business User"*, *"IT"*, *"IT-Security"* and *"User"* according to the role schema shown in Fig.15.

State of Implementation

This paper discusses how such a process can be implemented. But as today, this process is drafted using Metasonic Suite but not integrated and therefore not executable yet.

6   Conclusion and Outlook

The Neural Approach provides a very agile and adaptive way of generating tailored business applications. The conjunction with the Open Control Cycle provides the necessary agile control mechanism, goal orientation and compliance. A full integration with modeling tools and execution engine will erase the border between process model creation and execution. When the creation of a new process connection is easier than writing an e-mail, ad-hoc process improvement becomes absolutely dynamic. According to Gartner's Pace Layers [15] which defines three levels of application paces: the *Layer of Innovation*, the *Layer of Differentiation* and the *Layer of Record*, we implemented the layer of innovation first. This process is executable but not integrated at all. This means that all modeling, definition and validations have to be done manually. The process guides the user through the software development cycle and provides information about the activities closed the status of the process and the activities and responsibilities which have to be done to finalize the process development. The vision is to integrate this process fully with the existing modeling and execution tools as there are Metasonic Touch, Metasonic Build, Metasonic Proof and Metasonic Flow which can be achieved if the process shows the expected results and can pass from the Layer of Innovation to the Layer of Differentiation and finally to the Layer of Record. A fully integrated Neural Approach would no longer use forms which have to be entered manually. What the user would get to see is only a simple button on the actual form "add field" which fires the requirement of an additional piece of information and a "New message" button in Metasonic Flow which fires a new subject connection which results in a "Message Request" menu at the partner subject. The „add field-request which fires the Meta process to establish a new data connection.

Because the Open Control Cycle is a Meta-process and no hardcoded application, the improvement needs no time-consuming traditional software modification. It can be improved just by moving or adding some tangible elements on the Metasonic Touch or dynamically during execution. So the whole process modeling will be improved and tailored to customer needs by daily experience.

Acknowledgement. We would like to thank all the colleagues from Metasonic and Metasonic partners discussing with us their and our ideas on business process modeling meta-models. Those discussions contributed valuable pieces to the combination of Neural Approach and Open Control Cycle presented in this paper.

References

1. Fleischmann, A., Schmidt, W., Stary, C., Obermeier, S., Börger, E.: Subject-Oriented Business Process Management. Springer, Heidelberg (2012)
2. Rolland, C., Prakash, N., Benjamin, A.: A Multi-Model View of Process Modelling. Requirements Engineering 4(4), 169–187 (1999)
3. Rolland, C.: A comprehensive view of process engineering. In: Pernici, B., Thanos, C. (eds.) CAiSE 1998. LNCS, vol. 1413, pp. 1–24. Springer, Heidelberg (1998)
4. Turetken, O., Demirors, O.: Business Process Modeling Pluralized. In: Fischer, H., Schneeberger, J. (eds.) S-BPM ONE 2013. CCIS, vol. 360, pp. 34–51. Springer, Heidelberg (2013)
5. Schmelzer, H., Sesselmann, W.: Geschäftsprozessmanagement in der Praxis – Kunden zufriedenstellen, Produktivität steigern, Wert erhöhen, 8th edn. Carl Hanser Verlag, München (2013)
6. Smith, P.L.: An Introduction to Neural Networks (1996),
   http://www.cs.stir.ac.uk/~lss/NNIntro/InvSlides.html
7. Hendrickson, E.: Agile Testing - Nine Principles and Six Concrete Practices for Testing on Agile Teams. Quality Tree Software, Inc. (2008)
8. Bank for International Settlements, Basel III: A global (December 2010),
   http://www.bis.org/publ/bcbs189.pdf
9. Allweyer, T.: Geschäftsprozessmanagement. Herdecke, Bochum (2005)
10. Becker, J., Kugeler, M., Rosemann, M.: Prozessmanagement - Ein Leitfaden zur prozessorientierten Organisationsgestaltung, 7th edn. Springer, Berlin (2012)
11. Cabanillas, C., Resinas, M., Ruiz-Cortés, A.: Introducing a Mashup-Based Approach for Design-Time Compliance Checking in Business Processes. In: Bajec, M., Eder, J. (eds.) CAiSE Workshops 2012. LNBIP, vol. 112, pp. 337–350. Springer, Heidelberg (2012)
12. School of Computer Science, Fudan University, China, Detecting Runtime Business Process Compliance with Artifact Lifecycles. Springer
13. Metasonic AG, "MetasonicSuite," PlanetCreativ GbR,
    http://www.metasonic.de/metasonic-suite (accessed October 01, 2013)
14. Metasonic AG, MetasonicTouch, PlanetCreativ GbR,
    http://www.metasonic.de/touch (accessed September 12, 2013)
15. Kosil, E.: Organisation der Unternehmung, Wiesbaden (1962)
16. Gartner Inc., IT Glossary (2013),
    http://www.gartner.com/it-glossary/citizen-developer/
    (accessed October 01, 2013)
17. Gartner, Pace Layers (2010)

Managing Knowledge-Intensive Business Processes by Harnessing Collective Practical Experience without Codification

Andreas Fink and Simon Vogt

Institute of Computer Science
Faculty of Economics and Social Sciences,
Helmut-Schmidt-Universität Hamburg,
Holstenhofweg 85,
22043, Hamburg, Germany
{andreas.fink,simonvogt}@hsu-hh.de

Abstract. This work focuses on the execution of knowledge-intensive business processes by harnessing collective intelligence without codification. Trying to automate processes that are neither completely predictable regarding pre-defined structure and activities but instead require the decisions of experts, traditional workflow management reaches its limits. Having recognized this deficit, several new business process management concepts and techniques arose, drawing upon the advantages of Enterprise 2.0 and social software to face the complexity of knowledge-intensive processes. These elements offer cooperative coordination but always require linguistic codification to enable the knowledge transfer. This article untangles the various terms and concepts, derives requirements and develops a set of metrics that lead to a social, design-by-doing, machine-learning tool that harnesses the collective intelligence without the need for codification.

Keywords: Social BPM, Case Management, Machine Learning Tool, Knowledge-Processes, Design-by-Doing.

1   Introduction

"The answer is not to make all the decisions ahead of time, but rather to put the right resources in the hands of the workers, so they can make the right decisions at the right time" (Jacob P. Ukelson [20]).

Knowledge-intensive processes themselves are not novel. They have existed ever since, describing a goal-oriented sequence of activities and decisions that require experience, knowledge and expertise. In the business context, knowledge-intensive processes are likely to contain the value creation that leads to the comparative advantage or forms the uniqueness of a company. During the past decades, information technology soared and created opportunities to support or even execute business processes automatically. Focusing on knowledge processes, the recent years spotted the limits of Business Process Management (BPM) according to the traditional

C. Zehbold (Ed.): S-BPM ONE 2014, CCIS 422, pp. 107–121, 2014.
© Springer International Publishing Switzerland 2014

workflow management concepts – with the quest for automation – and revealed the need for new approaches. Pre-designed, fully automated workflows are not capable of facing the complexity of high-value knowledge-intensive processes [2].

The importance of Business Process Management is undisputable. Placing the focal point on the optimization of processes within businesses and companies has foiled the Tayloristic view of their organization. The automation of repeating, structured and predictable processes has become a critical factor of success in various business branches, enabling optimization and outsourcing. But, as BPM advanced and has been adopted in different contexts, it has become more and more obvious that traditional workflow management concepts are not able to cover the whole scope of business processes, at least not in its current state of advance.

As a result, new branches developed within the generic discipline of BPM, aiming at the support of knowledge-intensive processes, but differing in their perspectives and toolsets. The latter may therefore include (but is not limited to) tools of project management, groupware, Web-2.0 / Enterprise-2.0, document management, and cloud-technology, each of them relying on the transfer of codified knowledge. Sharing experience, expertise and knowledge about processes has become the key factor to deal with complex flows. At the same time the need to verbally express thoughts and decisions requires time and effort and may lead to information overhead.

2   Methodology

The purpose of this work is to further clarify the variety of terms and concepts in the context of knowledge-intensive process management as premise to spot commonalities and possible deficits in dealing with complex process cases and in accessing common intelligence. By subsequently deriving the resulting requirements, this will lead to a tool and metric to support the execution of such kinds of processes, harnessing the collective knowledge without the need of codification.

This work follows a three-step-approach of design science as described in [15][7], starting with a survey of the current state of research and untangling the different concepts and terms in current literature. As second step, conventional techniques and algorithms of process mining and design are examined to develop a metric that enables the use of machine-learning, design-by-doing tools that support the execution of knowledge processes at runtime. Finally, an exemplary implementation and a use case are presented.

3   Managing Knowledge-Intensive Processes

3.1   Definitions and Related Work

Knowledge-intensive (work) processes are unique [18][4]. They are neither completely predictable nor repeatable. Each knowledge-intensive process is routed by the decisions taken by experts under special situational awareness. To a high extent, such processes are among the core processes of many businesses since they include the

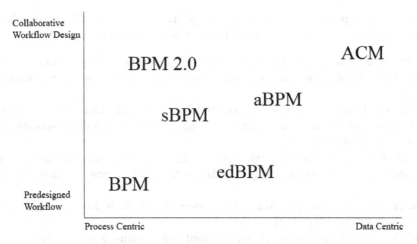

Fig. 1. Classification of Case Management Concepts

creativity, experience, and knowledge (or even wisdom) of the involved employees. "(…) As knowledge work proceeds, the sequence of actions depends so much upon the specifics of the situation (…) necessitating that part of doing the work is make the plan itself" [18]. There still is a certain amount of preplanning, considering the information which is available at the start. But the emphasis is now placed on the design during execution (technically spoken: at runtime).

In contrast to fully structured and predictable routine work, the traditional workflow management techniques and methods of BPM cannot easily be applied to knowledge-intensive processes and therefore require different approaches that can be summarized as "Case Management".

Case management in general is no new appearance. It has been discussed under various names and in different contexts at least during the last decade, mainly driven by two disciplines: Case management as an extension to BPM on the one hand and case management as a new use case scenario for enterprise-content-management on the other [14]. Common expressions include "case handling" [21][24][17], "Dynamic Case Management" (DCM) [13][14] and most recently "Adaptive Case Management", responding to the issue that knowledge-intensive processes as integral part of today's economic environment need special scientific appraisal [14][18]. The foundation of the letter term, Adaptive Case Management (ACM), has been laid during a meeting in 2009, leading to Swenson's publication "Mastering the Unpredictable" in 2010 [8]. This book introduces tools, procedures, and techniques for case management; its successor "Taming the Unpredictable" is a collection of various exemplary cases and collected practices [19]. Furthermore, intersections with "Social BPM", "subject-oriented BPM" (sBPM) and "adaptive BPM" (aBPM) occur, focusing on case management as an extension to the process-centric view of BPM. Figure 1gives an orientation over the most common concepts and terms. BPM and ACM are regarded as opposite sides of a two-dimensional continuum considering the perspective (data centric vs. process centric) and the design (predesigned vs. collaborative design at runtime) of cases. The continuum includes the listed elements:

- BPM: The common methodology according to workflow management concepts; aiming at a complete automation of control of repeatable, structured workflows [22].
- edBPM: Event-Driven BPM; combining BPM with elements of Service Oriented Architecture and Event-Processing, leading to a higher flexibility and responsiveness [25].
- S-BPM: Subject-Oriented BPM; emphasizing on the exchange of messages and natural languages between subjects, placing technical aspects in the background [5].
- BPM 2.0 (also social BPM): Adding elements of Web 2.0/Enterprise 2.0 to common BPM-tools [5][12].
- aBPM: BPM that provides techniques to deal with unplanned exceptions [3].

Forrester defines case management as "a highly structured, but also collaborative, dynamic, and information-intensive process that is driven by outside events and re-quires incremental responses from the business domain handling the case" [14].

This diversity of terms and perspectives concerning case management impedes the aggregation to a comprehensive precise definition. Accordingly, the two dimensions of the classification Figure 1 can be extended. Huber et al. extract common principles of current literature that form the outlines of case management [8], as presented in Figure 2. In addition to data centricity and collaboration, they propose goal orienta-tion, emergence and case templates as further common criteria.

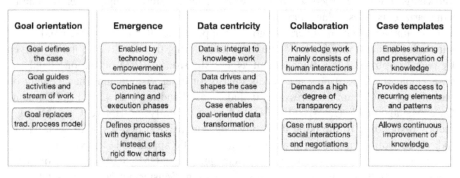

Fig. 2. Five Principles of Case Management [8]

3.2   Taming the Complexity of Knowledge-Intensive Processes

The main reason why knowledge-intensive processes require special tools and prac-tices is their complexity. Interdependent decisions, uncertain circumstances and assumptions based on experience and knowledge of its participants prohibit full antic-ipation and pre-modeling. Ukelson, author of the chapter "What to do when modeling doesn't work" in [18], therefore concludes that decisions should be made by the included workers at the right time, giving them the resources and tools to do so (as quoted from [18] in section 1 of this article). This paradigm change especially addresses collaboration as well as the need for a time shift and delegation of emerging decisions. Academic researches and commercial businesses have reacted to meet these requirements. Several tools have been developed and launched containing different features for collaboration, co-creation and (social-) networking.

ACM-software varies in architecture, scope, features and functionality. Standard software solutions exist as well as custom tailored toolsets. However, commonalities such as document management elements in order to keep all case-related content at one central place can be found. The need for collaboration is covered by the implementation of groupware features (e.g. E-Mail, team calendars), chats, collaborative document editors and social network functionality (status-posts, activity-streams, etc.). Additionally, to enable designing the process at runtime, wikis can be implemented. Especially the latter two elements provide a platform to discuss the upcoming events and decisions [14][16].

But these types of collaborative tools also increase the information- as well as the discussion-overload. Harnessing collective intelligence and knowledge of employees, experts, and other participants to make a decision on what to do next is the only way to cope with the complexity. But most of these tools require a knowledge-transfer via codification mainly in terms of written words (chat, wikis, comments, status-posts) or verbal discussion (video-chat). Enabling this transfer of knowledge requires additional platforms, tools and communication channels overlaying the process-/case-management-tool itself. An inherent attribute of knowledge-transfer via written or verbal codification is that experts need to explain their thoughts and steps in their own words. A direct exchange of the taken action itself without describing an explaining is neither supported nor the aim of these tools. The following disadvantages are the consequence:

- Meta-discussion about single process-steps requires additional time
- Especially complex scenarios and decisions with multiple valid results require a high amount of explanation

Different approaches are demonstrated by commercial ACM-software supplier Isis-Papyrus, and Herbst et al., as both introduce machine-learning tools to in the context of knowledge-processes. The latter use a machine-learning component to support the acquisition and adaption of workflow models by evaluating trace-logs of workflow executions to lead to a definite workflow model that may later be imported into workflow engines [6]. One module of Isis-Papyrus' ACM-suite is the so called "User-Trained Agent" (UTA). The company itself describes the UTA as "first solution to use real-time machine learning for automated business process discovery and continuous process optimization and adaptation" [9]. Even though further information about the detailed functionality of UTA remains hidden, the use of a learning machine (software) that observes the taken decisions and executed events to generate recommendations for the next time that another participant (of a different process instance) faces a similar situation, seems to be a promising approach to harness collective knowledge, expertise, and experience without having to start a (verbal or written) discussion. The premise is to enable "design-by-doing" instead of "design-by-discussion". Taking that idea as a frame to be filled with scientific content, this article now derives requirements to knowledge-process-management software and then develops and discusses metrics that enable machine-learning in knowledge processes.

3.3   General Requirements to Knowledge-Process-Management Tools

Analyzing the current market, Forrester developed a list of key factors that determine case management software and describe their character. The results may also be used as requirements for future development. The following three points are regarded as most important [13]:

- Case management allows more runtime and design-time changes.
- Case management platforms allow case workers to select predefined case steps.
- Case management provides information in context.

The first requirement, the need for runtime and more design-time changes, has already been described above. The second one may also be interpreted as contribution to 1., since runtime changes can especially be accelerated by offering predefined artifacts or patterns. These may be derived from previous case-instances, cases that are only partially comparable to the current one, and from pre-designed workflows. Khoyi and Swenson define templates in the context of case management as "collection of prebuild components" [11]. In contrast to templates as used in BPM solutions, the components included in case management templates "may be modified, or adapted, by the case owner to the specifics of the situation". The third requirement aims at a high level of integration to underlying systems to deliver data and information that supports the knowledge worker in his activities and decisions. This is what Ukelson summarizes as putting "the right resources in the hands of workers". Especially in complex knowledge-intensive processes that may even require fast or immediate decisions, the supply of only the essential information needed in that current context is the central task of any tool that tries to support the execution of these decisions and processes.

4   Metrics for Runtime Routing in Knowledge Processes

4.1   Process Mining

A solid base of fundamental work concerning metrics in business processes can be found in the area of "process mining". This discipline of BPM provides algorithms, techniques, metrics, and tools to determine the structure of existing business processes. The general goal of process mining is to generate an explicit process model of the observed behavior to achieve the highest possible alignment of business processes and their supporting IT. This technique therefore extracts information from event logs in order to capture the business as it is being executed [23]. Accordingly, process mining already considers that process design is not just something that happens previously but also during runtime. But in contrast to ACM, it tries to improve the existing model of a process, mainly assuming that one definite model has to exist. However, metrics and techniques introduced by process mining have been undergoing a solid level of research and prove of functionality in practice. Methods and metrics to analyze and evaluate processes can either follow algorithmic or statistical approaches [23][10]. Considering that strict and fully automated algorithms tend to lead to a definite process model and therefore might dismiss valuable (but infrequent) paths, statistical metrics provide a more adequate procedure to convert live workflow-logs into recommendations.

4.2   Frequency and Sequence of Executed Events

A common and intuitive method to analyze and evaluate the interdependency of executed tasks and related events in processes is their frequency in combination with the sequence. Frequency in this case describes the total count of executions of a specific event. The considered timeframe can be undefined or set to a definite period. The frequency only focuses on the event itself, ignoring the respective predecessor or successor. These are covered by analyzing the sequence of events. Van der Aalst et al. represent these measurements by a "dependency/frequency table" [26][27], while "dependency" is used synonymously to "sequence". They use it as first step to induct a definite dependency/frequency graph, according to the goals of BPM. However, the frequency/dependency table can also be applied to a learning machine that offers recommendations in flexible knowledge-intensive processes. It generates four different metrics using workflow logs (for each task A):

1. the overall frequency of task A (notation #A),
2. the frequency of task A directly preceded by another task B (notation #B<A),
3. the frequency of A directly followed by another task B (notation #A>B),
4. a local metric that indicates the strength of the dependency relation between task A and another task B ($A→B^L),
5. a more global metric that indicates the strength of the dependency relation of A and B, considering intermediate tasks ($A→B(g)$).

Metric 4 is composed as follows: $A→BL = (\#A>B - \#B>A) / (\#A>B + \#B>A + 1)$, with $A→BL$ in [0.0 … 1.0]. A higher value represents a higher level of strength regarding the local (direct) relation between A and B. Metric 5 includes intermediate tasks. If, in an event stream, task A occurs before task B and n is the number of intermediary events between them, the $A→B$-dependency counter is incremented with a factor $(\delta)n$. δ is a dependency fall factor ($0 \leq \delta \leq 1$). Exemplary values are given in Table 1.

Table 1. D/F-table for event T6 (i.e., A=T6) [27]

B	#B	#B<A	#A>B	$A→B$L$	$A→B
T10	1035	0	581	0,998	0,803
T5	3949	80	168	0,353	0,267
T11	1994	0	0	0	0,193
T13	1000	0	0	0	0,162
T9	1955	50	46	-0,041	0,161
T8	1994	68	31	-0,370	0,119
T3	3949	146	209	0,177	0,019
T6	1035	0	0	0	0,000
T7	959	0	0	0	-0,011
T12	994	0	0	0	-0,093
T1	1000	0	0	0	-0,246
T2	1994	0	0	0	-0,487
T4	1994	691	0	-0,999	-0,825

These metrics appear simple but already provide a versatile toolset to harness data from workflow logs. Further proceedings and research focused on reducing noise to lead to the so-called perfect workflow models (alpha algorithms). As pointed out before, this is not necessary in the context of knowledge-intensive processes and a design-by-doing paradigm.

4.3   Time between Events

The time of execution of a certain task and the related time between events (timespan after finishing task A and the start of task B) as recorded in workflow logs have so long been used as performance indicator to find possible bottlenecks or room for improvement [1]. Considering a suggestion-based tool, it becomes a handy metric. Given a specific event with multiple successors (based on event logs), the ones with the shorter time lag are regarded as more important. The shorter that interval, the more urgent and correlated is that sequence. A proper dimension for measuring the time between events in knowledge processes is minutes. Fully automated workflows, executed by machines and computers may require the scale "seconds", whereas decision and execution times in knowledge-intensive processes may range from seconds to hours. Minutes provide a balance between precision and scope. Therefore the numeric expression for the explanations above is aggregated by the urgency indicator u:

$$u = \frac{1}{\ln(TbE[m])} \tag{1}$$

Table 2. Exemplary calculation of u for event T6

Event Name	TbE [min]	u
T5	<=3	1
T12	200	0.189
T14	15	0.369
T3	8	0.481
T8	33	0.286
T4	50	0.256
T9	180	0.162

Table 2 shows the average time between events (TbE) from the completion of event T6 to the start of the respective successors. A TbE below three minute is set to u=1 by default. The inverted logarithm ensures that the value of u increases disproportionately high to the decrease of the time between events. The basic assumption underlying that logic is that if decisions and events have to be performed quickly, five minutes between events have a different significance than in workflows that include spans of hours. The time of execution that each task requires will not be considered in this context, since it is not possible to derive a level of importance form the duration itself.

4.4 Relevance of Predesigned Patterns

Knowledge-intensive process management requires design-by-doing. Still a predesign of certain steps and sequences is not completely obsolete (see second requirement in Sect. 3.3 and [11]). Some use cases may require a static and fixed sequence of several events, not allowing any deviations (inside the considered sequence). Furthermore it may be useful to implement predesigned fragments as a guideline. That will allow flexible routing but ensure that a previously set sequence is always regarded as one of the top suggestions (but not necessarily the only alternative). We therefore introduce a further factor:

$$p, 0 < p \leq 1. \tag{2}$$

If patterns are predesigned, the value of p has to be set manually. The lower the value of p, the lower is the weight in the suggestions list. A value of p=1 implies that no other route than the predesigned can be taken.

4.5 Post-design and Rating of Patterns

Analogously to Sect. 4.4, a factor for "post-design" is now being introduced. Post-design is a synonym for constructive evaluation after an instance has been completed or finished. Especially knowledge-intensive processes tend to vary in each process instance and follow different or new routes to reach the same goal. They therefore require some kind of post-evaluation of the taken actions. Examining the taken path from the retrospective may lead to different assessments of the decisions made previously. This will be included by implementing

$$e, \ 0 \leq e \leq 1. \tag{3}$$

This metric can only be manipulated after a process instance is completed. Participants may then change its value within the given range. Lowering e towards e=0 means that the decision to, for example, continue with event C after completing A turned out to be not recommendable. In contrast, e=1 implies that the sequence of the two considered tasks will be recommended for future cases without constraints.

4.6   Combined Metrics for Knowledge-Intensive Processes

Aggregating the previous sections 4.2 to 4.5, we introduce a combined metric that builds the core of a machine learning recommendation tool to support the execution of knowledge-intensive processes. The resulting formula models the level of recommendability for possible next steps/events in a knowledge-intensive process. It consists of the following elements:

- ($A \rightarrow B^L$) as empirical value that represents the strength of a relation between events by previous decisions,
- $u = 1/\log(TbE)$ represents the time span between the completion of an event and the start of its successor, also based on previous decisions by evaluating logs,
- an element that includes the importance of predesigned sequences or patterns, $p=x$, and
- an element e that analogously implies retroactive rating of the taken path.

These four elements are combined as follows: If a couple of events have been predesigned without allowing deviation, the recommendation value is $r = 1$. Otherwise, if it has been predesigned but different routes are allowed ($p < 1$), then

$$r = \frac{\frac{(\$A \rightarrow BL) + \frac{1}{\ln(TbE)}}{2} + p}{2}. \tag{4}$$

The post-rating is added after completion of the knowledge-intensive process instance, so

$$r = \frac{r+e}{2}. \tag{5}$$

The following section illustrates the use of the developed concept in an exemplary software artifact.

5   Prototypal Artifact Design

5.1   Implementation Types

The developed concept can be used in multiple tools in order to be applied in various use cases. It may as well be integrated into a complex ACM-suite (as demonstrated by the Isis-Papyrus-Suite) or even be a standalone assistant. Seizing to the relevant, the latter option is followed for demonstration purposes. The resulting software artifact will be an assistant that runs in a web browser or as a smartphone application. This ensures that it is always available to recommend courses of action when needed.

5.2   Artifact Architecture

Before a user is able to select between several options, at least a basic number of initial data has to be inserted into the systems database. A process type has to be created (for example, "emergency room: new patient"). This named container includes the fundamental steps or patterns (which may be configured with the parameter p). A task is characterized by a name, description, and an executing resource. The executing resources at this juncture are solely human since we contemplate knowledge-intensive processes. A task contains basic status information like "started"/"done" or "active"/"inactive".

The technical implementation is be realized by using relational databases. Every task will be represented by a table containing entities to every other task of the process (at first only filled with the initial data), and the value of r, computed as described in the previous section. The user interface of this tool displays the recommendations based on r. The higher the value of r, the higher the considered task will be ranked in this list. If none of the recommended tasks fits the situation, the user may create a new one, entering the respective attributes (name, description, resource).

5.3   Use Case Scenario

To illustrate the use of the tool and the developed metrics, an emergency room will now be taken as exemplary use case, focusing on one main knowledge process: the reception and further treatment of incoming patients. This process has a few sequences that remain fixed, but also variable parts that differ from case to case and require the expertise of the human resources. We assume to have the following roles as human resources:

- Nurses on duty,
- Surgeons on duty,
- Emergency doctors.

Every person carries a smartphone running the "Stapp"-application. They log-in by choosing the corresponding role as listed above. We observe the following situation: A nurse takes over a patient from the ambulance car. The first event is always similar:

the patient needs to be transported inside to some sort of reception point. As soon as this activity is finished (by tapping the "done" button), she automatically gets the recommendations for the further procedure.

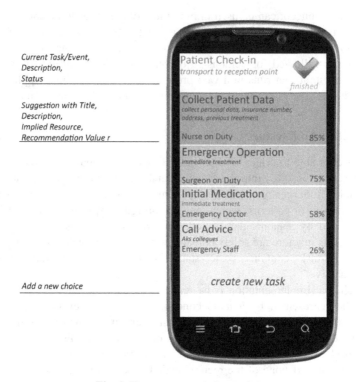

Fig. 3. The recommendation tool

Figure 3 shows the respective screenshot of this situation. The patient check-in is marked as finished. The task "Collect Patient Data" is listed on top with r = 0.85. This is the most common next step because in the majority of the cases, the patients are responsive and they do not need to be treated as soon as possible. The option "Emergency Operation" is listed second, rated r = 0.75. Even though these cases are the minority, they are characterized by a short time between events and the task has been given a comparatively high value of p during the predesign of this process. By selecting one option, the recommendation value r for this task is raised by the introduced formula. If the initially included tasks do not offer a proper solution, the nurse may also enter a new task. The more executions of a process instance are done, the more does the machine learn to map the possible paths and respective weighting. Different persons may add different steps and routes to reach the goal of a knowledge-intensive process. Using the introduced metrics in combination with this exemplary tool makes the wisdom of individuals reclaimable to the crowd. The tool may be implemented in several scales: Within a department of a company, within the whole company or even within a complete branch or sector. In reference to this use case example, the tool may harness the wisdom of every emergency room worldwide (since they are generally no business competitors).

6   Future Work

This article gives an overview over the current and emerging trends in the fast moving field of research dealing with knowledge-intensive process management. It collects insights, methods, and techniques from related and neighboring work to develop a metric that helps to manage the complexity of knowledge-intensive processes by harnessing collective wisdom without the need of codification.

This article illustrates that providing the information in context is the crucial challenge for tools that support the execution of knowledge-intensive processes. We conclude that adding collaboration features to existing process management software is no sufficient solution for the challenging complexity of knowledge-intensive processes. A knowledge worker who has to make a decision under complex circumstances or/and even in limited time needs clear options and suggestions instead of a started discussion. The implementation as presented in section 5 is a prototypal artifact. As a consequence, further effort needs to be put in the empirical evaluation of this tool, but especially in its core – the developed formula for calculating the recommendation value. The introduced metrics arise from theoretic considerations. They are meant to build a frame for future discussion, research and design in the context of case management. As soon as the demonstrated tool is ready for operation within a system environment it will be used to evaluate the metrics. As mentioned above, it can be implemented in different scales: inside a small business with just 10 employees or harnessing the practices of every emergency room worldwide. Since knowledge-intensive processes often are the key assets of business, the willingness to share might be restricted.

Taking the idea of a personal, crowd-learning suggestion tool a few steps ahead (leaving the business context), various opportunities spring up from that idea. Combining it with the functionalities of smart devices (smartphones, smartwatches, smartglasses, or augmented reality devices) may lead to a tool that offers perfectly tailored suggestions (based on GPS-location, movement profiles, phone-interaction, etc.) for daily life situations. Knowledge-intensive processes exist everywhere. At any place where humans are acting and interacting, they have to make decisions on what to do next. As universal as knowledge-intensive processes are, as universal are the possible use cases for a learning personal agent that provides options and suggestions based on experiences and practices that other humans made in comparable situations. To facilitate this development, we will evaluate the designed metrics and tool by testing it in groups of knowledge workers, iterate the results, and refine the design of the artifact.

References

1. Anupindi, R., Deshmukh, S.D., Van Mieghem, J.A., Zemel, E.: Managing Business Process Flows. Prentice Hall, Upper Saddle River (1999)
2. Davenport, T.H.: Process management for knowledge work. In: Handbook on Business Process Management 1. Springer, Heidelberg (2010)
3. De Leoni, M.: Adaptive process management in highly dynamic and pervasive scenarios. In: EPTCS, vol. (2), pp. 83–97 (2009)
4. Drucker, P.F.: Knowledge-worker productivity: The biggest challenge. California Management Review 41(2), 79–94 (1999)
5. Fleischmann, A.: What Is S-BPM? In: Buchwald, H., Fleischmann, A., Seese, D., Stary, C. (eds.) S-BPM ONE 2009. CCIS, vol. 85, pp. 85–106. Springer, Heidelberg (2010)
6. Herbst, J., Karagiannis, D.: Integrating machine learning and workflow management to support acquisition and adaptation of workflow models. In: Proceedings of the Ninth International Workshop on IEEE Database and Expert Systems Applications (1998)
7. Hevner, A.R., March, S.T., Park, J., Ram, S.: Design Science in Information Systems Research. MIS Quarterly 28(1), 75–105 (2004)
8. Huber, S., Hauptmann, A., Lederer, M., Kurz, M.: Managing Complexity in Adaptive Case Management. In: Fischer, H., Schneeberger, J. (eds.) S-BPM ONE 2013. CCIS, vol. 360, pp. 209–226. Springer, Heidelberg (2013)
   ISIS-Papyrus Software: ISIS Papyrus V7 Enterprise Communication and Process Platform Enables Consolidated Service Delivery for Customer-Focused Quality and Collaboration (2008), http://www.isis-papyrus.com/e10/pages/pressreleases/2/PR20080421.htm (Retrieved on August 01, 2013)
9. Khodabandelou, G., Hug, C., Deneckère, R., Salinesi, C.: Process Mining Versus Intention Mining. In: Nurcan, S., Proper, H.A., Soffer, P., Krogstic, J., Schmidt, R., Halpin, T., Bider, I. (eds.) BPMDS 2013 and EMMSAD 2013. LNBIP, vol. 147, pp. 466–480. Springer, Heidelberg (2013)
10. Khoyi, D., Swenson, K.D.: What to do when modeling doesn't work. In: Swenson, K.D. (ed.) Mastering the Unpredictable: How Adaptive Case Management Will Revolutionize the Way That Knowledge Workers Get Things Done. Meghan-Kiffer Press, Tampa (2010)
11. Kurz, M., Fleischmann, A.: BPM 2.0: Business Process Management Meets Empowerment. In: Fleischmann, A., Schmidt, W., Singer, R., Seese, D. (eds.) S-BPM ONE 2010. CCIS, vol. 138, pp. 54–83. Springer, Heidelberg (2011)
12. Le Clair, C., Miers, D.: The Forrester Wave: Dynamic Case Management, Q1, Forrester Research (2011)
13. Le Clair, C., Moore, C.: Dynamic Case Management — An Old Idea Catches New Fire. Forrester Research (2009)
14. March, S.T., Storey, V.C.: Design Science in the Information Systems Discipline: An Introduction to the Special Issue on Design Science Research. MIS Quarterly 32(4), 725–730 (2008)
15. Neumann, G., Erol, S.: From a social wiki to a social workflow system. In: Ardagna, D., Mecella, M., Yang, J. (eds.) Business Process Management Workshops. LNBIP, vol. 17, pp. 698–708. Springer, Heidelberg (2009)
16. Reijers, H.A., Rigter, J.H.M., van der Aalst, W.M.P.: The case handling case. International Journal of Cooperative Information Systems 12(3), 365–391 (2003)
17. Swenson, K.D.: Mastering the Unpredictable: How Adaptive Case Management Will Revolutionize the Way That Knowledge Workers Get Things Done. Meghan-Kiffer Press, Tampa (2010)

18. Swenson, K.D., Palmer, N., Silver, B.: Taming the Unpredictable. Future Strategies Inc., Lighthouse Point (2011)
19. Ukelson, J.P.: What to do when modeling doesn't work. In: Swenson, K.D. (ed.) Mastering the Unpredictable: How Adaptive Case Management Will Revolutionize the Way That Knowledge Workers Get Things Done. Meghan-Kiffer Press, Tampa (2010)
20. Van der Aalst, W.M.P., Berens, P.J.S.: Beyond workflow management: product-driven case handling. In: Proceedings of the 2001 International ACM SIGGROUP Conference on Supporting Group Work. ACM, New York (2001)
21. Van der Aalst, W.M.P.: Business Process Management: A Comprehensive Survey. ISRN Software Engineering (2013)
22. Van der Aalst, W.M.P., Weijters, J.M.M.: Process mining: a research agenda. Computers in Industry 53(3), 231–244 (2004)
23. Van der Aalst, W.M.P., Weske, M., Grünbauer, D.: Case handling: a new paradigm for business process support. Data & Knowledge Engineering 53(2), 129–162 (2005)
24. Von Ammon, R., Emmersberger, C., Ertlmaier, T., Etzion, O., Paulus, T., Springer, F.: Existing and future standards for event-driven business process management. In: Proceedings of the Third ACM International Conference on Distributed Event-Based Systems. ACM (2009)
25. Weijters, A.J.M.M., Van der Aalst, W.M.P.: Process mining: discovering workflow models from event-based data. In: Proceedings of the 13th Belgium-Netherlands Conference on Artificial Intelligence (BNAIC 2001). CWI, Amsterdam (2001)
26. Weijters, A.J.M.M., Van der Aalst, W.M.P.: Rediscovering workflow models from event-based data using little thumb. Integrated Computer-Aided Engineering 10(2), 151–162 (2003)

Short Papers

The contributions selected as short papers mostly refer to S-BPM language extensions, and to applying subject orientation in various domains, including learning and education.

In the first paper Matthes Elstermann and Jivka Ovtcharova present an early draft for a concept of using abstract layers to extend the modeling capabilities of the subject-oriented graphical process-modeling language PASS (Parallel Activity Specification Schema).

In an additional contribution the same authors present a graphical editing concept to extend the PASS capabilities, with respect to ad-hoc instance extension and alternative exception handling mechanisms.

Eray Uluhan and Mehmet N. Aydin look at Complex Adaptive Systems (CAS) theory as an alternative to better capture the complexity of business dynamics than existing BPM paradigms do.

The article of Ramtin Mesbahipour, André Nursinski and Michael Spiller gives a first impression of how the communication-oriented S-BPM approach relates to enterprise architecture management according to The Open Group Architecture Framework (TOGAF).

Christoph Piller and Walter Wölfel show how to use S-BPM to implement production planning for small and medium-sized enterprises (SME).

The work of Kai Michael Höver and Max Mühlhäuser explores the suitability of S-BPM for modeling collaboration scripts used in computer-supported learning environments.

In the last paper Georg Weichhart, Johanna Pirker, Christian Gütl, and Christian Stary present a virtual 3D world, based on a teaching approach following constructivist learning principles and facilitating S-BPM education.

Abstract Layers in PASS – A Concept Draft

Matthes Elstermann and Jivka Ovtcharova

Karlsruhe Institute of Technology (KIT)
Institute for Information Management in Engineering,
Bldg. 20.20, KIT Campus South, 76131 Karlsruhe, Germany
matthes.elstermann@kit.edu

Abstract. In this paper we present a first draft for a concept of using abstract layers to extend the modeling capabilities of the subject-oriented graphical process-modeling language PASS. The concept is nonintrusive to existing PASS specification. It is argued how the Abstract Layered PASS (ALP) concept can be used to manage and integrate challenges and requirements found in subject-oriented and general process management research. Also a holistic discussion of similar or related approaches within and outside S-BPM is given.

Keywords: process modeling, S-BPM, PASS, layered modeling, ALP.

1   Introduction

The basic idea of abstract layers[1] is to enable the defining of incomplete, but still useful descriptions of processes or process elements, and thus allow their flexible usage and reusability. In combination with standard PASS and the layered extension mechanism, the concept is supposed to let the level of abstraction[2] in process modeling become gradient and variable according to requirements of given circumstances.

2   Abstraction

Abstraction is a widely used term and concept. A rough description for it is "To leave something out", in order to focus on aspects of a problem that are important or to solve a problem more easily. Abstraction is present in many areas of computer science as is discussed in the following passage to define its meaning for this work.

2.1   Abstraction in Programming

Abstraction, as a concept or vocabulary, is prominently featured in object oriented programming (OOP), where data-types/classes can be specified using the concept of the abstract-data-type (ADT), extensively described in [1].

---

[1] For a basic introduction to PASS and the layer and layered editing concept based on the arbitrator pattern approach we refer to [15] available in the same publication.

[2] Levels of abstraction are distinguished from each other by the level of detail necessary to complete a description so it can be usefully applied in a context.

C. Zehbold (Ed.): S-BPM ONE 2014, CCIS 422, pp. 125–136, 2014.

Such specifications allow defining names, as well as input and output parameters for methods of (data) objects. The well-known *inheritance* and *polymorphism* mechanisms[3] allow refining or extending these specifications in order to reuse them in different, specialized contexts. The inheriting data types must adhere to the specification of the ADT. It is left to the programmer how specific or abstract the original first ADT is. The originating ADT can be modified to 'implement' the specification of another ADT. This way a great flexibility in the matter of choosing a level of abstraction is provided. The criteria for "proper", supposedly abstract, description of such data-types/classes according to Bertram Meyer in [1] are:

- The descriptions should be precise and unambiguous.
- They should be complete – or at least as complete as we want them in each case (we may decide to leave some details out).
- They should not be "overspecifiying".

So the means for specifying, while being precise, need to allow for a certain degree of flexibility in order to not require a full detailed description all the time, because there are circumstances and reasons where not all details are wanted or needed. Yet with great flexibility comes the ability to abuse the specification possibilities and spend too much effort in specifying something to a detail, so it cannot be used elsewhere.

Summarizing, it can be said that the base intention of a specification in OOP is to state or declare what an (abstract) unit *should be able to do* or what it *will do*. It does not *imperatively* state how things are to be done in detail. Neither it is required that an abstract description is holistic and exclusive, so that no further specifications are allowed. The details of *how to do something* are left to the concrete implementation in form of classes that may be defined to adhere to the specification of an ADT.

2.2   Abstraction and Process Modeling

Process modeling differs from OOP, but the necessity or possibility of leaving aspects out of a process model are well stated and implemented into several graphical process modeling languages, as is extensively described by Schonenberg et. al. in [2]. They give an overview and definitions over abstract process description mechanisms and their main purpose: Process Flexibility. Process Flexibility is an attribute essential to advanced process modelling and execution, as is stated not only in [2], but also required in [3] for the handling of deviations or unexpected circumstances, or for general agility of process models, as is defined by [4].

Schonenberg classifies mechanisms which allow flexible usage of process models according to the following principles. *Late Binding:* choosing and substituting pre-defined process fragments into another process description[4]. *Late Modeling*: creation

---

[3] See [1] or any reference work on Object Oriented Programming.

[4] Predefined process fragments are akin to "traditional modular structures", an approach where routines (aka. methods) are created and stored in a library. Bertram Meyer notes on that: "the routine library approach indeed seems to work well when you can identify a (possibly large) set of individual problems, subject to the following limitations: 1. It must be possible to characterize every problem instance by a small set of input and output arguments. 2. Clearly distinct sets of problems 3. No complex data structure" [1, p. 89].

of new process models modification of existing models during runtime. Both are being further described as either *static* – when such modification is done once and valid until the next explicit change – or are considered to be *dynamic,* if changes are applied upon every execution – assuming the model is being executed in a workflow engine.

More importantly, Schonenberg et.Al. distinguish in their taxonomy between *imperative* and *declarative* approaches with imperative approaches referring to classical process models that use completely connected graphs to state which tasks are to be done in exactly what order. In contrast, "a declarative approach focuses on what *should be done* instead of how. It uses constraints to restrict possible task execution options. By default, all execution paths that do not violate the constraints are allowed. In general, the more constraints are defined for a process, the less execution paths are possible, i.e., constraints limit process flexibility. In declarative languages, constraints are defined as relations between tasks. Mandatory constraints are strictly enforced, while optional constraints can be violated, if needed." [2, p. 18]

Schonenberg continues with a comparison between several process description languages and concepts such as ADEPT [5] or YAWL [6]. To a larger or smaller degree, those languages have mechanisms to allow for the required flexibility in form of more or less abstract process definitions. Except for the process language called Declare ([7], [8]), all compared modeling approaches are defined as *imperative.*

The widely used Business Process Modeling Notation (BPMN) was not considered by Schonenberg, but it also features approaches to allow process model flexibility. Examples are the *ad-hoc sub-process* notation build into the standard [9] or the concept of "process fragments" [10] where extensive research is done.

2.3   Abstraction and/or Flexible Mechanisms in PASS

For PASS, while at the core being an *imperative[5]* language itself, there are several flexibility or abstraction mechanisms, which go beyond the standard X-OR-choices (*Flexibility by Design* [2]) and allow for non-complete or partly non-deterministic descriptions of processes.

The first mechanism lies in the core concept of PASS and subject-orientation itself with subjects as the distinguishing factors on Subject Interaction Diagrams (SID) and Subject Behavior Diagrams (SBD). On the level of the SID it is only specified what communication is allowed between the abstract actors in a given context. How and in what order the communications and actions occur is being defined in the individual SBD-graphs. How often such an individual SBD-process is occurring in a process instance is not necessarily predefined. The according *multi-subject* mechanism allows for variability in terms of multiple sub-process instances. It is not included in other process description languages [11].

The *external-subject* mechanism functions as a connector or *interface* to other process models. In consequence, this allows leaving out the description of a subject's

---

[5] *Imperative* is not necessarily meant as in *imperative* programming language. A detailed discussion about similarities or differences of the concepts is not done at this point.

behavior in one model and up to the definitions in another. This enables for a simple way to flexibly map a subject to different SBDs or different connected processes with only the defined messages to an external-subject as a specification to adhere to (late binding). A practical implementation in this direction is the jCPEX approach that uses this idea to allow for remote execution of process parts in another process engine. In [12] the non-standard usage process models containing external-subjects – so called interface processes – are being used to specify the allowed interaction process.

In SBD view, two other mechanisms allow for flexibility in process description. One is the macro concept described in [13] with a first implementation described in [14]. It is related to the guard mechanism and is kind of a graph substitution mechanism, allowing the definition of placeholders which can be filled with process elements defined elsewhere – usually repetitive tasks or patterns that can be executed again and again. Yet the context of a given process model is never left and thus macros are, in theory, bound to a single process model.

The other flexibility mechanism on SBD level is the – so far only envisioned – "*checklist-operator*". It allows defining sequences of equally important steps, which can be done in any particular order, and thus are said to be "*worked on*" or completed at the same time. It does not necessarily break the concept of non-parallelism within single subjects. The checklist-operator rather allows for different combinations in the order that tasks are executed, while the tasks themselves are given and fixed.

Finally, as a conceptual contribution, the before mentioned layer mechanism (see [15]) introduces *late modeling* capabilities to PASS.

2.4   Abstract Layers in PASS

The previous section described the existing possibilities PASS offers to enable process flexibility. All are, in the terms of Schonenberg, considered as *imperative*. The contribution of the abstract layer concept is to introduce *declarative* means to subject-orientated process modeling that can be used to guide and support flexible modelling.

The general idea is to have two tiers of modeling akin to the two tiers in OOP, where they are represented by declarative ADTs and imperative concrete classes[6]. The interaction of the two concepts enables flexibility in the choice of the abstraction level, ranging from using only abstract specifications in a system concept to the functional programming of simple classes. Any shade of 'abstraction' or 'concreteness' in-between is possible as well. Figuratively, in the domain process modeling, standard imperative process modelling would be equivalent to the programming of normal classes, while the declarative specification of a process on an abstract declarative layer would be equal to using means for ADT definition (interfaces, contracts) to specify a class/system without predefining the exact content.

---

[6] Our hypothesis: only together both concepts give OOP the expressive power that makes that paradigm so successful. This is indicated by the fact that the described mechanisms exist and have been in practical use for over two decades.

A workflow system implementing the abstract layer concept will offer different possibilities: 1. Warn, if a process model is not adhering to a given specification. This means using abstract layers as guidelines for process modeling, guaranteeing their adherence, if necessary. 2. Execute predefined tasks, which have been specified for an abstract state, when an accordingly mapped state on a concrete behavior layer is executed. 3. Using a mechanism akin to the *polymorphism* concept from OOP, states or state sequence in different models can be treated the same way, if they implement the same concepts or state from an abstract layer.

Possibilities 2 and 3 combined will enable the system to reuse abstract elements.

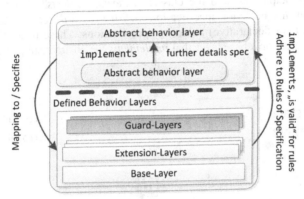

Fig. 1. Interaction/Meaning of abstract layers for layers with defined behaviors

2.5   Specification Possibilities in Abstract SIDs

Abstract layers adhere to the base principle of PASS with its split between Subject Interaction Diagrams (SID) and Subject Behavior Diagrams (SBD). But in order to specify a process, abstract layers need a slightly different model semantic. There are several levels or possibilities that an abstract/declarative PASS should offer in SID view. Each level gives means for more detailed specification or restrictions.

The first specification level in any subject-oriented process model is the definition of subjects itself. On a normal layer the subjects define that these, and only these, are the discerned abstract-actors for this process. On an abstract layer the definition of a subject means that specialized subjects should exist and be concerned with; but not exclusively. Other subjects are allowed to exist in an implementing model.

The next concept that can be specified in an SID is which of the subjects communicates with whom. In standard SIDs only the modeled communication is allowed. On abstract layers, by default, any communication is allowed and restrictions can be introduced in two possible ways: Either by forbidding explicit communications between subjects, using a *message restriction arc,* or by defining an *exclusive communication connector* that forbids all but the specified communication *from* the originating subject.

The third step of the modeling process of abstract SIDs is the specification of possible message types that are used in the communication. In general this is done by defining a list of messages used in a process (as in standard SIDs). Or more specific, by assigning specific messages to specific communication between subjects. The use of the *standard message connector* from PASS on an abstract layer has the connotation of *must* be in the process, although not exclusively in contrast to messages assigned to an *exclusive communication connector*. In order to declare possibilities of minor importance, an additional *Abstract Message Connector* is introduced with a *can/should* connotation[7].

The final step in standard SIDs is to model the behavior of subjects. On an abstract layer three different possibilities can be defined: 1. *Subjects* – "normal subjects" in the terms of PASS requires a complete underlying SBD. Placing a normal subject on an abstract layer has the semantic meaning of specifying that the subject including its behavior must be used *exactly as specified* in the process context. 2. *Interfaces Subjects* – in principle equal to the classic "*external subjects*". They are basically subjects without any behavior specification. 3. *Abstract Subjects* – a subject which contains abstract (or declarative) behavior specifications. These restrict the behavior of a standard subject on a base layer that *implements* the abstract subject[8].

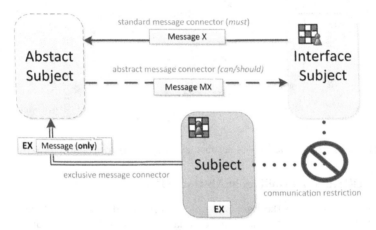

Fig. 2. Notation possibilities for SIDs on abstract layers

2.6   Specification Possibilities in Abstract SBDs

Standard Subject Behavior Diagrams (SBDs) are classic, completely connected, process graphs that determine which state *must exist* and which state *must come directly before or after* another state (*defined states* and *transitions arcs*).

On abstract layers this standard imperative PASS notation can be used as well. But in order to have declarative expression means in the process specification, further notions must be introduced.

---

[7] Whether this differentiation is necessary or not is not yet 100% determined. There are situations where the *should/can*-semantic is necessary. But it also complicates SIDs with a partly probabilistic concept. An alternative approach would be to have only a differing between *must* and *exclusive* in abstract layer SIDs.

[8] An additional idea is to allow that two abstract subjects can be implemented by one defined subject on a standard layer. This is an extrapolation of the S-BPM concept to have one actor or processer executing more than one subject in a process context. Here the principle is on higher abstraction layer and akin to the concept of multiple inheritances in OOP.

First is the notion of *abstract states* in contrast to the *defined states* in standard PASS. An example of this mechanism is already in standard PASS. It is the implicit declaration of at least one receive- and at least one send-state for each in- or outgoing message in an SID. Neither name nor position in a subject's behavior process is predefined, but these states *must* exist in one form or another.

An *abstract state* denotes that the description or function of the state *must* be implemented in one form or another, but not exactly how or when. A state on a defined behavior layer must be *mapped* to the abstract state expressing that it *implements* or *represents* that state and as thus the modeler has *'taken care of'* the requirement to implement it. A single defined state can *implement* more than one abstract state. On the other hand, an abstract state is not necessarily required to be implemented or represented by a single defined state, but can be implemented by a sequence or block in defined behavior layer[9]. This can also be done on another abstract layer that further specifies details. Should an abstract state contain a *refinement* – a function call to an ambient IT-system – the refinement is executed when the implementing state is activated. If a defined state implements more than one abstract state with a refinement, the refinements are executed in the hierarchical order of the position of their according layers in the layered modeling system. Since refinements are akin to methods in object oriented programming, it is supposed that an implementing state should have the option to overwrite the function call if needed.

In PASS a state can be repeated in a cycle, or similar states can be done multiple times. The notion of *abstract states* does not implicitly carry any restriction in that regard. If only a limited number or no such reoccurrences is required, it must explicitly be expressed that a state does *not occur within cycles (single occurrence)*, has a *max/min occurrence* on an implementing layer. These existential restriction types can also be applied to defined states or process fragments on abstract layers.

The second notion to be added for abstract SBDs is the notion of *order restrictions*. The *standard transition arc* can be seen as a restriction that defines that a state must come *directly after* or *directly before* another state. A softer restriction in this manner is to define that a state must come *sometime after* or *before* another state. An even softer restriction is the *response* or *trigger* relation that defines that a succeeding state must be executed, *if* the preceding state has been triggered. Otherwise the succeeding state is not mandatory.

These three options are inspired by the possibilities in the DECLARE modeling language [8]. DECLARE has more restriction types then the three concepts defined here. An example would be a *non-coexistence* relation between states. But in this first draft those capabilities are not included and it is left to further research to say which of those are necessary and practical for subject-oriented process modeling.

---

[9] Since a 'state' in PASS comes with the implicit definition that it can be *entered* or *reached*, is *'being executed'*, *'in processing'*, or has been *'completed'* there is no problem to *implement* an abstract state in a sequence or process block that also can be entered, traversed through, or finished and exited.

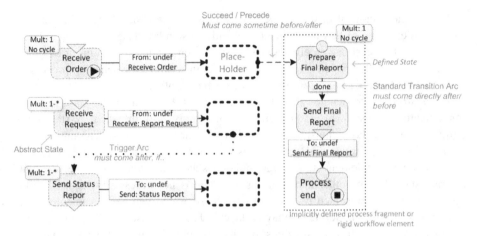

Fig. 3. Example of declarative process description in an SBD on an abstract layer

2.7   Mappings of Abstract States, Subjects, and Messages

In order to express that a basic model adheres to a specification, all subjects and states of an abstract layer must be adopted or *implemented* by states in the base layer that is to be executed. This task is expected to be done in semi-automatically with user interaction. Fig. 4 shows how an according GUI to map or match states with abstract states could look like in SBD view for one subject. The general idea there is to drag and drop states over an according matching state. Links and their graphical representation can be generated automatically. Crosses and checkmarks denote, whether a state of an abstract layer has been matched correctly or not. For SIDs the interface would look similar with the functionality to match subjects.

Such matching or implementation specification must also be done for messages and business objects (BOs), if they are declared abstractly. Since both can be considered as data objects or data types, they can be specified with the means of OOP and it is possible to use the according mechanisms to check for consistency or to handle them.

2.8   Ad-Hoc-Process-Instantiation and Modeling by Restriction

The standard PASS process interpreter can only execute complete PASS process graphs. In order to use abstract layers, at least an additional rule engine is necessary to verify that a normal PASS process model adheres to the specifications. This, though, still would not execute the disconnected graphs of abstract layers. A simple approach would be to automatically generate rigid process models from an abstract layer that simply contain all combinatorial-possible execution paths allowed by the spec. Such models would not be legible for humans, but are executable on the existing engine.

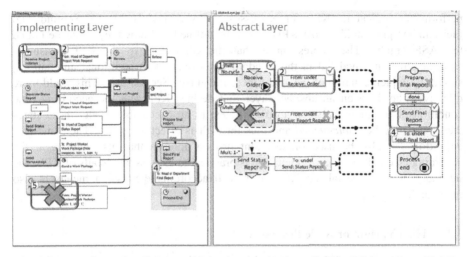

Fig. 4. Layout of mapping dialogue with implementation layer (left) and abstract layer (right): Same color/number boxes with green checks are validly mapped. Crosses denote invalid maps.

More elegant and, as has been shown with Declare [7], possible would be a workflow engine that dynamically calculates the according possibilities for the status of each subject, using one or even more abstract layers as the basis for execution restrictions. The according research and development could proof to be very interesting and would provide a real implementation of the concept of *"Modeling by Restriction"* as described by Fleischmann in [13]. Or rather: *"Execution with Restrictions"*.

3   Eligibility and Usage Scenarios

3.1   Target Processes and Process Variance Handling

One direct use for the abstract layer concept is to define target processes that, because of their speculative forward looking nature, should never be 100% predetermined. On an abstract layer a target process can be modeled as a set of restrictions to sketch out the workflow without fixing it. Separated from that, and at a later time or location an executable process model, or rather several version of it can be created. As long as they adhere to the general spec, they all are considered valid by the process engine and are treated as instance of the same abstract process in terms of information management or process mining. This can be of relevance for globally operating companies with branches in several countries where the same basic process needs to be executed, but with different detailed characteristics or additional steps to face local requirements based on culture or work habits.

3.2   Possibilities for KPI Management

The layer mechanism ([15]) in general, and the abstract mechanism in particular have the potential to be very effective when defining, modeling and handling key performance indicators (KPI) for processes in PASS models. In [16] Schmidt and Fleischmann give an idea how KPIs should be defined and how they could be bound to PASS graphs. The impression is that the connectors to the KPI measuring functionalities are modeled in the standard SBD plane with additional annotations, similar to implementation of the guard mechanism (see Section 2.3). This could more effectively be done on an abstract layer that defines KPIs and the according time conditions as relations between abstract states. In an executable model these states then must only be *implemented* and thus the KPI is effective in use. The same KPI definition can also be used on different process models that also *implement* the according layer. If a specialized notation is practical to express the details of KPIs, the introduction of a specialized KPI-Layer with according expression means is also imaginable.

3.3   High Variant or Agile Processes

The goal of the ADISTRA project [17] is to describe a reference process model that guides the usage of a set of methodologies in the domain of strategic product planning and innovation management for small and medium enterprises. The same reference model is also to be implemented and run in an "agent based" workflow engine. The abstract layer concept was developed with the challenges of that research project in mind. There is a combinatorial multitude of factors as boundary condition for the process description, such as varying company size, industry or product types, types of innovation, thematically overlapping of some methodologies, and the handling of their conditional or combination usage, among other aspects.

Due to this highly variant situation, it is hard to describe a functional process model with standard *imperative* means. Of the reviewed approaches only a declarative language seems practical to meet the requirements in this or similar cases. The abstract layer concept would add exactly that mechanism to PASS. It can be used to easily define single process elements, from participants to the sub-process of methodologies, on several separated abstract layers and formulate conditions for their usage. These can then be combined in more defined layers or finally in an executable process model. An abstract-layer-enabled process engine could evaluate whether a given derived variant model adheres to the general spec and thus is valid. Or it could, assuming an engine with the capabilities described in 2.8, use the ad-hoc instantiation mechanism to create process instance on the fly.

3.4   Extended Interface Process – The Ability to Specify Service Details

Section 2.3 discussed the interface processes used by the CJPEX-Approach [12]. An interface process only contains external subjects and thus defines *what* they communicate. This in itself can be considered as a simple, abstract process specification that can be distributed to different workflow engines which must adhered to the spec in order to work together. But only specifying input and output of subjects is more akin to object orientated data modeling than process description. Using the abstract layer approach, this concept can be improved and extended. The declarative mechanism allows sketching intended behavior or boundary conditions such as order of message reception and reply. It would give actual control over a process without completely taking away the freedom of a remote service. An abstract interface process model can thus be used as the base for service orchestration and the creation of process network over the nodes of two or more separated process engines.

4   Final Thoughts and Outlook

The abstract layer concept combines both, *imperative* and *declarative* BPM approaches for different usage scenarios. It can be considered as hybrid BPM methodology, where the level of abstraction can be scaled continuously and adjusted to given circumstances to allow a maximum of flexibility.

In contrast to other process modeling languages like BPMN or YAWL, it keeps different concerns separated on different layers. In the form of base layers, the standard PASS model can always be used and executed, while specialized layers can be used to add further notation elements to PASS, e.g. notations for defining and applying business rules or KPIs.

As a restraining thought: Layers, by their very nature, form a hierarchy. But the layer concept is explicitly not meant as a *top-down* modeling approach forced onto PASS, which is generally used *bottom-up*. The mechanisms of the layer concept can and should be used to extend the modeling capabilities of PASS in situations, where it is required and useful and not always by default, they are technical concepts and do not represent e.g. organizational hierarchy levels.

The ideas presented here are of theoretical nature. If efforts into future research are made, the concept could contribute to the conceptual foundation of S-BPM. In order to actually implement the concept, several issues need be addressed by future research. Among them is the question of a data format to exchange such models (the goal is to make the concept part of an open-source meta-specification of PASS), or how and which of the logical details for declarative workflow models can be adopted for the abstract layered PASS concept.

References

[1] Meyer, B.: Object-oriented software construction, 2nd edn. Prentice Hall PTR, Upper Saddle River (1997)
[2] Schonenberg, H., et al.: Process flexibility: A survey of contemporary approaches. In: Dietz, J.L.G., Albani, A., Barjis, J. (eds.) CIAO! 2008 and EOMAS 2008. LNBIP, vol. 10, pp. 16–30. Springer, Heidelberg (2008)
[3] Kurz, M., Fleischmann, A., Lederer, M., Huber, S.: Planning for the Unexpected: Exception Handling and BPM. In: Fischer, H., Schneeberger, J. (eds.) S-BPM ONE 2013. CCIS, vol. 360, pp. 123–149. Springer, Heidelberg (2013)
[4] Heininger, R.: Requirements for Business Process Management Systems Supporting Business Process Agility. In: Oppl, S., Fleischmann, A. (eds.) S-BPM ONE 2012. CCIS, vol. 284, pp. 168–180. Springer, Heidelberg (2012)

[5] Reichert, M., Rinderle, S., Dadam, P.: ADEPT Workflow Management System. In: van der Aalst, W.M.P., ter Hofstede, A.H.M., Weske, M. (eds.) BPM 2003. LNCS, vol. 2678, pp. 370–379. Springer, Heidelberg (2003)

[6] The YAWL Foundation, YAWL Homepage, http://yawlfoundation.org/ (accessed September 23, 2012)

[7] Pesic, M., Schonenberg, M.H., Sidorova, N., van der Aalst, W.M.P.: Constraint-Based Workflow Models: Change Made Easy. In: Meersman, R., Tari, Z. (eds.) OTM 2007, Part I. LNCS, vol. 4803, pp. 77–94. Springer, Heidelberg (2007)

[8] Eindhoven, T.: Declare - Homepage, http://www.win.tue.nl/declare/

[9] OMG: Business Process Model and Notation (BPMN) - Version 2.0. Object Managment Group, Needham (2011)

[10] Eberle, H., Unger, T., Leymann, F.: Process Fragments. In: Meersman, R., Dillon, T., Herrero, P. (eds.) OTM 2009, Part I. LNCS, vol. 5870, pp. 398–405. Springer, Heidelberg (2009)

[11] Börger, E.: Approaches to Modeling Business Processes. A Critical Analysis of BPMN, Workflow Patters and YAWL,
http://www.di.unipi.it/~boerger/Papers/Bpmn/EvalBpm.pdf

[12] Meyer, N., Feiner, T., Radmayr, M., Blei, D., Fleischmann, A.: Dynamic Catenation and Execution of Cross Organisational Business Processes - The jCPEX! Approach. In: Fleischmann, A., Schmidt, W., Singer, R., Seese, D. (eds.) S-BPM ONE 2010. CCIS, vol. 138, pp. 84–105. Springer, Heidelberg (2011)

[13] Fleischmann, A., Schmidt, W., Stary, C., Obermeier, S., Börger, E.: Subjektorientiertes Prozessmanagement: Mitarbeiter einbinden, Motivation und Prozessakzeptanz steigern. Hanser, München (2011)

[14] Strecker, F.: New Modeling Concepts in S-BPM: The First Implemenation of the "Message Guard" and "Macro" Behaviour Extension. In: Oppl, S., Fleischmann, A. (eds.) S-BPM ONE 2012. CCIS, vol. 284, pp. 121–134. Springer, Heidelberg (2012)

[15] Elstermann, M., Ovtcharova, J.: An Editing Concept for PASS Layers. In: Zehbold, C. (ed.) S-BPM ONE 2014. CCIS, vol. 422, pp. 137–146. Springer, Heidelberg (2014)

[16] Schmidt, W., Fleischmann, A.: Business Process Monitoring with S-BPM. In: Fischer, H., Schneeberger, J. (eds.) S-BPM ONE 2013. CCIS, vol. 360, pp. 274–291. Springer, Heidelberg (2013)

[17] ADISTRA Projekt,
http://www.produktionsforschung.de/verbundprojekte/
vp/index.htm?VP_ID=3302

An Editing Concept for PASS Layers

Matthes Elstermann and Jivka Ovtcharova

Karlsruhe Institute of Technology (KIT)
Institute for Information Management in Engineering,
Bldg. 20.20, KIT Campus South, 76131 Karlsruhe, Germany
matthes.elstermann@kit.edu

Abstract. In this paper we present a graphical editing concept to extend the capabilities of the subject-oriented process-modeling language PASS. The concept builds up on the arbitrator-pattern-inspired PASS-interpreter and clarifies its ad-hoc instance extension and exception handling mechanisms. The paper thereby proposes the arbitrator pattern as a possible alternative for the PASS guard mechanism.

Keywords: process modeling, S-BPM, PASS, layered modeling, ad-hoc, guard.

1   Background Motivation

The Parallel Activity Specification Schema (PASS) is one of the cornerstones of subject-oriented Business Process Management (S-BPM). It has been effectively applied to capture the requirements for business process management in several domains ([1] or [2]). It also has been proven to be well understandable [3] and is considered to be appropriate to capture and model the essence of (business) processes and can functions as an adequate basis for general process improvement.

PASS was first presented by Fleischmann in [4]. A formal and precise definition of PASS exists in form of an interpreter model, specified as an abstract state machine (ASM) ([5], [6]), allowing PASS to be directly executed in work flow engines. The only known implementation to execute PASS is the S-BPM engine in the Metasonic S-BPM suit [7].

1.1   Basic Terms and Descriptions of PASS

In contrast to other graphical process modeling languages, the Parallel Activity Specification Schema (PASS) is comprised of two different diagram types with different expressions. Both types are connected to each other.

First is the Subject Interaction Diagram (SID): the 'upper' level of a PASS diagram representing all involved subjects[1] in a process and the communication between them via Message Connector Arrows (MCA). The MCA are annotated with a list of

---

[1] Subjects can be considered as abstract processors (active entities) in a process.

C. Zehbold (Ed.): S-BPM ONE 2014, CCIS 422, pp. 137–146, 2014.

allowed messages, defining the possible communication between the entities. Received messages are considered to be saved in a subject's *message box* and as such represent asynchronous communication possibilities if not specified otherwise.

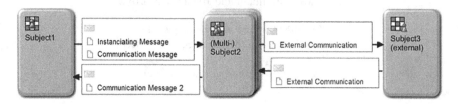

Fig. 1. Example Subject Interaction Diagram (SID)

Each subject is linked to an individual underlying Subject Behavior Diagram (SBD). The SBD is composed of transition-arcs between three possible states: *send state*, *receive state* and *function state*. An SBD is considered to define a sequential process with only XOR branching. In a workflow engine each subject instance is supposed to be executed or managed by an individual user /agent/processor. It is explicitly allowed for one agent (e.g. a human user) to execute the task of more than one subject. This responsibility for one subject can also change between agents at runtime.

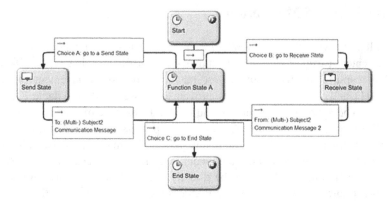

Fig. 2. Example for a Subject Behavior Diagram (SBD) – for Subject 1

Also the declaration of subjects as *multi-subjects* is possible to allow multiple instances of subjects/sub-processes within one process instance. And it is also possible to insert '*external subjects*' (subjects without underlying SBDs) that can be used as connectors to other PASS processes or as interfaces to external systems.

1.2   Ad-Hoc Extension Mechanism

In [8] a mechanism and a specification were introduced that allow *ad-hoc* extensions at runtime for PASS processes models in work-flow engines based on the formal interpreter model for single SBDs presented in [6]. The basic idea was to use the arbitrator pattern to manage ad-hoc process instantiation.

The arbitrator pattern stems from the field of robotics and was introduced by R.C. Arkin in [9] to allow for fast and effective programming of independent robots in non-predefined environments.

The basic principle assumes a robot with input and output equipment (sensors and motors), which need to be interpreted and controlled to result in 'intelligent' behavior. Instead of programming a single large complex program to control the machine, there is one arbitrator deciding which of many smaller behavior programs (short "behaviors") is currently to be executed. These behaviors may contain only simple instructions like "move forward". Which behavior is currently controlling the robot is determined by a dynamically computed priority list that is evaluated based on the sensor inputs. As soon as external events (e.g. the robot hitting a wall) require a change, the priority is shifted and the arbitrator executes a different behavior, which has the necessary information for the next action.

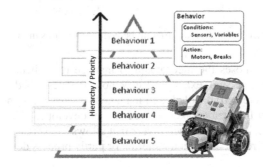

Fig. 3. Depiction of behavior priorities in the arbitrator pattern

The concept for adapting this pattern for *ad-hoc* process extension in a PASS-workflow-engine is to have an arbitrator in control of each subject, with the sending and receiving capabilities of a subject as the equivalent of sensors and actuators. Altered or deviating process versions would be put 'on top' the behaviors defined in the SBDs of an original PASS process as a new layer. The mechanism of the arbitrator pattern would allow the execution of these behavior extensions, if they are applicable for a current status of a subject and as such are considered to be executable.

A higher-priority behavior would become executable when the subject is in a state that is described in both, in the original behavior, as well as in the behavior extension. Since an SBD is individual for each subject and since the description of how to reach such a state is not required by a PASS interpreter, it is implied that a behavior extension is not necessarily a complete process graph with all information of the original behavior. Instead it can be a light weighted, short description that may affect only two or even one subject[2] and only extends them where deviation is needed.

---

[2] The PASS interpreter model ([6]) describes an abstract state machine for single subjects/SBDs. The arbitrator pattern is also applied to individual subjects. Hence a complete process model including SIDs and SBD for many process model is not necessary to extent a behavior already containing all information.

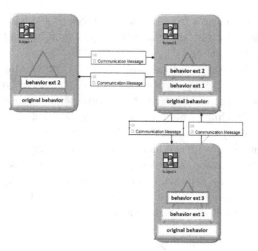

Fig. 4. Schematic depiction of different behavior extensions in different subjects

But while [8] proposes the mechanism to manage these behavior extensions and their execution, it does not exactly specify how the described process extensions themselves can be created, handled, and managed or what rules should apply to their usage. In this paper the idea is taken up and further developed. The goal is to derive a concept for graphical editing of such *layers* that allows to express and to easily handle ad-hoc process extension, exception handling or partly process descriptions.

2   Modelling Extension and Guard Layers

2.1   Extension Layers

The graph of an extension layer is basically a normal SBD that deviates from the original behavior and has a higher execution priority. Thus an extension behavior does not need to be a complete SBD-graph, as long as it can refer to a base layer containing a complete process. This requires *mappings* of states in the extension layer to states in the underlying base behavior, from where the deviation is intended or where it should end.

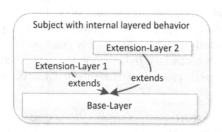

Fig. 5. Basic layer and extension layers

In order to navigate through the layers and selectively modify them, it is proposed to use an element from digital image manipulation software such as Photoshop or GIMP: a layer pallet or layer navigator. It allows selecting which layers are shown and which layer can currently be edited (Fig. 6). The graph of the underlying behavior can be shown as if seen through a translucent foil[3] to allow easy and intuitive determination or mapping of states from the base behavior layer to an extension behavior layer. When editing layers, the process modeler can choose to hide other layers or set them to be *visible* as he requires using the layer pallet.

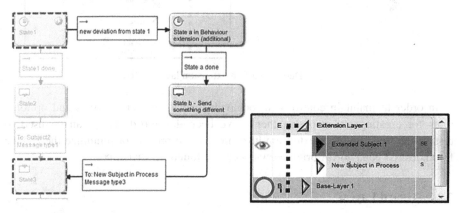

Fig. 6. Rendering of an extension layer with underlying base layer & layer navigating panel

The mechanism described here is focused on SBDs. For graphical process modeling the notion of layers must also be applied to the SID view. Fig. 7 shows how such an SID view of extension layers indicates that subjects either contain extension behaviors for existing underlying subjects, or contain new subjects introduced only for the extension. For new subjects, the SBD specified in the extension layer will be the base-layer and as such must necessarily fulfill all completeness requirements for an SBD.

The extensions to process models are mainly needed to modify running process instances *ad-hoc*. If such an extension should be deemed a good addition to the general process model (the base layer) for future instances, a mechanism is proposed to *flatten* or *merge* all wanted layers into one single PASS model to be used for the future process instances[4].

---

[3] The analog analogy are transparent sheets or foils that can be put atop a basic drawing and additional things can be drawn on it. The original image is not destroyed and can partly be seen. The digital analogy of the concept is that of the layers in digital image processing programs as Adobe Photoshop or the open source image manipulation Software GIMP.

[4] Each layer is considered to be an independent model that could be saved in a separate resource file. But models such as incomplete extensions layers refer to complete models that as a consequence must be known to the modeling and the interpreting environment. Therefore it is practical to save especially guard layers (see section 2.2) and extension layers in the same resource (file). Abstract layers are more suited to be stored independently.

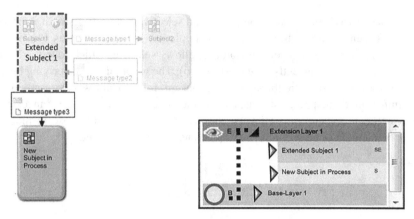

Fig. 7. Depiction of an extension layer in SID

In order to maintain control over behavior extensions, certain rules and optional rules for creating and applying them have been developed. They can be used to restrict the freedom of an extension layer in order to prevent or minimize the chance for undesired behavior. A brief overview can be found in Appendix 2.

2.2   Guard Layers

The concept of layers and the arbitrator interpreter mechanism can also be used as an alternative for the PASS guard or exception handling mechanism described in [5] and [10] with a first implementation described by Strecker in [11].

A *guard* is a special process description to handle an event – in PASS this is usually the reception of a special exception message – that is not designated in the normal workflow at a predetermined time specified in an SBD. In the existing concept, guards are modeled as normal process elements with special annotations in the standard SBD plane for each subject.

Using the layer-concept, guards will be modeled in their own "guard-layers" that, by default, have a higher execution priority than any other layer. In contrast to extension layers, the first state of a guard layer must not correspond with a state in an underlying SBD graph, but start in a special annotated receive state that deems the layer executable as soon as the according event has been triggered (aka. the according message has been received).

In the layer pallet every guard layer should be displayed directly at its corresponding subject in the corresponding base or extension layer (Fig. 9). But since they are higher in execution priority (see Fig. 8), the layer pallet should also display the guard layers above the normal behaviors (see smaller alternative in Fig. 9). This is also needed to display and manage the SID view of guard layers. The SID view can be used to unify and group, and keep an overview over cases, where the exception behaviors for more than one subject need to be coordinated.

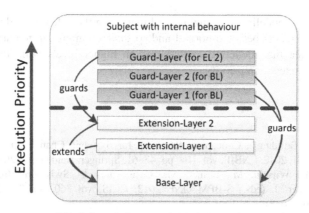

Fig. 8. Layers in execution priority order

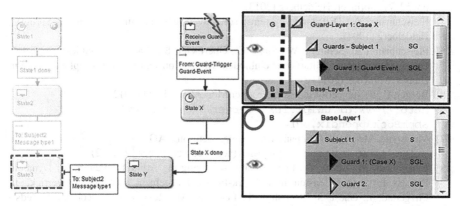

Fig. 9. Rendering of a guard layer with underlying base layer and non-dynamic mapped return-to-state + two different possibilities to display guard layers in the layer navigating panel

If an extension layer is not completely covering the base layer (complete cover rule), the *guards* of the base layer are still above the extension layer and must be overwritten, if they are meant to not be effective.

3   Final Thoughts

Layered editing has been proven in image manipulation, where it is a powerful and widely used concept. But it is an advanced feature not taught to beginners. The same, supposedly, will be true for extension/guard layers and the according editing feature.

Adding ad-hoc extensions to an existing and running process instance should and probably will be done mostly by experienced and in the special cases under special circumstances. In contrast, describing guards is expected to be more common in every day process modeling. In both cases though, the layer concept could prove advantageous for modeling, organizing, and managing these features, due to the clear separation of concerns between normal and specialized modeling features, as well as the intuitive idea that modeling expressions on higher levels coincides with them having a higher execution priority.

References

[1] Augl, M.: Building a Conceptual Roadmap for Systemic Change. In: Stary, C. (ed.) S-BPM ONE 2012. LNBIP, vol. 104, pp. 43–61. Springer, Heidelberg (2012)

[2] Walke, T., Witschi, M., Reiner, M.: Case Study @ Swisscom. In: Fischer, H., Schneeberger, J. (eds.) S-BPM ONE 2013. CCIS, vol. 360, pp. 264–273. Springer, Heidelberg (2013)

[3] Weitlaner, D., Guettinger, A., Kohlbacher, M.: Intuitive Comprehensibility of Process Models. In: Fischer, H., Schneeberger, J. (eds.) S-BPM ONE 2013. CCIS, vol. 360, pp. 52–71. Springer, Heidelberg (2013)

[4] Fleischmann, A.: Distributed systems: software design and implementation. Springer, Heidelberg (1994)

[5] Fleischmann, A., Schmidt, W., Stary, C., Obermeier, S., Börger, E.: Subjektorientiertes Prozessmanagement: Mitarbeiter einbinden, Motivation und Prozessakzeptanz steigern. Hanser, München (2011)

[6] Börger, E.: A Subject-Oriented Interpreter Model for S-BPM (2012), http://www.di.unipi.it/~boerger/Papers/Bpmn/ SbpmBookAppendix.pdf

[7] Metasonic, Metasonic Company Homepage, Metasonic AG, http://www.metasonic.de/en/ (accessed September 12, 2012)

[8] Elstermann, M., Seese, D., Fleischmann, A.: Using the Arbitrator Pattern for Dynamic Process Instance Extension in a Work-Flow Management System. In: Derrick, J., Fitzgerald, J., Gnesi, S., Khurshid, S., Leuschel, M., Reeves, S., Riccobene, E. (eds.) ABZ 2012. LNCS, vol. 7316, pp. 323–326. Springer, Heidelberg (2012)

[9] Arkin, R.C.: Behavior-based robotics. MIT Press, Cambridge (2000)

[10] Kurz, M., Fleischmann, A., Lederer, M., Huber, S.: Planning for the Unexpected: Exception Handling and BPM. In: Fischer, H., Schneeberger, J. (eds.) S-BPM ONE 2013. CCIS, vol. 360, pp. 123–149. Springer, Heidelberg (2013)

[11] Strecker, F.: New modeling concepts in S-BPM: The first implementation of the "Message guard" and "Macro" behavior extensions. In: Oppl, S., Fleischmann, A. (eds.) S-BPM ONE 2012. CCIS, vol. 284, pp. 121–134. Springer, Heidelberg (2012)

Appendix: Additional Images for the Concept

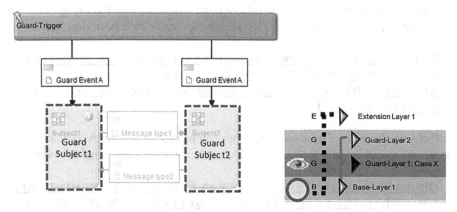

Fig. 10. Guard Layer in SID view

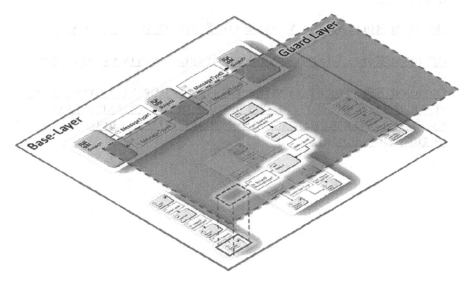

Fig. 11. Isometric depiction of a guard layer covering a base layer with according mapping

Appendix 2: Possible Rules for Implying Process Extensions

In order to maintain a certain control over the extension the following rules for creating and applying extensions (if they are allowed at all) have been developed.

RULE: A VALID BEHAVIOR EXTENSION LAYER MUST HAVE AT LEAST ONE VALID MAPPING TO AN UNDERLYING BASE LAYER
RULE: IN SIDS AN EXTENSION LAYER MUST CONTAIN AT LEAST ON MATCHING SUBJECT

There are also a set of optional rules. They can be used to restrict the freedom of an extension layer in order to prevent or minimize the chance for undesired behavior.

OPTIONAL RULE: THE WORK-FLOW OF AN EXTENSION LAYERS MUST END IN A MAPPED STATE (IT AUTOMATICALLY MUST START AT A MAPPED STATE)

OPTIONAL RULE: NO SENDING OR RECEIVING OF MESSAGES ALLOWED IN EXTENSION

OPTIONAL RULE: NO NEW MESSAGES OR SUBJECTS ALLOWED IN SIDS.

OPTIONAL RULE: NO LOOPS OR LOOPING STRUCTURES IN AN EXTENSION

OPTIONAL RULE FOR STATE INTERPRETATION: COMPLETE COVERING - IF A STATE IS MAPPED ONLY THE CONNECTORS OF THE EXTENDED STATE ARE VALID, THE INTERPRETING AGENT IS NOT ALLOWED TO CHOOSE THE PATH OF THE ORIGINAL STATE.

Complex Adaptive Systems Theory in the Context of Business Process Management

Eray Uluhan[1] and Mehmet N. Aydin[2]

[1] BPMTurkey, Istanbul, Turkey
eray.uluhan@bpmturkey.org
[2] Department of MIS, Kadir Has University, Istanbul, Turkey
mehmet.aydin@khas.edu.tr

Abstract. Organizations require agility, adaptiveness, and flexibility to survive and to deal with complexity in business ecosystems and business processes are recognized as cornerstones of successful organizations. Paradigms underlying existing business process management (BPM) methods and solutions have been questioned for their ability to capture the complexity of business dynamics. The basic trust of this research is to search for an alternative approach to better understand underpinnings of business process management. In this paper we contend that Complex Adaptive Systems (CAS) theory can be an alternative approach to better examine underpinnings of the very notion of business process. In this regard, we articulate the basic principles of CAS in the business process management context. It is this articulation that paves the way to establish an appropriate account for BPM.

Keywords: Business process management, process modeling, complex adaptive systems, complexity theory.

1   Introduction

Organizations today are faced with significant business challenges, intense competition, and rapidly changing markets. Both the internal and external business environments are evolving at a rapid pace with the advances in technology, and changes in customer requirements, markets and regulations. To survive in the global market organizations have to develop and improve their competencies. They have to be agile, adaptive, responsive to changes in both internal and external business environments.

An organization deliver its products or services through business processes. Conventional conceptualization of business process management (BPM) suggests that business processes can be defined as a collection of related, structured activities or tasks that produce a specific service or product for internal or external customers. This conceptualizations is limited, and need to be revisited with an alternative approach. Business processes provide the basis for organizations to align IT and business strategies. By managing processes efficiently and effectively organizations can improve their operational performance and create customer value.

C. Zehbold (Ed.): S-BPM ONE 2014, CCIS 422, pp. 147–156, 2014.

Underlying principles for traditional management approaches to business process improvement such as LEAN, total quality management (TQM), business process reengineering (BPR) mainly adopt principles from research fields like operations management and systems engineering that focus on how to optimize a process or system. However, business processes operate differently compared to manufacturing systems and assembly lines. They are often large, complex, unpredictable and require faster enactment. Traditional process models are created by applying different abstraction methods in which essential properties and key process indicators are preserved and insignificant details are left out [30]. Current issues and future challenges of business process modeling are studied in [31] which bring out three critical areas of concern, i.e. standardization of modeling approaches, identification of the value proposition of business process modeling and model-driven process execution. Process models are unable to cover the real dynamic structure of a business environment and the gap between abstract process models and reality create barriers to agility and adaptability. Organizations require agility, adaptiveness, flexibility, and have to be emerging and proactive to survive and business processes are recognized as cornerstones of successful organizations.

The focus of this paper is to introduce Complex Adaptive Systems (CAS) theory into the context of BPM. This research may question the way processes are modeled and enacted, thus offer a novel way of reconceptualizing business processes. In section 2, we provide a brief description of current business process modeling practices. Section 3 focuses on CAS Theory and outlines the properties of complex adaptive systems along with its possible implications into a process management domain. In Section 4, the implications of applying CAS Theory to BPM domain are explained. We conclude this paper and discuss future work in section 5.

2   Business Process Modeling Techniques

Early research on process improvement carried out in industrial revolution era but it is 1990s when BPM appeared as a separate discipline. In the early 1990s business process reengineering emerged as a management strategy focusing on the analysis and design of workflows and processes [1]. Even though business process management is one of the highest cited management approaches today, organizations face significant problems in business process implementation and maintenance.

Existing business process modeling techniques can be categorized as graph-based modeling techniques based on graph theory or its variants and rule-based modeling techniques based on formal logic [2]. Graphical modeling techniques (YAWL, FlowMake, ADEPT$_{Flex}$) are mostly aimed at business people for capturing and understanding processes and identifying business requirements and process improvement points. Rule-based modeling techniques (ADEPT, PLM$_{flow}$, AgFlow) are mostly used for process analysis, process execution [3], and process simulation. In addition, [4] explains that in considering how to model business processes, the decision of the type of notation (or modeling) to be used for process modeling is an important consideration. BPMN [5] is developed by Business Process Management Initiative (BPMI), aimed to serve as a common language used by both business users and technical users, for process design and execution.

The aforementioned modeling techniques describe the business process entirely in design time. That is, all activities and paths are provided, ordering constraints and sequence flows are predetermined. In [26], researchers examine how process modeling techniques have developed over time, comparing popular techniques such as Petri-Nets [6], ANSI flowcharts, DFD [7], EPC [8], BPML [9], BPEL4WS [9], BPMN.

In procedural modeling practices there is lack of capability to cover the dynamic structure of business processes. They pay primary attention to the enactment sequence of tasks. However, these processes are required to be updated regularly due to inconsistencies in real life and changes in their intended purpose. In addition, the processes also need to be updated because of changes in data, organization structure, procedures and legislations. Traditional process modeling techniques are more suitable for structured and well-defined processes.

[2] states that agent-based modeling is an alternate approach in rule-based modeling techniques. Due to complex and dynamic structure of business processes, it is not always possible to predict beforehand all the process comprehensively. Agent-based modeling provides a flexible infrastructure for incorporating dynamic changes to the executing process model [32]. In [33] a business process managed by an agent-based system, ADEPT (Advanced Decision Environment for Process Tasks), is described. Another, so called Adept project [34], aims to support business users in modifying an executing process, while maintaining its correctness and consistency.

Process modeling is widely used within organizations as a method to increase awareness and knowledge of business processes, and to reduce organizational complexity [10]. How to manage complexity instead of reducing it is a challenge for the management of contemporary organizations. Scholars including [11] argue for applying ideas of complex adaptive systems to managing organizations. An alternate approach derived from the notion of complex adaptive systems to model processes can provide more flexibility, agility and adaptability.

3   Complex Adaptive Systems Theory

The problems stated in Section 1 motivate us to search for alternative approaches to better understand business processes. We propose to look into characteristics of business processes along with the metaphor of a living organism. Like evolution and mutation in living organisms, organizational adaptability or agility is a core survival requirement. "The survival of the fittest" applies to both organisms, organizations in general and business processes in particular. Modern organizations have to keep evolving if they are to survive.

Complex Adaptive Systems (CAS) are special cases of complex systems. A complex adaptive system is a complex, self-similar collection of interacting adaptive agents. The study of CAS focuses on complex and emergent properties of the system. Due to the different applications in many domains, there is no clear definition of a complex adaptive system rather sets of principles and properties, which are defined by different researchers in their own terminology [12], [13], [14], [15], [16].

[17] is one of the first publications that state organizations are complex, variable-rich environments that can be studied from multiple perspectives. [18] adds that the behavior of complex systems is surprising and is hard to predict, because it is nonlinear. In [35], the author proposes to depict complex adaptive systems by hierarchical arrangements and boundaries and signals.

Key concepts of complex adaptive systems cited in [13] are agents with schemata, self-organization, coevolving agents, and system evolution. [20] states that complex adaptive systems can be summarized in terms of four properties and three mechanisms: aggregation (property), tagging (mechanism), nonlinearities (property), flows of resources (property), diversity (property), internal models (mechanism), building blocks (mechanism). CAS are occasionally modeled by means of agent-based models [21], [22], and complex network-based models [23], [24], [25]. Agent-based models are developed by various methods and tools primarily by first identifying the different agents inside the model.

CAS behave according to two key principles: order is emergent as opposed to pre-determined, and the state of the system is irreversible and often unpredictable [19]. The adaptation and non-deterministic, non-linear communication capabilities of agents promise that order to be emergent in the system. The change of the system is not limited to an entity but also occurs in entities around it and in the external environment. Implications of these principles for BPM are worth noticing.

Table 1. Traditional-Agent Based Modeling Approaches Comparison

	Traditional Approaches	**Agent Based Approaches**
Flexibility	Limited	More flexible
Interaction	Linear; need to be explicitly defined into the model	Usually strong and nonlinear; agents continually adapt to changing environment
change behavior	Model need to be updated regularly to keep up with the changes	Execution model updates are less frequent, changes are maintained descriptively.
Adaptation	None. The model is pre-determined.	Partial support of adaptation by means of agent properties.
Simplicity	Quite lucid.	More complex to model and analyze.

In both areas of interest (CAS and BPM), there is relatively extensive literature, however only few are overlapping. CAS is an emerging subject, and mostly used on biological, evolutionary complex organisms studies. Some CAS studies on Organizational Science are worth noticing [13], [20], but it has not been studied comprehensively in the process management perspective. Modern organizations are complex adaptive systems par excellence and need to be studied to understand the fundamental nature of non-linear, self-organized structures. As discussed earlier, there are different process modeling related studies in which some are closely related with complexity theory, such as agent and rule based techniques. However most of these studies do not derive from a rigorous theoretical account, rather aim to solve well-defined problems.

In Table 1, we summarize a comparison between traditional and agent-based modeling approaches with respect to flexibility, interactions, change behavior, adaptation and simplicity. Flexibility is the modeling capabilities related to exception handling and dynamic changes in resource levels. Interaction represents modeling of communication between participants, systems and other processes. Change behavior describes the required effort to make modifications in the process model and implementation. Adaptation is how the system reacts to changes and adjustments to extant conditions, conditions and external environment. The agent based approaches examined are mainly based on computational agent and simulation models. Simplicity is ability to understand and model processes by business people with ease. By adopting CAS properties into agent based process modeling approaches we aim to attain better and more reliable process models.

4   CAS and BPM: Theoretical Articulations

As discussed in previous section, there are different definitions and concepts related to CAS. In this section, we try to extract key concepts of CAS that can help us when modeling business processes. CAS properties related to business processes may be defined as self-similarity, emergence, and self-organization, continual adaptation, non-linearity, distributed control and interdependent agents. One of implications of the adoption of CAS as an alternative theoretical account for examining BPM is to put emphasis on the socio-technical underpinnings of BPM. That is, CAS contribution to better understanding of BPM is the need for exploring its essentials by taking into account social, organizational as well as technical characteristics [36].

Self-similarity is being exactly or approximately similar to a part of itself. Businesses are self-similar in respect to their organizational units and employees. Neither hierarchical nor process oriented or matrix organizations are able to mimic the real structure of business dynamics. In [27] scholars analyze an email network of a university and as a result they show the emergence of self-similar properties that suggest that "some universal mechanism" could be the underlying driving force in the formation and evolution of informal networks in organizations, as happens in other self-organized complex systems.

Emergence is the way complex systems and patterns arise out of a multiplicity of relative simple interactions. These patterns can formulate the workflows and process models. Emergence property of complex systems premises the adaptation of business processes. [19] states that a CAS behaves/evolves according to two key principles: order is emergent as opposed to predetermined, and the state of the system is irreversible and often unpredictable. The emergent patterns of dynamic, nonlinear interactions between agents are more than the sum of their parts. The change does not occur only in an entity itself, but also in entities around it, and in the external "environment".

Self-organization can be defined as a system of cooperative elements whose patterns of global behavior are distributed (no single element coordinates the activity) and self-limiting in nature (limits its own growth). [28] define the concepts of self-organization and emergence in multi-agent systems and the associated properties and characteristics. Accordingly, self-organizing behavior is characterized by three properties, i.e. absence of explicit external control, decentralized control and dynamic operation.

Table 2. Properties of Complex Adaptive Systems

Properties of Complex Adaptive Systems	
Property	**Definition**
Self-Similarity	The same structural motifs are present at many scales
Emergence	Emergence is a feature in CAS which derives from adaptation
Self-Organization	Order emerges from the interaction of simple entities without explicit external command
Continual Adaptation	Change to accommodate variations in the environment.
Non-linearity	Interaction possibilities of entities are non-linear and not known a priori, rather than planned and designed.
Distributed Control	Control is not assigned to a single entity and is not centralized but each entity has its own control.
Interdependent Agents	Autonomous agents cooperating for emergence

To describe complexity approach in economics, [29] proposes a definition of complex systems with six properties and refer these systems as 'adaptive nonlinear networks'. According to *Continual adaptation* feature the system constantly adapts as the individual agents accumulate experience through changes in the environment. Agents adopt their strategies over time in response to their past actions."Out-of-equilibrium Dynamics" feature of adaptive nonlinear networkssupplements continual adaptation by the definition that continual change and adaptation results the system to operate far from global optimum and equilibrium. Improvements are always possible and regularly occur.

In CAS, the flow of information within and between organizations is not predetermined. [13] suggests that CAS models enable analyzing complex systems without abstracting away their interdependencies and *nonlinear interactions*. When the nonlinear interactions are abstracted for the sake of mathematical models, the emergence patterns are ruled out. However, the business environment is dynamic, unpredictable in nature and interactions offers new possibilities and opportunities.

In organizations *Distributed Control* helps enhancing reaction speed and robustness. The control is not assigned to a single entity but each entity has its own control. Each entity has its own goals and acts accordingly that results self-organization of the system. Self-organization is a collective result of local yet nonlinear interactions among entities. Cause and effect are not proportional, i.e. small causes can have big effects.

An organization consists of different organizational units, managers, and employees. Each of these are the *interdependent agents* of a complex adaptive system. Interdependent agents must rely on one another to share information and resources and have a common goal for the system. Interdependent agents cooperate to accomplish the aim of the system.

In Table 3, we relate some key process modeling concepts with CAS properties. When thinking on BPM concepts listed on the left, we can make use of the definitions of CAS properties listed right side of the table. Collaboration is unpredictable in terms of modeling and it fits perfectly to the non-linearity notion of CAS. Similarly activities and flows modeled in business processes follow similar characteristics with self-organization and non-linearity properties of CAS. Considering BPM Concepts with their CAS properties gives us ability to view the problems faced in BPM from a different perspective and extensions that can be made applying these properties onto the problems.

Table 3. Sample BPM Concepts mapped into CAS Properties

BPM Concept	CAS Properties Counterpart
Collaboration	Non-linearity, Interdependent Agents
Events	Distributed-Control, Self-Organization
Activities / Flows	Self-Organization, Non-linearity
Participants	Interdependent Agents
Sub-Processes	Self-Similarity, Distributed Control, Non-linearity
Pools and Lanes	Interdependent Agents, Distributed Control, Non-linearity

By applying CAS theory into BPM domain based on these properties we expect to obtain following results. Process modeling does not have to be done exclusively prior to implementation. Models can be modifiable, and process instances can execute on the fly. Action can be taken when new or exceptional cases are lived through. In procedural modeling, the rules that restrict how a process should work are set. However, to better manage and monitor processes we need to observe how the process works in reality, not vice versa.

It is argued that after a complete BPR project, the adaptation of processes is more likely to happen not that often. However, in some business environments organizations prefer commencing small process improvement projects rather than complete BPRs. In addition, the need for a change arises even after a BPR project due to government regulations or procedures, i.e. the external business environment is not stabilized and also rapidly changing.

Traditional business process modeling approaches require a detailed design considering all possibilities, thoroughly testing and verification of performance, and implementation of prototypes. This approach is more suitable for well-understood, predictable and relatively simple environments. Aligning underlying principles of CAS theory with BPM domain promises to be beneficial in approaching the mentioned research problem.

5   Conclusion and Future Work

In conclusion, the proposed account is considered as an alternative approach to better understand the underpinnings of BPM and expected to be an alternative solution to model agile and adaptive business processes. To support our theoretical work, we aim to demonstrate and articulate CAS properties in a real business process management case that will provide us important feedback on the opportunities offered and further research direction.

Current business process management systems tend to offer monitoring and management capabilities but are lack of capturing the complexity of business dynamics. This is crucial especially for enterprises in which processes are becoming more and more complicated and businesses require faster response times. In order to realize such business requirements it is necessary to model and execute business processes with agile and adaptation capabilities. This research aims to create a novel way of modeling agile business processes and finally, this research is expected to produce a useful artifact for businesses, basing its roots on rigid theoretical background, and demonstrate the outputs of synthesizing CAS theory and BPM.

References

1. Hammer, M.: Reengineering work: Don't automate, obliterate. Harvard Business Review 68(4), 104–112 (1990)
2. Phalp, K.T.: The CAP Framework for business process modelling. Information and Software Technology 40(13), 731–744 (1998)
3. van der Aalst, W.M.P., ter Hofstede, A.: YAWL: Yet another workflow language. Information Systems 30(4), 245–275 (2005)
4. Rosemann, M.: Potential pitfalls of process modeling: Part A. Business Process Management Journal 12(2), 249–254 (2006)
5. Business Process Model and Notation, http://www.bpmn.org/
6. van der Aalst, W.M.P.: Three good reasons for using a Petri-net-based workflow management system. In: Navathe, S., Wakayama, T. (eds.) Proceedings of the International Working Conference on Information and Process Integration in Enterprises (IPIC 1996), Cambridge, Massachusetts, November 14-15, pp. 179–201 (1996)
7. Huckvale, T., Ould, M.: Process Modeling – Who, What & How: Role Activity Diagramming. In: Grover, V., Kettinger, W. (eds.) Business Process Change: Reengineering Concepts, Methods and Technology. Idea Group Publishing (1995)
8. Keller, G., Nüttgens, M., Scheer, A.-W.: Semantische Prozeßmodellierung auf der Grundlage "Ereignisgesteuerter Prozeßketten (EPK)". In: Scheer, A.-W. (ed.) Veröffentlichungen des Instituts für Wirtschaftsinformatik. Heft 89, Saarbrücken (1992)
9. Shapiro, R.: A Comparison of XPDL, BPML and BPEL4WS. Draft version 1.4. Cape Visions (2002), http://xml.coverpages.org/Shapiro-XPDL.pdf (accessed June 2013)
10. Bandara, W., Gable, G.G., Rosemann, M.: Factors and Measures of Business Process Modeling: Model Building Through a Multiple Case Study. European Journal of Information Systems 14(4), 347–360 (2005)

11. Lissack, M.: Complexity: the science, its vocabulary, and its relation to organizations. Emergence 1(1), 110–126 (1999)
12. Sutherland, J., van den Heuvel, W.: Enterprise application integration and complex adaptive systems. Communications of the ACM 45(10), 59–64 (2002)
13. Anderson, P.: Complexity theory and organization science. Organization Science, 216–232 (1999)
14. Rhodes, M., MacKechnie, G.: Understanding public service systems: Is there a role for complex adaptive systems theory? Emergence 5(4), 57–85 (2003)
15. Janssen, M., Kuk, G.: A complex adaptive system perspective of enterprise architecture in electronic government. In: Hawaii International Conference on System Sciences, vol. 39, p. 71. IEEE (2006)
16. Gell-Mann, M.: What is Complexity? In: Curzio, A.Q., Fortis, M. (eds.) Complexity and Industrial Clusters, pp, pp. 13–24. Physica-Verlag, Heidelberg (2002)
17. Daft, R.L., Lewin Arie, Y.: Can organization studies begin to break out of the normal science straitjacket: An editorial essay. Organizational Science 1(1) (1990)
18. Casti, J.: Complexification: Explaining a Paradoxical World Through the Science of Surprise. Harper Collins, New York (1994)
19. Dooley, K.: A complex adaptive systems model of organizational change. Non-linear Dynamics, Psychology and the Life Sciences 1(1), 69–97 (1997)
20. Holland, J.H.: Hidden order: How adaptation builds complexity. Helix Books (1995)
21. Jennings, N.R.: An agent-based approach for building complex software systems. Communications of the ACM 44(3), 35–41 (2001)
22. Forrest, S., Jones, T.: Modeling complex adaptive systems with Echo. In: Stonier, R.J., Yu, X.H. (eds.) Complex Systems: Mechanisms of Adaptation, pp. 3–21. IOS Press, Amsterdam (1994)
23. de Nooy, W., Mrvar, A., Batagelj, V.: Exploratory social network analysis with Pajek. Cambridge University Press, Cambridge (2005)
24. Junker, B.H., Screiber, F.: Analysis of biological networks. John Wiley & Sons (2008)
25. Batagelj, V., Mrvar, A.: Pajek-Program for large network analysis. Connections 21, 47–57 (1998)
26. Rosemann, M., Recker, J., Indulska, M., Green, P.: A study of the evolution of the representational capabilities of process modeling grammars. In: Martinez, F.H., Pohl, K. (eds.) CAiSE 2006. LNCS, vol. 4001, pp. 447–461. Springer, Heidelberg (2006)
27. G.R., Danon, L., Diaz-Guilera, A., Giralt, F., Arenas, A.: Self-similar community structure in a network of human interactions. Physical Review E 68, 065,103 (2003)
28. Di MarzoSerugendo, G., Gleizes, M.-P., Karageorgos, A.: Self-Organisation in MAS. Knowledge Engineering Review 20(2), 165–189 (2005)
29. Brian Arthur, W.: Introduction: Process and Emergence in the Economy. In: Brian Arthur, W., Durlauf, S., Lane, D.A. (eds.) The Economy as an Evolving Complex System II, Addison-Wesley Pub. Co., Reading (1997)
30. Weske, M.: Business Process Management: Concepts, Languages, Architectures. Springer (2007)
31. Indulska, M., Recker, J.C., Rosemann, M., Green, P.: Business process modeling: current issues and future challenges. In: van Eck, P., Gordijn, J., Wieringa, R. (eds.) CAiSE 2009. LNCS, vol. 5565, pp. 501–514. Springer, Heidelberg (2009)
32. Ehrler, L., Fleurke, M., Purvis, M., Tony, B., Savarimuthu, R.: Agent-based workflow management systems (WfMSs). Journal of Information Systems and E-Business Management 4(1), 5–23 (2005)

33. Jennings, N.R., Faratin, P., Johnson, M.J., O'Brien, P., Wiegand, M.E.: Using intelligent agents to manage business processes. In: Crabtree, B., Jennings, N.R. (eds.) Proceedings of the First International Conference on Practical Applications of Intelligent Agents and Multi-Agent Technology (PAAM 1996), pp. 345–360. Practical Applications Company Ltd. (1996)
34. Reichert, M., Dadam, P.: Adeptflex—Supporting dynamic changes of workflows without losing control. Journal of Intelligent Information Systems 10(2), 93–129 (1998)
35. Holland, J.: Signals and Boundaries: Building Blocks for Complex Adaptive Systems. MIT Press (2012)
36. Fischer, G., Herrmann, T.: Socio-technical systems: a meta-design perspective. International Journal of Sociotechnology and Knowledge Development (IJSKD) 3(1), 1–33 (2011)

Architecting the Enterprise along Communication Paradigm Using the TOGAF® Framework

Ramtin Mesbahipour, André Nursinski, and Michael Spiller

Detecon International GmbH, Sternengasse 14 – 16, 50676 Köln, Germany
{ramtin.mesbahipour,andre.nursinski,
michael.spiller}@detecon.com

Abstract. The hidden paradigm behind modelling the enterprise capabilities is based on Ford's and Taylor's idea of sequencing activities and taking the best in class approaches. It has once proven to be suitable for mass production of goods. While the paradigm is still the basic modelling assumption for shaping enterprise capabilities, the environmental and social basis for enterprises have changed. The business has moved from mass good production to massive individualized services around goods, where customers can place unpredicted change requests almost at any time. The fact that such events occur unpredicted does not mean they occur rarely. The exception to the lucky path is basically the routine. How the reaction to such unpredicted events look like is shown by the inflationary usage of e-mails, instant messages, phones, and meetings. It seems that communication is about to become the new paradigm. Putting massively personalized services on top of complex products asks for fitting architectural structures. Ford's hidden paradigm fails to master the resulting architectural complexity due to the lack of the concept of "communication". What enterprises need to master is an enterprise architecture driven by communication. The proposed paper discusses a methodology to create an enterprise architecture that promotes the communication-centric paradigm using the TOGAF[1] framework. We describe how the role of individuals within an enterprise and the communication paths between them are used to create an enterprise architecture that is easily understood and accepted by end-users. We also show how architecture planning on business, application, and data is performed using the concepts of subject-oriented business process management (S-BPM) in rapid architecture cycles, creating greater agility.

Keywords: TOGAF, S-BPM, Enterprise Architecture, Communication.

1 Introduction

At the beginning of the 20th century the two economists Frederick Winslow Taylor (20.03.1856 - 21.03.1915) and Henry Ford (30.07.1863 - 07.04.1947) revolutionized the methods of producing goods. Taylor introduced the scientific management, also called Taylorism, to analyze and synthesize production workflows. His major goal

---

[1] TOGAF is a registered trademark of The Open Group.

C. Zehbold (Ed.): S-BPM ONE 2014, CCIS 422, pp. 157–163, 2014.

was to improve labor productivity through separation of management and operations, according to his assumption, that the workforce doesn't have the intellectual ability to shape their daily work on their own. Ford brought assembly-line work to perfection during introducing an industrialized and standardized form of mass production. With this type of so called Fordism he was able to produce a high number of items for a small price not only to increase the shareholder's value but also to pay good salaries [1, p. 1283 f.].

Concerning these innovations the modern production follows the core paradigm, that tools and necessary qualifications should be placed where they are needed into the assembly chain. Therefore high qualified workforce can be eliminated by breaking down complex work into smaller steps. According to these techniques the former known all-rounders develop to specialists in their production step and no one in the assembly chain need to know the big picture.

In a further iteration these "small steps" can be hand over to machines and the scope of human action is narrowed down to the necessary minimum of high qualified tasks or control of the machines. Doing this one can create highly scalable assembly chains where you can double your production output by simply adding another assembly line into the production construct.

Because the paradigm is so understandable, we carried it forward for decades. Until the present age we follow the basic principle of division of labor and assembly chains. We arrange our entire way of working according to this paradigm. And also processes are seen as hidden assembly chains, which focus on scale.

Fordism and Taylorism has become hidden paradigms in our way of production.

Concerning this perception we systematically translate the paradigm into our application and technology landscapes and we wonder why inflexible IT-Systems came into existence creating a high IT landscape complexity. As an approach frameworks such as the TOGAF framework were developed to provide powerful tools for managing the resulting complexity.

2   Development to Communication-Based Paradigm and the Way to Manage It

Today a social development to a strong accentuation of individualism took place. The individual very often is not satisfied with a standard product, which was produced by mass production, but wishes a special "own" version of it, which satisfies the individual requirements.

Furthermore no product will be produced in just one fabric anymore. Instead lots of partners, suppliers and service providers located worldwide are involved into the assembly chain. These various supplier relations and global collaboration ask for a tight alignment.

As a third point today's production processes are not linear. Very often you need to leave the lucky way and branches, exceptions and the way back are the routine. Therefore the complexity managing processes and IT increases rapidly.

2.1   Role of Communication Concerning Individualization

The hidden paradigm concerning economies of scale has already been more or less broken by adding the dimension "individualization" to the current "scale only" dimension. The way how to approach this dimension is visible in the way people act in nearly any business of today. They write a tremendous amount of emails with information added to them as attachments; they meet and make lot of phone calls and phone conferences. They communicate!

To achieve individualization, a common understanding of customer requirements and the appropriate solutions on how to approach them is necessary. Hence the solution seems to be to enable communication between individuals, a systematic way of "directing" the communication needs to be established.

Exactly the subject orientation of S-BPM focuses on these communication relations and therefore brings flexibility into interaction. But not only processes need to be adapted to react on the new challenges into business. Also IT needs to be adapted to support the business requirements.

Current approaches to manage enterprise architecture, the way people, processes, and IT interoperate, attempt to create an alignment between the way products and processes are organized in an enterprise and to translate this organization and flow into IT. But how will they apply when the basis of a today's enterprise is still built on "scale" but the processes are suddenly changing to the communication enforcing paradigm? Will the methods still apply?

We observed the deployment of S-BPM on enterprise level while considering the aspects of enterprise architecture in such a deployment.

2.2   Enterprise Architecture at Communication Intensive Processes

A well-known framework to direct change in enterprise is TOGAF, an Open Group standard. TOGAF was first published by The Open Group in 1995. The TOGAF standard builds on the terminology of ISO Standard 42010 and is an architectural framework, which "provides the methods and tools for assisting in the acceptance, production, use, and maintenance of an enterprise architecture."[2, p. 9]

For development and management of enterprise architectures, the TOGAF framework provides a set of tools, classification schemas and also the Architecture Development Method (ADM), an iterative management process that consists of eight phases starting by the architecture vision until the end of implementation of the architecture and getting ready for a next architecture change iteration. A core preparation phase is meant to initialize the execution of EA management, whereas the central activity of requirements management provides input to all phases.

The TOGAF ADM cycle starts with the preliminary phase (see fig. 1, lower left), which prepares and initializes the enterprise architecture management cycle. After preparation and initialization activities are performed, the scope of the enterprise architecture management endeavor is defined within the architecture vision phase (A). In the following phases (B), (C) and (D) the business architecture, information systems architecture, and technology architecture are developed.

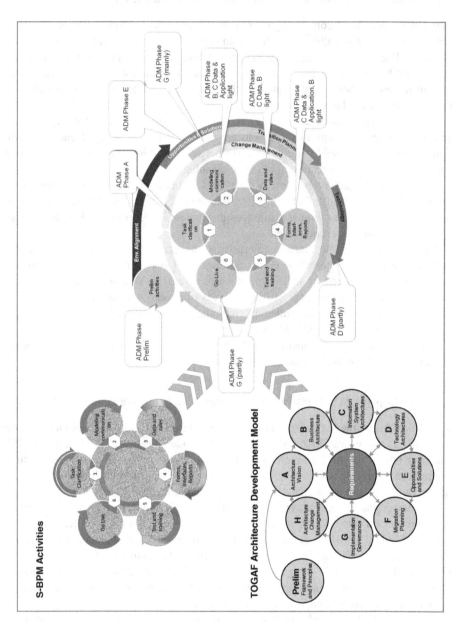

Fig. 1. Interaction of S-BPM and TOGAF ADM

The fundamental course of action of these phases is very similar: Initially, the baseline architecture (current state of the enterprise architecture) is described. Based on this and taking into account the architecture vision, the target architecture is developed. Phase opportunities and solutions (E) is concerned with linking the separated business, information system, and technology architecture and deriving projects and programs, which describe the transformation from current to target architecture via intermediate transition architectures (planned states). The transition architectures form the input of the migration planning phase (F), which is concerned with the formulation of an implementation and migration plan that schedules and realizes some or all of the planned architectures. In phase implementation governance (G) projects selected for realization in the preceding phase are executed. Final phase (H) architecture change management concludes an ADM cycle and prepares the initiation of the next iteration. As part of the phase, the changes of the architecture are assessed.

Beside the TOGAF approach the S-BPM deployment approach promotes a sequence of pragmatic activities (see fig. 1, upper left). Therefore the S-BPM activities "Task clarification", "Modeling communication", "Data and rules", "Forms, interfaces, reports", "Test and training" and "Go Live", which represent the process of a S-BPM project [3] could be very much accompanied by the phases promoted by the TOGAF ADM.

When S-BPM is used in the context of enterprise architecture, we observe a certain interaction between the phases promoted by the TOGAF ADM and the approach of S-BPM. The right part of figure 1 illustrates this interaction.

The S-BPM activities can be used in the known sequence because they are already optimized for communication intensive environments they build the core of a S-BPM centric enterprise architecture (Figure 1, steps 1-6). Due to our observations the traditional sequence of the TOGAF ADM phases rearranges individual or iterative communication sequences. The traditional sequences, which were used to develop classical enterprise architectures, are transformed to accompanying activities enveloping the S-BPM activities. Especially the phase implementation governance, opportunities & solutions and migration planning cannot be placed any longer at the end of an architecture process, where architectures will be implemented into IT. Instead they are observed already in early phases of the process. Reason for this paradigm change is that the barriers between process, architecture and IT development are unsustainable. A turn from a top down approach to an integrative procedure takes place.

With respect to the communication paradigm the different architecture levels business architecture, information systems architecture and technology architecture cannot be separated into several phases, which will be assessed step by step. Instead with different levels of detail activities for all architecture levels in the process modeling phases of an S-BPM project can be found.

An important aspect in setting up enterprise architecture is to get aware about gaps in the current state of the architecture and to close them in a future state. Based on the specific modeling of S-BPM based architectures, three steps are needed to plan a new architecture with subject orientation as illustrated in figure 2. The figure shows the approach of building a new target architecture (illustrated by the lower right figure) based on an As-Is architecture (illustrated by the lower left figure) as an example.

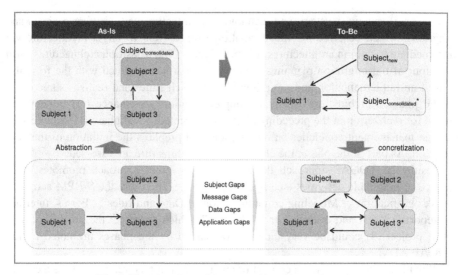

Fig. 2. Planning the architecture with subject orientation

There are two different concepts that are used to build the target architecture. First one is the concept of abstraction. The given As-Is architecture normally describes subjects and their communication is a very detailed level, thus building a new target architecture becomes complex. The abstraction condensates subjects and their communication into subject-clusters and simplifies the communication. This step requires a good understanding of the business domain in order to create sense making clusters. Abstraction can be performed multiple times in order to create a view which can be shared and communicated at the necessary stakeholder level. Based on the abstraction, new elements of the intended target architecture are incorporated and hence build the target architecture, also on an abstract level.

In a second step the abstract target architecture is broken down to a concrete level of subjects. This is done by subsequently replacing subject clusters by concrete subjects and their communication paths. The step of concretization also requires a high level of business domain understanding and will involve individuals who will be involved in the future shape of the communication. The step of concretization will also be executed multiple times until all subject clusters have been replaced.

Gaps between the As-Is and the target architecture are determined by comparing the two states and will serve as input to build up the architecture roadmap elements. The list of gaps that can be determined contain: Subject gaps, Data gaps, communication gaps (message and data) as well as gaps in integration of applications.

3   Conclusions and Next Steps

As described in preceding chapters the switch to communication paradigm requires an adaption of existing enterprise architecture frameworks to satisfy customer needs and provide necessary flexibility. Therefore the existing phases of TOGAF ADM can be combined with the activities of an S-BPM project.

Though the effect in using TOGAF ADM has been examined in S-BPM projects, a series of TOGAF related artifacts still need to be evaluated in determine whether they would apply out of the box or if adoptions to them are necessary. Such an analysis will primarily focus on the assessment of following components:

- ADM Guidelines and Techniques
- Architecture Content Framework
- Enterprise Continuum an Tools
- TOGAF Reference Models
- Architecture Capability Framework

References

1. Campus Management. Campus Verlag, Frankfurt (2003)
2. The Open Group: Open Group Standard TOGAF Version 9.1. Van Haren Publishing, Zalt-bommel/NL (2011)
3. Fleischmann, A., Schmidt, W., Stary, C., Obermeier, S., Börger, E.: Subjektorientiertes Prozessmanagement. Hanser, München (2011)
4. Berneaud, M., Buckl, S., Fuentes, A., Matthes, F., Monahov, I., Nowobilska, A., Roth, S., Schweda, C.M., Weber, U., Zeiner, M.: Trends for Enterprise Architecture Management and Tools. Technical Report, Köln (2012)

Production Planning for SMEs – Implementation of Production Planning with Subject-Oriented Business Process Management (S-BPM)

Christoph Piller and DI Walter Wölfel

UAS Technikum Wien, Höchstädtplatz 6, 1200 Vienna, Austria
{iw12m002,walter.woelfel}@technikum-wien.at, chpiller@gmx.net

Abstract. In this paper a subject-oriented solution for Production Planning (PP) for a small and medium-sized enterprise (SME) in the craft sector is developed. Many SMEs have limited financing options and do not have the knowledge to use PP correctly. PP is introduced at the beginning of this paper, in order to provide an overview of objectives and challenges. After presenting an exemplary company and its problems with implementing PP, the subject-oriented approach of PP for this company is exposed. Therefore the single steps of PP are only seen as modules. With this view of PP, the whole PP process can be customized and simplified. Furthermore it is shown that even strategic linking with this new approach is possible. The result is a favourable and lean usage of PP, especially for the exemplary SME.

Keywords: Production Planning, Process Management, Subject-Oriented Business Process Management, Change Management.

1   Introduction

Today, systematic planning and forecasting are factors of success in every company. Business objectives should be determined, in order to achieve them; furthermore measures for the achievement of these objectives and the preparation of these selected measures are important steps to be oriented on them and therefore achieve them. It is important to discover several opportunities and use them. This is called strategic planning and is an important foundation of a company [6], [11].

Production Planning itself is an operational planning instead of a strategic planning, but the objectives of Production Planning are built up on strategic planning [20]. The main focus lies on the required resources, i.e. required materials, types of materials, number of employees, delivery dates, etc. At this planning stage a production plan is created, in order to be oriented on predetermined objectives and achieve them. For this many calculations and mathematical-logical systems are necessary. Generally there are various PP systems, which are used by companies, in order to execute PP correctly [4], [7].

However PP as it is generally known is difficult to implement in SMEs. SMEs have less money to invest and less knowledge to use PP systems in the correct way

C. Zehbold (Ed.): S-BPM ONE 2014, CCIS 422, pp. 164–173, 2014.

[17]. This means, that a PP system for SMEs should at least not cost anything and should be understandable and user-friendly.

In this thesis a new approach to PP, especially in SMEs, is investigated. First of all, a brief overview about PP as it is generally known is given, in order to provide an understanding of this complex process. Then the company is presented in which PP was implemented with the help of S-BPM. Therefore the single steps of PP were broken down into several modules. Due to this view on PP, the process can be described with just one subject behaviour; that made the PP process understandable in the company. Furthermore the modules could be easily used in an excel document, so the costs for this approach were minimal.

Finally it should be said that there are neither explanations of the historical development of PP nor derivations of mathematical formulas, which are used. Also the different PP systems are not investigated. The approach does not include a new application of a PP system. This still has to be investigated in further studies. In this thesis an alternative and subject-oriented approach, especially for the exemplary SME, is presented.

2   Production Planning

PP is generally divided into Primary Requirements Planning, Secondary Requirements Planning as well as Date and Capacity Planning [3], [10].

2.1   Production Planning Process

Primary requirements planning deals with the types of products a company wants to produce. Therefore planning periods should be implemented and the length of such a planning period should be determined [2]. In summary, it can be said that companies engaging in Primary Requirements Planning want to know which types of products should be produced, in which time they should be produced, and their exact amount. The result of this calculation is called a production plan [10].

After Primary Requirements Planning has been completed, *Secondary Requirements Planning* should follow [4]. The data from the Primary Requirements Planning are used in this subsequent stage. First, the gross requirements are calculated, representing all products that are needed to finish a production plan. After that the net requirements are calculated, which represent all products which have to be ordered [3], [10]. Based on the result of these calculations as well as on the expenditure of these calculations, the inventory policy may be revisited [3].

Once Primary and Secondary Requirements Planning have been executed, *Date and Capacity Planning* will be the next and the last step of Production Planning [4]. In this step a timely order of a previously defined time period is made. Therefore start and finish dates of each order are investigated. In addition, necessary measures for capacity adjustments are investigated [3].

In order to guarantee a quick and understandable overview of the single steps of PP, the PP process is described with an event-driven process chain (EPC) (Fig. 1) [17].

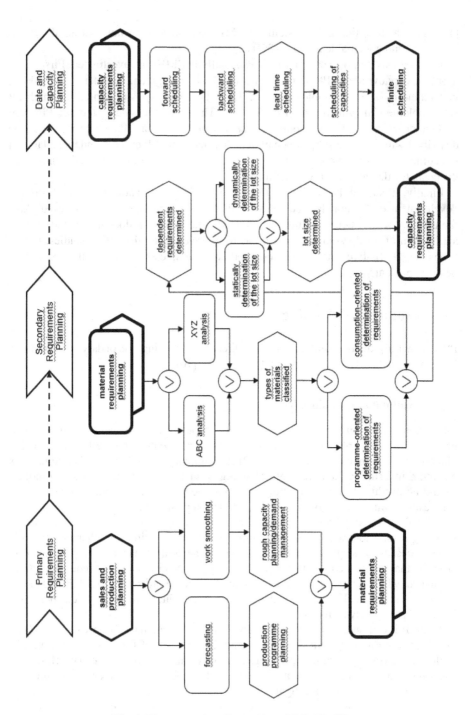

Fig. 1. PP process described with an EPC ([3], [9])

Even though there are many IT programmes and the three steps of PP seem to be simple, it is difficult for SMEs to implement and use PP in the correct way. The reasons are discussed in the next subchapter.

2.2   Implementation Problems of SMEs

Because of the limited financing options of SMEs and the limited utilisation of modern management methods [17], PP itself is used rarely by SMEs. They do not have the money to invest in a PP system; furthermore there is no knowledge to use such systems in the correct way [19]. "Some writers have argued forcefully that formal strategic management procedures are particularly inappropriate for small and medium-sized firms which have neither the management nor financial resources to indulge in elaborate strategic management techniques." [1], p. 7. Another problem is that SMEs in the craft sector often have short-term orders. Furthermore, the orders are often customer-dependent; i.e. the customer determines what she/he wants and when she/he wants it. Additionally, changes and interruptions of fixed orders (by the customer) are very likely. In literature this production is called market-oriented production. As a result, SMEs have to fight with random order entries, so a forecast is difficult to make and has only weak significance [3]. However the main focus of SMEs is a full utilisation of all employees. Furthermore the product is often a service or often includes a service in which the customer and his satisfaction are of main focus [14]. This focus suggests that the PP process should be more subject-oriented; that there is a lot of communication with subjects.

In order to provide a better understanding for these problems, the challenges for implementing PP in the exemplary company are presented below.

First of all, as mentioned before and typically for an SME, the new PP system should be free of charge, because the CEOs argued that the company has no money to invest in such a system.

In addition, the new system had to be simple to use and understand. PP, especially PP systems, had not been used before. In order to minimize the training period, the system needed to be as simple as possible; without losing the effectiveness and efficiency of PP.

Moreover the system had to be customisable. The company had to fight with random order entries and with frequent changes and interruptions of fixed orders. In order to be able to react to such circumstances quickly and flexibly, the new PP system itself had to be flexible, and also customizable.

Finally, the product offered was mainly a service. There was a lot of communication with all stakeholders, i.e. the subject itself and its behaviour were of primary importance for the company. For that reason it seemed obvious to develop a subject-oriented approach, which is presented in the next chapter.

3   Production Planning with S-BPM: Case Study

First of all the company in which this subject-oriented approach of PP was implemented is introduced, in order to show the difficulty of implementation and not only the subject-oriented solution but also the strategy linking solution.

3.1   Company

The company is a metalworking shop with 24 employees, two CEOs (one for operative the other for administrative area) and one secretary, who supports both CEOs. The single departments are responsible for a turnover of nearly two million Euros per annum. Considering this basic information, it should be clear that this company is an SME.

The strategy and framework of the company is shown in Fig. 2. The core processes are divided into the acquisition and initial support of customers, the three main activities (represented by departments) and finally the support of customers. The supporting processes, marketing, human resources, accounting and controlling, provide support for the core processes over the entire product life cycle.

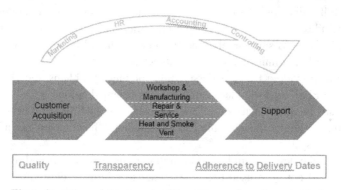

Fig. 2. Strategy and framework of the company from the case study

The vision of the company and the long-term objectives of the company are quality, transparency and adherence to delivery dates. That means that the metalworking shop wants to provide better quality than its direct competitors. It wants to offer total transparency of the production for the customer; therefore, the CEO invested a lot of money for new software, which is now hardly used. Finally, the company wants to provide adherence to delivery dates for every single order. Considering this initial situation of the company, the challenges listed in chapter 2.2 were present two years ago. Considering the challenges of the company the subject-oriented approach is shown in the next chapter.

3.2   Subject-Oriented Production Planning Process

The activity in processes is performed by persons who are involved in these processes, the subjects. The subject is put in the centre of considerations; thus the subject will receive a greater focus [8]. Therefore the single steps of PP are seen as single modules, in order to simplify PP as well as use only these steps of PP, which are necessary. In this subchapter, the new approach for the Service and Repair Department is presented.

The department's main fields of activity are repairs and maintenances of locks, door closers, fittings and so on, the service of a typical locksmith as generally known. The amount of orders and the order entries can be seen as linear, because there are not great fluctuations. With this knowledge a subject-oriented solution can be investigated.

The PP process is shown in Fig. 3. As mentioned before, the single steps of PP have been transformed to several modules. In the service and repair department, three modules were used, in order to perform PP: forecasting, linear optimization and inventory policy.

Every week the company gets between 74 and 114 orders. Each order is similar to a previous one and executes no more than two hours. These facts make the calculation of a forecast useful for PP. To calculate a forecast for this department the mathematical method of the moving average is offered. There is a constant development of the amount of orders and every amount of the past has the same weighting. With the result from the moving average[1] a forecast can be made for this department [3].

As already mentioned in the theoretical part of this paper, Secondary Requirements Planning is used to calculate the requirements, which have to be ordered to finish the production plan. In the service and repair department it is difficult to make an ABC or an XYZ analysis, calculate gross requirements and net requirements. The product offered in this department is a service. That means this department does not need a lot of products or materials. So the main focus is placed on the inventory policy. A good beginning would be the implementation of a reorder system. But the inventory policy is not the area of this thesis and can be ignored here.

Finally, the linear optimisation is done regularly, because the results of the forecast as well as the capacity[2] are known. With the result an optimal lot size for the daily order release can be given [3]. If there are changes of the processing time of some orders capacity coordination has to be done. For example outsourcing of some orders is possible. The lot size can also be changed or some overtime has to be made, which means a change in working time. But this capacity coordination is only short-term, because irregularities of these orders are rare.

After performing the most important PP modules the orders are either released to an employee or stored until their releasing date.

---

[1] The moving average is used to eliminate random irregularities. Contrary to the arithmetic average, only the latest values are considered.

[2] The capacity of human resources and machinery can be seen as constant in this department.

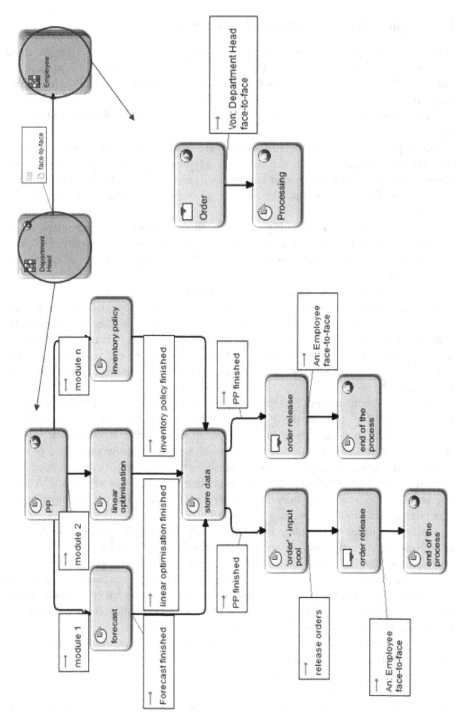

Fig. 3. Subject behaviour of the PP process

To sum up it can be said that the calculation of the forecast, the linear optimisation and an inventory policy are the main modules of PP in this department. The usage of these tools should be repeated in defined time periods. These periods can be different for every module.

3.3   Results

This new subject-oriented approach of PP was successfully implemented at least in the Service & Repair department. Based on this approach, a strategic link to the company's vision was established as well, and a kind of Balanced Scorecard was developed and implemented. The average of delays, the amount of new and finished orders, the amount of complaints and the turnover per employee were calculated. With a decrease of the complaints and a decrease of the delays, the quality of the product (which is mainly a service) and the transparency for the customer would be increase. The numbers for the delays are easily to calculate, because important dates, e.g. delivery dates, are known because of PP. The numbers of new and finished orders should be known, if a forecast and a linear optimisation is done regularly; likewise, the turnover per employee should be known, if a linear optimisation is completed.

After nine months of using PP in the Service & Repair department, delays in delivery decreased from 4.5 days to 0.75 days per contract, the complaints decreased from 10 to two per week and the turnover per person increased by 20%. Furthermore PP was used and understood by the participants of the PP process. This means that the complex PP process could be made understandable with the help of S-BPM. Every employee knows what she or he should do to use PP correctly. Furthermore S-BPM helped to break down the entire PP process into single modules, which made it as simple as possible and as complex as necessary.

Nonetheless, PP, and in particular this approach of PP, is not accepted by every employee; today PP is not used any more in this company.

4   Discoveries and Outlook

4.1   Case Study

As mentioned in the last chapter, PP is not used any more in the company; for several reasons. First of all, during the entire project of developing a new PP approach and implementing this approach, there has been minimal commitment by the executives and lack of support from other department heads. It has become evident that none of the decision makers wanted to invest time and money in PP, although they themselves made the decision to implement PP at the beginning.

Furthermore the lack of know-how, time and documentation in the company made it hard to finish this "change management" project and satisfy every stakeholder.

Nevertheless, a new approach of PP could be developed with the help of S-BPM. It was possible to implement PP, make it understandable and establish a direct strategy linking. As a result several key figures have been clearly improved.

The big issue, especially in this company, is change management itself. Without the necessary support from the executives, it seemed to be impossible to implement a new management method in this SME.

4.2   General

Fig. 4 shows the BPM activity model [18]. Due to the fact that SMEs play a more important role in economy[3] today, even SMEs have to follow such an activity model to ensure a sufficient service [12].

First of all, it is important to define a strategy from which the policy, the IT environment and the organisation should be derived. On this strategic basis operational steps can be done. Performances can be analysed, processes can be created, optimised and implemented.

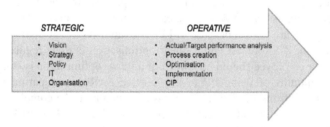

Fig. 4. Activity Model

In order to achieve objectives and fulfil the predefined strategy, it is important that every person of the company act in concert. The successful implementation of a process system or a PP system is not a task for an IT technician; it is a task for every person, especially the top management [5].

5   Conclusion

This thesis presents a new approach to PP. In order to put the main focus on the subject, the methods of Primary Requirements Planning, Secondary Requirements Planning and Date and Capacity Planning have been transformed into one PP process with several modules. By describing and defining this process, PP is defined for the employee and can thus be applied. As shown in the example, this process is simple to understand and to create.

One factor must not be forgotten: PP is a small piece of production logistics and production logistics is a small piece of logistics. So it is important that an overview in terms of supply chain management is kept in mind. Furthermore the process PP is only a sub process of the complete process model and the process model should be oriented to the vision and the strategy of a company. So the overall concept and the core processes should always be kept in mind if sub processes are created.

---

[3] In Germany 99.6% of all enterprises are SMEs.

This approach needs more practical investigations and practical verification. On that account the studies will be continued and it will be tried to find more SMEs, which want to cooperate. Finally, not only PP for SMEs has to be investigated, but also the analysis of process management for SMEs in general should be prioritised.

References

1. Analoui, F., Karami, A.: Strategic Managemen. In: Small and Medium Enterprises. Thomson, London (2003)
2. Arnold, D.: Handbuch Logistik. Springer, Heidelberg (2008) (in German)
3. Buzacott, J.A.: Produktionsplanung und Steuerung. Oldenbourg, Munich (2010) (in German)
4. Dangelmaier, W.: Theorie der Produktionsplanung und –steuerung. Springer, Heidelberg (2009) (in German)
5. Davenport, T.H.: Putting the Enterprise into the Enterprise System. Harvard Business Review (July-August 1998)
6. David, F.R.: Strategic Management. Pearson Education, New Jersey (2011)
7. Dickersbach, J.T., Keller, G.: Production Planning and Control with SAP® ERP. Galileo Press, Bonn (2011)
8. Fleischmann, A.: Subjektorientiertes Prozessmanagement. Oldenbourg, Munich (2010) (in German)
9. Fleischmann, A., Schmidt, W., Singer, R., Seese, D. (eds.): S-BPM ONE 2010. CCIS, vol. 138. Springer, Heidelberg (2011)
10. Gansterer, M.: Produktionsplanung. Vorlesungsskript, UAS Technikum Wien, Vienna. MIWI, vol. 2 (2013) (in German)
11. Grünig, R., Kühn, R.: Process-based Strategic Planning. Springer, Heidelberg (2011)
12. Kletti, J., Schumacher, J.: Die perfekte Produktion. Springer, Heidelberg (2011)
13. Koether, R.: Taschenbuch der Logistik. Carl Hanser, Munich (2011) (in German)
14. Lanninger, V.: Prozessmodell zur Auswahl Betrieblicher Standardanwendungssoftware für KMU. Josef Eul, Cologne (2009) (in German)
15. Mac an Bhaird, C: Resourcing Small and Medium Sized Enterprises. Springer, Heidelberg (2010)
16. Mittendorfer, M.: Open Source Business Intelligence in SMEs, Vienna, UAS Technikum Wien, International Business and Engineer. Master Thesis (2013)
17. Monk, E.F., Wagner, B.J.: Concepts in Enterprise Resource Planning. Course Technology Cengage Learning, Boston (2009)
18. Schmidt, W. (ed.): S-BPM ONE 2011. CCIS, vol. 213. Springer, Heidelberg (2011)
19. Schroeer, S.: Internationalisierung von KMU – Problemfelder und Chancen. Grin, Norderstedt (2009) (in German)
20. Slack, N., et al.: Operations and Process Management. Financial Times Prentice Hall, Harlow (2009)

Can We Use S-BPM
for Modeling Collaboration Scripts?

Kai Michael Höver and Max Mühlhäuser

Technische Universität Darmstadt
Dept. of Computer Science
64289 Darmstadt, Germany
{kai,max}@tk.informatik.tu-darmstadt.de

Abstract. S-BPM is a well-known approach for modeling business processes. Collaboration processes in form of computer-supported collaborative learning (CSCL) scripts are apparently similar to business processes as they also define sequenced activities of subjects and interaction between them. Therefore, S-BPM is analyzed with regard to its suitability to model CSCL scripts, because a formal description of such learning processes is still missing. In order to address the requirements of those processes, a subject-oriented interpreter model is presented that facilitates the change of subjects' behavior during the execution.

Keywords: S-BPM, CSCL, Collaboration Scripts, ASM.

1 Introduction

Subject-oriented Business Process Management (S-BPM) is an evolving paradigm of modeling business processes [1, 2]. It uses a puristic set of graphical symbols in contrast to other approaches like BPMN with over 50 graphical symbols, describes processes in a natural language like manner, and has a strong focus on subjects in the modeling phase defining their behavior and their interaction among each other [3]. As its name reveals, the purpose of S-BPM is the description of business processes. However, as we will see in the following sections, collaborative learning processes are very similar to business processes, but have also some differences. Like business processes, collaborative learning processes describe the behavior of learners and their interaction with each other. In order to describe and execute such learning processes a formal description language is necessary. However, languages and tools for modeling and deploying computer-supported collaborative learning (CSCL) scripts are still missing. Specification like IMS Learning Design [1] (IMS LD) are still insufficient languages for the requirements of CSCL scripts [4], although there has been work done for extending IMS LD [5–7]. Another motivation for a formal language of CSCL scripts is that they are usually informally described by natural language. This, however, makes it difficult for the stakeholders (teachers, learners, software programmers) to unambiguously understand CSCL scripts due to a lack of execution semantics.

---

[1] http://www.imsglobal.org/learningdesign/

C. Zehbold (Ed.): S-BPM ONE 2014, CCIS 422, pp. 174–187, 2014.
© Springer International Publishing Switzerland 2014

In this paper, we enquire if it is possible to model learning processes (especially collaboration scripts) with S-BPM. After a short introduction to CSCL scripts we reveal missing concepts in S-BPM that are required for CSCL scripts. We address these missing features by extending the S-BPM interpreter model developed by Egon Börger [8, 9]. We finish with a summary and provide an outlook on future work.

2   CSCL Scripts

As "social constructivists tell us that learning is a social process" [10, p. 7]. Exchanging opinions, views, and discussing about concepts with other learners help to construct knowledge and to clear up misconceptions. However, collaborative learning is often ineffectively organized. So called *collaboration scripts* provide scaffolds to improve learning between two or more learning partners [4, 11, 12]. Although such scripts can be applied for face-to-face learning without computer support, they are often used in distributed learning settings with computer mediation for collaboration purposes. In this context we refer to CSCL (computer-supported collaborative learning) scripts.

2.1   Scripts Examples

To give an idea of collaboration scripts (sometimes also called "cooperative" depending on the outcome), we present examples of scripts in this section.

The MURDER Script. A well-known and one of the simplest cooperative scripts is the MURDER script [13] (the acronym stands for "mood", "understand", "recall", "detect", "elaborate", "review" and describes the script's sequence). It puts up scaffolding for the interaction between two learning partners learning from a text. In an initialization step the text is subdivided into paragraphs. Starting from the first paragraph, the script defines repeating rounds with assigning roles and actions to the learners, and defining interactions between them for each of the paragraphs. The process steps of the MURDER script are:

1. *Assigning roles*: the MURDER script defines two roles: the *summarizer* and the *listener*. One learner slips into the role of the summarizer, the other one takes over the role of the listener.
2. *Mood and understanding*: Both learners set the mood for studying. Afterwards, both read the selected text paragraph in order to understand its content.
3. *Recall and Detection*: The summarizer recalls the content of the read paragraph and writes a summary that contains important aspects of the content from her point of view. In a CSCL environment the summarizer sends her summary to the learning mate (listener). The listener reads the summary, tries to detect errors, misconceptions etc., and sends her feedback to the summarizer.

4. *Elaborate*: Both summarizer and listener elaborate on the read passage. Afterwards, these process steps are repeated with the next paragraph if there is one left and with changed roles, i.e., the summarizer becomes the listener and vice versa.

Finally, both *review* the read passages and reflect what they have learned.

A variation with more than two learners is also possible. In this case, one could take over the role of the summarizer and sends her summary to the set of listeners who will provide feedback in return. Afterwards the roles are changed and one of the listeners becomes the next summarizer.

The Maze Script. The Maze Script was applied to the field of learning robot programming [6, 14]. In particular, students should learn to create rules for controlling a robot in order to autonomously find the exit out of a maze. The script was applied in a class with 24 students. The process steps of the Maze script are:

1. Divide students into groups: 24 students are divided into 6 groups, 4 students each.
2. Each group is divided in 2 subgroups à 2 persons: the *maze builders* and the *strategy developers*.
3. The strategy developers create rule sets to control the robot, which are tested by the maze builders. So the strategy developers send their rule sets to the maze builders of their group.
4. The maze builders test the received rule sets of the group mates.
5. One member of the 6 groups sends the first results of the group to the other 5 group members. The groups exchange their results with the other groups.
6. Each group starts again working on rules and testing them, but this time the members of the subgroups change their roles: the maze builders become the strategy developers and vice versa. As the groups have now the rule sets and mazes of the competitor groups, they can learn from the others' rule sets by applying them with their mazes, and create mazes that are hard to solve for the competitor groups and their rule sets.
7. The script continues with step 3 to 5. An end state could be entered if a group could solve all mazes with their rules.

Many more examples of CSCL scripts can be found in literature, e.g., [4, 12, 15–19]. Next, we analyze the characteristics of presented scripts.

3   Analysis

In this section, we analyze the characteristics of CSCL scripts and derive modeling requirements. Subsequently, we discuss how far these characteristics are supported by S-BPM.

3.1 Characteristics of CSCL Scripts

According to Kollar et al. [11], collaboration scripts have at least five conceptual components:

- *learning objectives*: like business processes learning processes also pursue a purpose that should be achieved after their execution
- *type of activities*: several activities are defined to accomplish a learning goal
- *sequencing*: these activities are performed in a certain sequence
- *role distribution*: during the execution of a process (script) the participants adopt to several roles with activities that are assigned to these roles
- *type of presentation*: for guiding users, a script can be presented in many different ways, either orally, textual, or graphical.

Kobbe et al. [15] identify the following components of collaboration scripts:

- *participants*: scripts define their participants. Sometimes their number or type are predefined, like an even number or divisible by three, or participant characteristic data like nationality or grades
- *activities*: participants are engaged in certain activities carried out in a certain sequence and defined by a script.
- *roles*: roles are assigned to certain activities or resources, legitimizations, etc.
- *resources*: participants access, create, modify, exchange virtual or physical objects
- *groups*: groups consist of participants or smaller groups; participants can be members of more than one group, and even have different roles in a group (see the Maze script, section 2.1).

Dillenbourg [20] defines five attributes that describe the different aspects of collaboration scripts: *type of task* to be accomplish, *group formation* (which participant is in which group), *distribution of the tasks* (who is doing what), *type and mode of interaction* (synchronous or asynchronous, text-based or voice-based, etc.), and *timing of the phases*.

Although every of the presented analysis of identifying characteristic components lists five items, there are both differences and similarities between them. We will discuss this in the subsequent section.

3.2 Requirements of CSCL Scripts

After the identification of characteristics of cooperation scripts, we derive requirements with a focus on modeling of this kind of learning processes.

Key aspects of cooperation scripts are activities and their order of succession. Resources may be involved in activities and are exchanged between participants exchanging messages. Further, activities are assigned to roles, and participants can be members of one or more groups. Cooperation scripts also have different repeating phases in which participants may be assigned to other roles and thus change their behavior. Therefore it should be possible to model:

- activities
- participants and groups
- communication between participants
- a sequence of activities
- assigning behavior to roles
- assigning participants to roles and groups during the execution

What makes the modeling of CSCL scripts a challenging task are the following aspects:

- Groups and roles
- Changing the behavior of individuals and groups during the execution phase
- Unknown number of participants
- Behavior is assigned to both groups and subjects
- Subjects change groups and thus their behavior during the execution of a CSCL script process
- Alternating changes between individual activities and activities in a group

3.3   CSCL Scripts and S-BPM

When considering the elicited requirements with regards to S-BPM (especially the S-BPM language PASS (Parallel Activity Specification Schema) [1]), we can see both similarities and differences. A sequenced execution of activities is one of the main features of business process modeling. S-BPM defines three kinds of activities: send, receive, and internal actions or functions. Activities are performed on (business) objects which are transported by messages. S-BPM also supports multi-processes which facilitate the simultaneously or sequentially execution of (sub)processes multiple times. Therefore, multi-processes are suitable if the number of subjects with the same behavior is unknown in the modeling phase. One big difference, however, is the change of behavior during execution which is not explicitly supported by S-BPM. It can only be achieved by modeling each of the different behaviors for every subject. However, this is only possible if the different behavior changes can be foreseen and modeled in advance. This approach thus is not very flexible and not always possible in case of dynamic changing behaviors.

The results of the analysis are summarized in table 1.

4   A Subject-Oriented Interpreter Model for CSCL Scripts

In this section we provide an overview of our basic interpreter model for S-BPM processes that is a simplified[2] version of the interpreter model developed by Egon Börger [9] using the method of Abstract State Machines (ASM) [21]. Afterwards, we describe how we extend our S-BPM interpreter model in order to address the requirements derived from CSCL scripts as presented in section 3.

---

[2] The basic interpreter model does not consider synchronous communication, input pool constraints, TryRounds, timeouts, and user abruption.

Table 1. Analysis results with regard to CSCL scripts requirements

Cooperation scripts requirements	S-BPM
Definition of activities	yes (function, send, receive)
communication types	yes (support of synchronous and asynchronous communication)
resources	yes (in form of business object)
groups	yes (multi-processes)
behavior	yes (behavior can be defined in subject behavior diagrams)
changing behavior/roles	no (description of behavior but not changing during execution)

4.1 The Basis Interpreter Model

Subsequently, we present the subject-oriented interpreter model we use for interpreting CSCL script processed. As mentioned above, we use the ASM method for the specification. ASMs have a finite set of transition rules of the form **if** *Condition* **then** *Updates* which transform abstract states. A *Condition* is a first-order logic formula. If it is true, then the *Updates* are executed, i.e., the values of defined functions are updated.

To be able to proof the defined ASM, we use the ASMETA Simulator[3] that facilitates the execution of ASM models [22, 23]. The subsequent code examples are provided in the ASMETA Language[4] (AsmetaL).

Subject Behavior

A S-BPM process defines the behavior of a set of subjects. A behavior can be modeled with a directed graph, the *subject behavior diagram* (SBD). *SID states* (Subject Interaction Diagram states) represent the state each subject is in. In the BEHAVIOR rule, a subject performs a certain *service* (send, receive, or function) of a state until it is completed. If the service is completed, then an outgoing edge satisfying an exit condition is selected to proceed to the next node of the behavior diagram.

```
BEHAVIOR(subj,state) =
if  SID_state(subj,state) then
   if  Completed(subj, service(state), state)  then
      let edge = select_Edge({e ∈ OutEdge(state)|ExitCond(e)(subj, state}))
      PROCEED(subj, service(target(edge)), target(edge))
   else
      PERFORM (subj, service(state),state)
   end if
end if
```

---

[3] http://asmeta.sourceforge.net
[4] http://fmse.di.unimi.it/asmeta/download/AsmetaL_quickguide.html

The corresponding code in AsmetaL is

```
rule r_behavior($s in Subject, $state in State) =
    if(sid_state($s) = $state) then
    seq
      if(completed($s, service($state),$state)) then
        let ($edge = exitCond ) in
          r_proceed[$s, service(target($edge)),target($edge)]
        endlet
      else r_perform[$s, service($state), $state]
      endif
      endseq
    endif
```

The PERFORM rule is a simplified version without try-rounds and user abruption. It mainly checks the type of service and proceeds with the execution of further rules.

```
rule r_perform($s in Subject, $service in Service, $state in
    State) =
  seq
    if serviceType($service) = FUNCTION then
        r_performInternalBehavior($s,$service,$state) endif
    if serviceType($service) = SEND or serviceType($service)
        = RECEIVE then r_tryAlternative[$s,$state] endif
  endseq
```

Alternative Send and Receive

If a state performs a communication act, alternative send or receive can be applied. If there are alternatives one can be selected and the messages are prepared for the selected alternative communication act (see also [2, chapters 5.5.4.3 and 5.5.4.4]).

```
rule r_tryAlternative($s in Subject, $state in State) =
  seq
    if ( waiting($s)=false ) then
      r_chooseAndPrepareAlternative[$s,$state]
    endif
    r_try($s,$state)
  endseq
```

In TRYALTERNATIVE(subj,state) an alternative is chosen (*let alt =
selectedAlternative(subj, state)*) and prepared if the subject is not already waiting for incoming messages. Otherwise it tries to perform the chosen alternative (TRY(subj,state)). The message(s) that should be (multi)send or (multi)received are stored in a set of messages that is stored in the function *MsgToBeHandled(subj,state)*.

In TRY((subj,state)) a message is chosen out of this set of message to be sent or received. In the first case (Send) the message(s) is/are put into the input pool(s) of the receiver(s) *(receiver(msg))* of the message. In the second case (Receive), the receiver waits for one or more expected messages. If it is found it is removed from the input pool and further processed.

```
turbo rule r_try($s in Subject, $state in State) =
  if (size(msgToBeHandled($s,$state))>0) then
    choose $msg in msgToBeHandled($s,$state) with true do
      par
        if ( serviceType(service($state))=SEND ) then
          seq
            r_insertMsg[$msg]
            msgToBeHandled($s,$state) := excluding(
                msgToBeHandled($s,$state),$msg)
            r_try($s,$state)
          endseq
        endif
        if ( serviceType(service($state))=RECEIVE ) then
          seq
            // set to waiting for messages
            waiting($s) := true
            // check if expected message is in inputpool
            if ( expectedMsgInPool($msg, inputPool($s)) )
              then
              seq
                // remove it from the to be handled messages
                msgToBeHandled($s,$state) := excluding(
                    msgToBeHandled($s,$state),$msg)
                // ... and from the input pool
                inputpoolMessages(inputPool($s)) := excluding
                    (inputpoolMessages(inputPool($s)),$msg)
                r_try($s,$state)
              endseq
            endif
          endseq
        endif
      endpar
    else
      par
        completed($s,service($state),$state) := true
        waiting($s) := false
      endpar
  endif
```

An expected message is found in the input pool if it matches the expected message type and sender of the message:

$$expectedMsgInPool(msg, pool) \iff$$
$$\exists m \in Message.\, type(m) = type(msg) \land sender(m) = sender(msg)$$

In this section we could only provide a short explanation of the interpreter model. However, we tried to focus on the most important aspects for the sake of better understanding. For further information we refer to [8].

4.2   The Scripts Interpreter Model

In the following, we suggest an interpreter model that is able to execute CSCL scripts. We explain the interpreter model along the example of the MURDER script with more than two participants.

Description of Roles

As we have seen in section 3.1, CSCL scripts define roles. Such roles represent the behaviors of participants. A subject is assigned to a certain role in order to perform a specific behavior. The idea is now that the behavior of roles is modeled using subject behavior diagrams (see section 4.1). Figure 1 depicts the behavior of both the Listener and Summarizer roles reduced to its core elements. They are like behavior diagrams but are assigned to subjects only during execution of the process. In this way a certain behavior is not tight to a subject, but can be assigned to it during execution and even be reused in different contexts.

Therefore, the subject behavior diagram that are assigned to roles do not contain any specific behavior yet, but a special state. In this state a subject waits for the assignment of a role, i.e., the behavior to be performed.

Assignment of Roles

At the beginning, subjects that participate in a script process and to whom a specific behavior is meant to be assigned are in a special state that is not an initial state but an *Assignment* state (see Figure 2). If a subject is inside such an assignment state the main rule of the ASM does not call the BEHAVIOR(subj,state) rule as long as a subject is assigned to an initial state of a role. After they have finished the behavior of a role they move on to an assignment state again where another role behavior can be assigned. Behaviors of subjects can be performed if no assignment is left. If all subjects are in a final state their *GroupAssignments* are reset to avoid old group assignments in the new assignment phase.

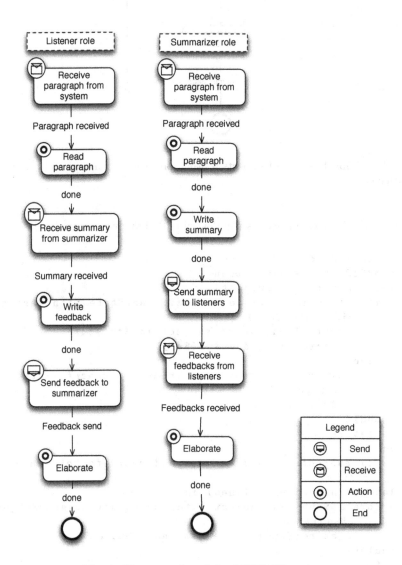

Fig. 1. The two roles of the MURDER script

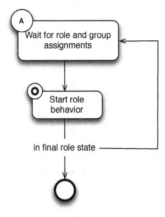

Fig. 2. The simple behavior of subjects waiting for a role assignment and running the role behavior

The ASM MAIN rule presents the described behavior in more detail.

```
main rule r_Main =
  if(endOfProcess=false) then
    let ($s = currentSubject) in
      if( not(exist $astate in AssignmentState with $astate=
          sid_state($s))) then
      // execute behavior of subject in its state
        r_behavior[$s,sid_state($s)]
      else
        // if the subject is not in an assignment state,
            assign Role and Groups
        r_doAssignment[$s]
      endif
    endlet
  else
    // if subjects should be assigned again to roles and
        groups
    let ($finished = finished) in
      forall $subj in Subject with (contains(assignedSubjects
          ,$subj)) do
        sid_state($subj) := a_assignmentState
    endlet
  endif
```

with

```
function endOfProcess =
    ( forall $s in Subject with notfinished($s)=false )
```

and

```
function notfinished($s in Subject) =
    ( forall $asubject in Subject with not( exist $astate in
        EndState with $astate=sid_state($asubject)
        and $s=$asubject ))
```

meaning that the process is completed if all subjects are in a final state.

Similar to the preparation of alternatives, role and group assignments need to be prepared before they can be applied. This is done in DOASSIGNMENT(subject)

```
rule r_doAssignment($s in Subject) =
  seq
    r_chooseAndPrepareAssignment[$s]
    r_tryAssignment[$s]
  endseq
```

In CHOOSEANDPREPAREASSIGNMENT(subj) roles and groups are selected, and a subject is assigned to at most one role as well as zero or more groups. These assignments are applied in TRYASSIGNMENT(subj). This means that a function maps a subject to a finite set of groups. Further, the assignment of a role means that the *sid_state(subj)* of a subject is set to the first state of the assigned behavior.

```
rule r_chooseAndPrepareAssignment($s in Subject) =
  seq
    let ($r = roleAssignmentToBeHandled($s)) in
      assignedRole($s) := $r
    endlet
    let ($g = groupsAssignmentToBeHandled($s)) in
      assignedGroups($s) := $g
    endlet
  endseq
```

5   Summary and Future Work

In this paper, we present a discussion about the question if it is possible to model CSCL scripts with S-BPM. After an analysis of characteristics of CSCL scripts we conclude that S-BPM has a lack of changing the behavior of subjects during the execution of processes. Therefore, we extend a basic version of Egon Börger's subject-oriented interpreter model in order to provide a formal model for assigning behavior to subjects during the execution of processes.

For the future we plan to complete the implementation of the interpreter model with ASMETA with regards to [8]. In the analysis the importance of learning (business) objects was emphasized. We plan to extend the interpreter model to support the description of such artifacts and how they are involved in the learning process.

In the current version of the S-BPM Scripts Interpreter, the assignment of subject instances to roles and groups is managed by a machine. This can be extended in form of triggering the creation of subjects and assigning roles by messages and rules to increase variability of system design and execution as suggested in [24].

To conclude, the contribution of this paper is twofold. First, an analysis of S-BPM is presented with regards to collaboration scripts. Second, a formal specification with the ASM method is provided to facilitate the change of subjects' behavior during the execution of collaboration processes.

References

1. Fleischmann, A.: What Is S-BPM? In: Buchwald, H., Fleischmann, A., Seese, D., Stary, C. (eds.) S-BPM ONE 2009. CCIS, vol. 85, pp. 85–106. Springer, Heidelberg (2010)
2. Fleischmann, A., Schmidt, W., Stary, C., Obermeier, S., Börger, E.: Subject-Oriented Business Process Management. Springer, Heidelberg (2012)
3. Singer, R., Zinser, E.: Business Process Management — S-BPM a New Paradigm for Competitive Advantage? In: Buchwald, H., Fleischmann, A., Seese, D., Stary, C. (eds.) S-BPM ONE 2009. CCIS, vol. 85, pp. 48–70. Springer, Heidelberg (2010)
4. Weinberger, A., Kollar, I., Dimitriadis, Y., Mäkitalo-Siegl, K., Fischer, F.: Computer-Supported Collaboration Scripts. In: Balacheff, N., Ludvigsen, S., Jong, T., Lazonder, A., Barnes, S. (eds.) Technology-Enhanced Learning, pp. 155–173. Springer, Netherlands (2009)
5. Harrer, A., Kobbe, L., Malzahn, N.: Conceptual and computational issues in the formalization of collaboration scripts. In: Proceedings of the 8th International Conference on Computer Supported Collaborative Learning, CSCL 2007, pp. 280–282. International Society of the Learning Sciences (2007)
6. Miao, Y., Hoeksema, K., Hoppe, H.U., Harrer, A.: CSCL scripts: modelling features and potential use. In: Proceedings of the 2005 Conference on Computer Support for Collaborative Learning: Learning 2005: The Next 10 Years! CSCL 2005, pp. 423–432. International Society of the Learning Sciences (2005)
7. Miao, Y., Harrer, A., Hoeksema, K., Hoppe, H.: Modeling CSCL Scripts — A Reflection on Learning Design Approaches. In: Fischer, F., Kollar, I., Mandl, H., Haake, J.M. (eds.) Scripting Computer-Supported Collaborative Learning. Computer-Supported Collaborative Learning Series, vol. 6, pp. 117–135. Springer, US (2007)
8. Börger, E.: A Subject-Oriented Interpreter Model for S-BPM. Hanser Verlag (2011)
9. Fleischmann, A., Schmidt, W., Stary, C., Obermeier, S., Börger, E.: A Precise Description of the S-BPM Modeling Method. In: Subject-Oriented Business Process Management, pp. 227–240. Springer, Heidelberg (2012)
10. Pritchard, A., Woollard, J.: Psychology for the classroom. Constructivism and social learning. Psychology for the classroom series. Routledge, Milton Park (2010)
11. Kollar, I., Fischer, F., Hesse, F.: Collaboration Scripts – A Conceptual Analysis. Educational Psychology Review 18, 159–185 (2006)
12. Dillenbourg, P., Jermann, P.: Designing Integrative Scripts. In: Fischer, F., Kollar, I., Mandl, H., Haake, J.M. (eds.) Scripting Computer-Supported Collaborative Learning. Computer-Supported Collaborative Learning Series, vol. 6, pp. 275–301. Springer, US (2007)

13. Dansereau, D.F., Collins, K.W., McDonald, B.A., Holly, C.: Development and evaluation of a learning strategy training program. Journal of Educational Psychology 71(1), 64–73 (1979)
14. Jansen, M., Oelinger, M., Hoeksema, K., Hoppe, U.: An interactive maze scenario with physical robots and other smart devices. In: Proceedings of the 2nd IEEE International Workshop on Wireless and Mobile Technologies in Education, pp. 83–90 (2004)
15. Kobbe, L., Weinberger, A., Dillenbourg, P., Harrer, A., Hämäläinen, R., Häkkinen, P., Fischer, F.: Specifying computer-supported collaboration scripts. International Journal of Computer-Supported Collaborative Learning 2, 211–224 (2007)
16. Weinberger, A., Fischer, F., Mandl, H.: Gemeinsame Wissenskonstruktion in computervermittelter Kommunikation. Zeitschrift für Psychologie / Journal of Psychology 211(2), 86–97 (2003)
17. Stegmann, K., Weinberger, A., Fischer, F.: Facilitating argumentative knowledge construction with computer-supported collaboration scripts. International Journal of Computer-Supported Collaborative Learning 2(4), 421–447 (2007)
18. Weinberger, A., Stegmann, K., Fischer, F.: Learning to argue online: Scripted groups surpass individuals (unscripted groups do not). Computers in Human Behavior 26(4), 506–515 (2010)
19. Fischer, F., Stegmann, K., Wecker, C., Kollar, I.: Online-Diskussionen in der Hochschullehre. Kooperationsskripts können das fachliche Argumentieren verbessern. Zeitschrift für Pädagogik 57(3), 326–337 (2011)
20. Dillenbourg, P.: Over-scripting CSCL: The risks of blending collaborative learning with instructional design, pp. 61–91 (2002)
21. Börger, E., Stärk, R.F.: Abstract State Machines: A Method for High-Level System Design and Analysis. Springer-Verlag New York, Inc., Secaucus (2003)
22. Gargantini, A., Riccobene, E., Scandurra, P.: A Metamodel-based Language and a Simulation Engine for Abstract State Machines. Journal of Universal Computer Science 14(12), 1949–(1983)
23. Gargantini, A., Riccobene, E., Scandurra, P.: Ten Reasons to Metamodel ASMs. In: Abrial, J.-R., Glässer, U. (eds.) Rigorous Methods for Software Construction and Analysis. LNCS, vol. 5115, pp. 33–49. Springer, Heidelberg (2009)
24. Fleischmann, A., Kannengiesser, U., Schmidt, W., Stary, C.: Subject-Oriented Modeling and Execution of Multi-Agent Business Processes. In: International Conference on Intelligent Agent Technology, IAT 2013. IEEE/WIC/ACM (2013)

3D Progressive Education Environment
for S-BPM

Georg Weichhart[1,2], Johanna Pirker[3], Christian Gütl[3,4], and Christian Stary[1]

[1] Communications Engineering - Dept. of Business Information Systems, Kepler
University Linz, Austria
{Georg.Weichhart,Christian.Stary}@jku.at
[2] Metasonic AG, Pfaffenhofen, Germany
Georg.Weichhart@metasonic.de
[3] Inst. for Information Systems and Computer Media,
Technical University Graz, Austria
{jpirker,cguetl}@iicm.edu
[4] Curtin Business School – School of Information Systems,
Curtin University, Australia

Abstract. The work described in this paper combines our existing work
on virtual 3D worlds and progressive education, applying it in order to
support tbe education of S-BPM. The application of the approaches results in a demonstrator developed for S-BPM-One 2014 conference. The
paper presents the underlying theory and motivation for the demonstrator. An outlook with respect to what is visible in the described e-learning
3D World is given.

Keywords: S-BPM, Virtual World, Progressive Education, 3D Learning Evnironment, Intelligibility Catcher.

1 Introduction

Modern information society requires learning environments (such as schools)
to not only prepare students to reproduce (isolated) facts, but also convey the
capability of self-organised learning, in order to allow students to cope with
the rapid changing technological and social environments. This is especially of
importance in order to satisfy the need for life long learning, where learning does
not only take place in classroom settings but where companies rely on workers
able to acquire skills needed for their day to day work [10].

Electronic learning environments provide the potential to satisfy the grow-
ing need for self-organised knowledge acquisition [6,8]. E-learning environments
that support autonomous learning enable learning of both, content and self-
organised content acquisition strategies. These environments are effective [8]
and efficient [1]. To elevate this potential, the teaching design needs to take into
account the potential of the technical environment [21]. A teaching approach,
based on constructivist learning principles, shows the most promising results in
terms of long-term knowledge acquisition [4]. However, progressive educational

C. Zehbold (Ed.): S-BPM ONE 2014, CCIS 422, pp. 188–197, 2014.

approaches like the Dalton Plan [15], despite being created hundred years ago, show similar properties, enabling and facilitating self-organised learning.

In the demonstrator described in this paper we apply the Dalton Plan approach within a virtual 3D world called Open Wonderland [9,14]. We show an implementation of a learning environment which enables self-organised learning.

Content-wise, the demonstrator will focus on Subject-oriented Business Process Management, as „there is a significant need for BPM skilled people" [12, p. 789]. The learning environment demonstrated in this paper supports the education of S-BPM for self-organised learners. The approach is sufficiently generic to be applied to educate BPM in general.

2 Didactic Approach to e-Learning

Progressive Education in general, is dedicated to support students in becoming self-organised learners. Didactic approaches following this paradigm, focus on allowing individualised approaches to acquire theoretical, and equally important practical capabilities [5]. Learners become members of learning groups, working collaboratively on open-ended tasks.

The Dalton Plan is an applied progressive education approach, which facilitates the design of self-organised learning environments [1,21]. Two instruments have been developed for the Dalton Plan [15]: (a) Assignments and (b) Feedback graphs. It has been shown that by transferring these instruments into the web, self-organised learning is supported even more as the "technological learning environment" makes the responsibilities of all actors (students, teacher) and their interaction transparent [23].

„The effective use of technology in education, however, is not instantaneous and must take into account that it must be used with thoughtful planning, design, reflection and testing." [3, p. 895]. *Intelligibility catchers* (ICs) have been derived from Dalton Plan assignments, simplifying the structure and giving special attention to technical features [20,21]. "In contrast to traditional assignments, ICs refer directly to the knowledge individualization and sharing features of semantic e-learning systems" [21, p. 203].

Assignments and *Intelligibility catchers* (ICs) guide learners by giving a motivation, an objective, and a work structure [15,20]. Additionally a project view on the learning work is given, by presenting deadlines, responsibilities and the planned effort for the work. By definition these instruments put the responsibility for planning work on the students. This implies that the tasks in section 3 (see below) include challenges where students have to develop their individual problem solutions. In addition, the written work /documented work section (3a) only shows how work is to be documented, but does not prescribe how the respective tasks are actually accomplished. IC's, in addition to assignments, include e-learning features to be used for documentation of the work done. This helps students to understand functionalities of the used e-learning system.

Assignments facilitate individual and group problem-solving strategies, but do not determine learning paths [24,23]. The following figure (Fig. 1) highlights the structure and the intentions of the IC's parts.

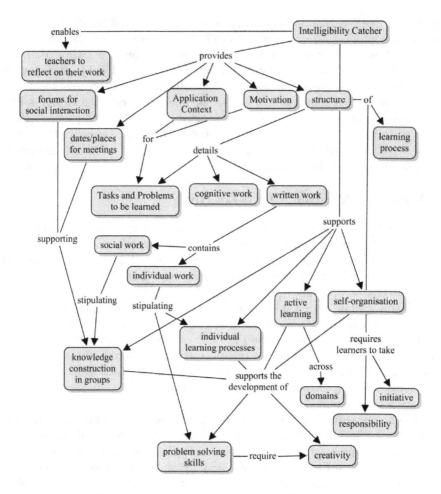

Fig. 1. Structure and intention of ICs [21, p. 212]

More specifically, ICs consist of the following parts [20,21]:

1. **Preface/Orientation:** Motivates learners through grounding the work in real world issues.
2. **Objectives:** General topic of this assignment.
3. **Tasks:** Students should be assigned reproduction, reorganisation, problem-solving tasks [19,22]. Work may be done individually or in groups
3a. **Documented/Written Work:** Shows how the work on the tasks is documented, and how the documentation is handed over to the teachers. This includes features specific to the learning environment [21].
3b. **Intellectual Challenge/Work:** Shows where students have to pay attention with respect to what should be learned.
4. **Conferences:** Meetings where learning groups collaborate, or documented work is handed in.

5. **References:** Guide to books and information resources, which help to solve the tasks.
6. **Bulletins:** Place where up-to-date information is found.
7. **Equivalents:** The planned effort which is later then documented in feedback graphs.

Fig. 2 shows the structure of a concrete ICs represented as Concept Map [13] implemented in a web-based e-learning environment for teaching S-BPM [23]. In [22] an example for an assignment about S-BPM is given.

The Concept Map navigation feature provides a non-linear navigation structure allowing the user to navigate to the theory (see mouse pointer in the centre of Fig. 2: context menu "Reference") and in the same menu to the S-BPM content (see context menu above the mouse pointer). This image highlights another aspect of web-based learning environments, these allow learners to structure their individual learning paths.

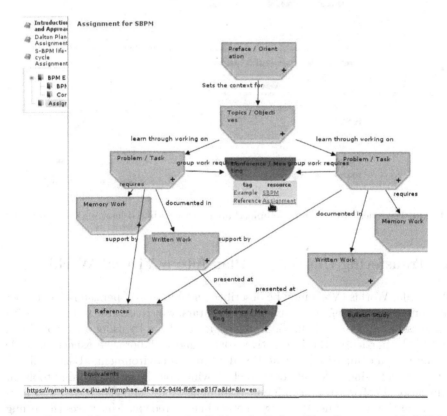

Fig. 2. Concept Map based navigation linking the Dalton Plan Structure with S-BPM content; the actual content for this assignment is presented in [22]

The second instrument created by Parkhurst to guide learners are feedback graphs [15]. These show the progress made by individual learners and the overall learning group. Fig. 3 shows a particular implementation of feedback graphs for the web. The blue lines show the progress students think they have made in the documented work sections of that particular intelligibility catcher (left part). After evaluation the teacher also draws a line, showing where she/he thinks the learner is (also left part). Icons show text comments and uploaded files that point to the work documented by students. The mouse in Fig. 3 (left part) hovers of such an icon, and the text from the student is shown below the cursor. Fig. 3 (right part) shows the area where learners submit their comments/work/files. Its these comments and files provided in this form that are shown with the graphs.

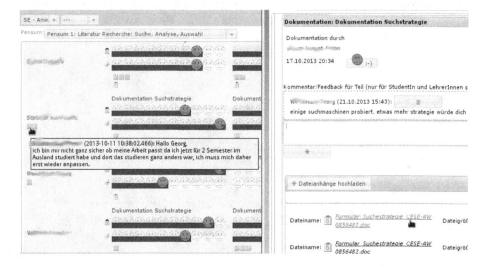

Fig. 3. Feedback graphs and the upload area in a web-based learning environment

3   Transfering the Dalton Plan into a Virtual World

3D Virtual Worlds (VW) may be described as "immersive, persistent multi-user environments representing individuals as avatars, which are able to interact with other users, objects, and the environment in real-time by using a network" [16, p. 12]. In particular the interactive, social, and collaborative aspects provide advantages in comparison to traditional e-learning environments. Users collaborate in-world using different tools (such as whiteboards, brainstorming-tools, or conventional software) and different communication channels (verbal and non-verbal) at the same time. Working together in a shared space increases the feeling of presence and enforces the communication with other users. In addition, the three-dimensional aspects enable new forms of learning content visualization [17,7,16,2,11].

Introducing a new technology to students is challenging. Learning the use of new software may lead to user frustration and might have impact on learning results. Therefore it is in particular important to focus on a good environment design, exciting user experience and advanced usability to attract students instead of discouraging them. Based on the design model introduced in [18] the integration of the individual pedagogical tools and concepts of the learning format should be in line with usability heuristics for VW environments, and with the pedagogical attractors of the Dalton Plan: (1) interactivity and creativity, (2) collaborative tasks, and (3) feedback and assessability. In addition to this, do the used Intelligibility Catchers support users in the virtual world by explicitly referencing the use of features available in the VW. Table 1 shows pedagogical features translated from the Dalton Plan (Assignments & Feedback graphs of 1924)[15] to the web (using Intelligibility Catcher, ICs) [20] and to the VW.

Table 1. Realisation of pedagogical features of the Dalton Plan in Web-based Intelligibility Catchers and in Virtual Worlds

Dalton Plan	Web-based IC	Virtual World Dalton Plan
Motivation Section	Hyper Text	Videos in World
Collaborative Work	Discussion Forum	Collaborative In-World Editor
Verbal Presentation	Upload Form, Chat	In-World Presentation
Feedback Paper Forms	Coloured Graphs	3D Objects

4   The Educational Virtual S-BPM World

The following integration of the pedagogical formats *Dalton Plan* and *Intelligibility Catcher* in a virtual world is constructed using the open-source virtual world toolkit Open Wonderland [14]. The content is based on existing assignments and intelligibility catchers described in [22,23].

The main objective of the education Virtual S-BPM World is to provide an online collaborative learning environment that integrates the pedagogical valuable components of the Dalton Plan to provide an environment for learning S-BPM. Being in line with the learning objectives the world is designed as an interactive, creative place, where students can work and learn together. The educational Virtual S-BPM World is separated into different areas with different purposes:

1. **Motivation Area.** In the *Motivation Area* (see Fig. 4) orientation material and bulletins are provided. In this area doors (e.g. on the right side, labelled "Go to Task 1") lead to the work area for the different tasks. In the example, videos (e.g. the four white windows in front of the students) provide motivational input to modelling with S-BPM. There also a concept map is shown on the left, which provides an overview of the tasks and the relationship between IC/assignment parts. This map serves as explanation of the pedagogical instrument used.

Fig. 4. *Motivation Area* where students (Johanna, Georg) find introduction materials and doors lead to areas where students work on individual tasks

2. **Work Area.** The *Work Area* (one for each task; see Fig. 5) is a wide place to support the students' creativity and interactive collaboration. The task's objectives, documented work description, and intellectual work are described in this area. In this area also reference materials required for working on the task are given. Students may brainstorm and work together on one of the tasks presented in the current Intelligibility Catcher. Collaboration tools such as whiteboards, sticky notes, or image uploaders provide students the possibility to create their own personalized shared working environment.

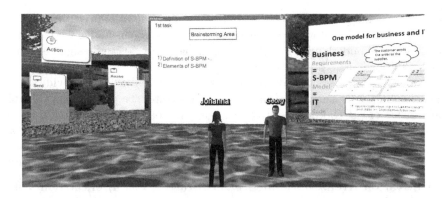

Fig. 5. The *Work Area* as a collaborative space for working on a task

3. **Feedback Space:** The last area is the *Feedback Space*, where each student can assess their own progress by interacting with an interactive representation using 3D-objects. Following the Dalton Plan's feedback graphs approach, teachers pile up blocks in order to provide feedback (see Fig. 6).

Fig. 6. *Feedback Space* where students can reflect on their learning and teachers provide feedback

As students are also required to provide their own assessment, the two piles next to each other highlight differences in assessment of the work by students and teacher. The collaboration possibilities may be used here to discuss the differences of the assessments.

5   Conclusions

Integration of technology in classroom settings provides teachers and students with new possibilities. Virtual Worlds facilitate collaborative distant learning. The nature of these 3D learning environments provides a good basis for self-organised collaborative learning as shown above.

The world described in this paper is an initial prototype, enabling explorative and creative learning of a single aspect of S-BPM, building on the Dalton Plan pedagogy [15]. Future worlds could enable learning possibilities for multiple aspects brought together in a large world through providing access to multiple intelligibility catchers.

In addition to the content, also the pedagogical underpinnings might be altered. Freinet Pedagogy makes use of ateliers where students work on assignments. These ateliers are one-stop-shops for the acquisition of capabilities with respect to a single topic. In addition to this, in this pedagogy students formulate their own assignments, and may in turn asses their own and other students work with only minimal teacher intervention [5]. Further work in this direction could be an In-World-Editor supporting students and teachers in creating ICs and Ateliers for the Virtual World (cf. [23]).

Acknowledgement. The research leading to these results has received funding from the European Commission within the Marie Curie Industry and Academia Partnerships and Pathways (IAPP) programme under grant agreement n° 286083. For more information on the IANES project see http://www.ianes.eu.

References

1. Auinger, A., Stary, C.: Didaktikgeleiteter Wissenstransfer - Interaktive Informationsräume für Lern-Gemeinschaften im Web. Deutscher Universitäts-Verlag/GWV Fachverlage GmbH, Wiesbaden (2005)
2. Bouras, C., Tsiatsos, T.: Educational virtual environments: design rationale and architecture. Multimedia Tools and Applications 29(2), 153–173 (2006), http://dx.doi.org/10.1007/s11042-006-0005-7
3. Casanova, D., Moreira, A., Costa, N.: Technology enhanced learning in higher education: results from the design of a quality evaluation framework. Procedia - Social and Behavioral Sciences 29, 893–902 (2011), http://www.sciencedirect.com/science/article/pii/S1877042811027807, the 2nd International Conference on Education and Educational Psychology 2011
4. Davis, E.J., Smith, T.J., Leflore, D.: Chaos in the Classroom - A New Theory of Teaching and Learning. Carolina Academic Press, Durham (2008)
5. Eichelberger, H., Laner, C., Kohlberg, W.D., Stary, E., Stary, C.: Reformpädagogik goes E-Learning - neue Wege zur Selbstbestimmung von virtuellem Wissenstransfer und individualisiertem Wissenserwerb. Oldenbourg, München, Wien (2008)
6. Friedman, R.S., Deek, F.P.: Innovation and education in the digital age: Reconciling the roles of pedagogy, technology, and the business of learning. IEEE Transactions on Engineering Management 50(4), 403–412 (2003)
7. Gütl, C.: The support of virtual 3d worlds for enhancing collaboration in learning settings. In: Pozzi, F., Persico, D. (eds.) Techniques for Fostering Collaboration in Online Learning Communities: Theoretical and Practical Perspectives, pp. 278–299. IGI Global (2011)
8. Jong, T., Weinberger, A., Girault, I., Kluge, A., Lazonder, A., Pedaste, M., Ludvigsen, S., Ney, M., Wasson, B., Wichmann, A., Geraedts, C., Giemza, A., Hovardas, T., Julien, R., Joolingen, W., Lejeune, A., Manoli, C., Matteman, Y., Sarapuu, T., Verkade, A., Vold, V., Zacharia, Z.: Using scenarios to design complex technology-enhanced learning environments. Educational Technology Research and Development 60(5), 883–901 (2012)
9. Kaplan, J., Yankelovich, N.: Open wonderland: an extensible virtual world architecture. IEEE Internet Computing 15(5), 38–45 (2011)
10. Laal, M., Salamati, P.: Lifelong learning; why do we need it? Procedia - Social and Behavioral Sciences 31, 399–403 (2012), http://www.sciencedirect.com/science/article/pii/S1877042811030023, world Conference on Learning, Teaching & Administration - 2011
11. Lucia, A.D., Francese, R., Passero, I., Tortora, G.: Development and evaluation of a virtual campus on second life: The case of seconddmi. Computers & Education 52(1), 220–233 (2009), http://www.sciencedirect.com/science/article/pii/S0360131508001243
12. Marjanovic, O., Bandara, W.: The current state of BPM education in Australia: Teaching and research challenges. In: zur Muehlen, M., Su, J. (eds.) BPM 2010 Workshops. LNBIP, vol. 66, pp. 775–789. Springer, Heidelberg (2011), http://dx.doi.org/10.1007/978-3-642-20511-8_69

13. Novak, J.D., Cañas, A.J.: The theory underlying concept maps and how to construct and use them. Technical Report IHMC CmapTools 2006-01 Rev 01-2008, Florida Institute for Human and Machine Cognition (IHMC) (2008), http://cmap.ihmc.us/Publications/ResearchPapers/TheoryUnderlyingConceptMaps.pdf (zugriff: December 04, 2010)
14. Open Wonderland Foundation: Open Wonderland Documentation Wiki (2013), http://openwonderland.org (last accessed: October 2013)
15. Parkhurst, H.: Education on the Dalton Plan. Nabu Press (1923, 2010)
16. Pirker, J.: The Virtual TEAL World - An Interactive and Collaborative Virtual World Environment for Physics Education. Master's thesis, Graz University of Technology (2013)
17. Pirker, J., Berger, S., Gütl, C., Belcher, J.W., Bailey, P.H.: Understanding physical concepts using an immersive virtual learning environment. In: Gardner, M., Garnier, F., Kloos, C.D. (eds.) Proceedings of the 2nd European Immersive Education Summit, pp. 183–191 (November 2012)
18. Pirker, J., Gütl, C., Belcher, J.W., Bailey, P.H.: Design and evaluation of a learner-centric immersive virtual learning environment for physics education. In: Holzinger, A., Ziefle, M., Hitz, M., Debevc, M. (eds.) SouthCHI 2013. LNCS, vol. 7946, pp. 551–561. Springer, Heidelberg (2013), http://dx.doi.org/10.1007/978-3-642-39062-3_34
19. Rozendaal, J.S., Minnaert, A., Boekaerts, M.: Motivation and self-regulated learning in secondary vocational education: information-processing type and gender differences. Learning and Individual Differences 13(4), 273–289 (2001)
20. Stary, C.: Intelligibility catchers for Self-Managed knowledge transfer. In: Seventh IEEE International Conference on Advanced Learning Technologies, ICALT 2007, pp. 517–521 (July 2007), http://dx.doi.org/10.1109/ICALT.2007.168
21. Stary, C., Weichhart, G.: An e-learning approach to informed problem solving. Knowledge Management & E-Learning: An International Journal (KM&EL) 4(2), 195–216 (2012), http://www.kmel-journal.org/ojs/index.php, special Issue on Supporting, Managing, & Sustaining Creativity and Cognition through Technology
22. Weichhart, G.: S-BPM education on the dalton plan: An E-learning approach. In: Oppl, S., Fleischmann, A. (eds.) S-BPM ONE 2012. CCIS, vol. 284, pp. 181–193. Springer, Heidelberg (2012)
23. Weichhart, G.: Der Dalton Plan im E-Learning: Transformation einer Reformpädagogik ins Web. Phd. thesis, Johannes Kepler Universität Linz, Sozial- und Wirtschaftswissenschaftliche Fakultät, Institut für Wirtschaftsinformatik - Communications Engineering (2013)
24. Weichhart, G.: The learning environment as a chaotic and complex adaptive system. Systems 1(1), 36–53 (2013), http://www.systems-journal.eu/article/view/130/138

Author Index

Aydin, Mehmet N.   147

Bonaldi, David   42

Demirörs, Onur   55

Elstermann, Matthes   125, 137

Fink, Andreas   107
Fleischmann, Christoph   21, 85

Gütl, Christian   188

Höver, Kai Michael   174

Kannengiesser, Udo   42
Kurz, Matthias   67

Lederer, Matthias   67
Lembcke, Ulricke   67

Mesbahipour, Ramtin   157
Meyer, Nils   21
Mühlhäuser, Max   174

Nursinski, André   157

Oppl, Stefan   3
Ovtcharova, Jivka   125, 137

Piller, Christoph   164
Pirker, Johanna   188

Rothschädl, Thomas   3

Salmanoğlu, Murat   55
Sobočan, Boris   21
Spiller, Michael   157
Stary, Christian   188
Stein, Gerhard   85

Totter, Alexandra   42
Türetken, Oktay   55

Uluhan, Eray   147

Vogt, Simon   107

Weichhart, Georg   188
Wölfel, DI Walter   164